May 3, 1997

To Wayne Evans:

With great hope that America can be reborn as a free nation!

"Steve"

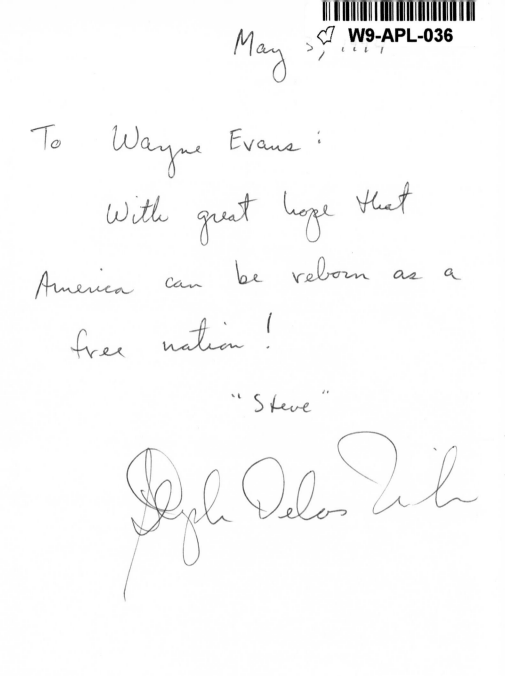

THE
BANKRUPTCY
of
AMERICA

Additional Comments Concerning
The Bankruptcy of America:

"Stephen Wilson's *The Bankruptcy of America* is an enlightening exposé of the 1980's financial mania that has created our current financial and economic problems. I believe that he is one of the first economists to clearly delineate how the decline of moral and ethical decision making help to create the financial dilemma of the 1990's."

> —O. C. Ferrell, Ph.D., Distinguished Professor
> of Marketing and Business Ethics
> Memphis State University

"*The Bankruptcy of America* is a readable explanation of the causes and effects of economic cycles and reinforces the theory of 'looking back to the future.'"

> —John Simpson
> *Memphis Business Journal*

"In the midst of the greed induced wreckage of the 1990's United States economy, Stephen Delos Wilson prophetically summons our society to a renewed commitment to moral responsibility. It is a summons which cannot be avoided any longer and *The Bankruptcy of America* takes the lead in focusing attention on the urgency of that summons."

> —Neil J. O'Connell, O.F.M., Ph.D., President
> St. Bonaventure University

"The *Bankruptcy of America* is a commendable book, closely reasoned, and brimming with details. As one who has spent much time thinking about the topics Dr. Stephen Delos Wilson covers, I nonetheless found his book most interesting for the way that it stimulated my thinking in a variety of directions. Good stuff—I hope he finds the broad audience that he deserves."

> —James Davidson, Chief Economist
> National Taxpayers' Union

THE
BANKRUPTCY
of
AMERICA

How the BOOM of the 80's
Became the BUST of the 90's

★ ★ ★ ★ ★

Stephen Delos Wilson

Ridge Mills Press
Germantown, Tennessee

Additional copies of this book may be ordered through bookstores
or by sending $19.95 plus $2.50 for postage and handling to:
Publishers Distribution Service
121 East Front Street, Suite 203
Traverse City, MI 49684
1-800-345-0096.

Copyright © 1992 by Stephen Delos Wilson

All rights reserved. No part of this book may be reproduced, by any means, without
permission in writing from the publisher, except by a reviewer who wishes to quote
brief excerpts. For information contact Ridge Mills Press, 8188 Wethersfield Drive,
Germantown, TN 38139-2430.

Publisher's Cataloging-in-Publication Data

Wilson, Stephen Delos, 1948-
       The bankruptcy of America : how the boom of the eighties became the
       bust of the nineties / by Stephen Delos Wilson. —Germantown, TN :
       Ridge Mills Press, 1992.
         p. cm.
         ISBN 0-9630358-1-9
    1. United States—Economic conditions—1981- 2. United States—Economic
    policy—1981- 3. Finance—United States. I. Title.

HC106.8.W55   1992
330.9'73'0927—dc20   91-62520

Manufactured in the United States of America

To my parents:

Murray Crowell Wilson

and

Mary Humphrey Wilson

With thanks for not betting the farm!

Acknowledgments

Though not in quite the same fashion as a certain literary character, I have always relied upon the kindness of strangers. Many of these have touched me only by their sympathy, their prayers, or by what Schumpeter called the "pre-analytic cognitive act" — their vision. To these I offer my thanks and I regret that they are only in the most general of terms. Turning to the practical aspects of writing this book, I have obtained most of the supporting data and anecdotal information from *The Wall Street Journal, Barron's,* or the *Federal Reserve Bulletin*. To have cited these sources each time a figure was quoted would have cluttered the text to no purpose, so I have noted the above sources only where the data or references are critical to one of the major themes of the book.

Several individuals have been kind enough to read early drafts of the manuscript and have provided helpful comments. Foremost among these is A. Gary Shilling, whose own economic forecasts have long foreseen the perplexed economy of the eighties and nineties, and for this I owe him a huge intellectual debt. Professor Otto Helweg of Memphis State University suggested that I clarify a number of important areas, and provided much-needed moral support while I was writing the first draft. Likewise, Robert W. Williams, Managing Director of Prudential Home Mortgage Company and a former colleague in mortgage banking, has long encouraged me to undertake a literary effort of this type. His friendship has been a great asset to me, as has that of Robert S. Welborn, President of Welborn Mortgage Corporation. Over the years, my continuing correspondence with Mr. Welborn has encouraged me to look beyond the more narrowly practiced discipline of economics in search of a deeper understanding of market behavior.

I would also like to express my gratitude to those who reviewed galley copies of the book and provided me the benefit of their comments and insights. These include David Levy, Director of Forecasting at the Jerome Levy Economics Institute; Brian Fabbri, Chief Economist at Midland Bank PLC of England; Richard Rahn, Chief

Economist of the U. S. Chamber of Commerce; O. C. Ferrell, Distinguished Professor of Marketing and Business Ethics at Memphis State University; Father Neil J. O'Connell, President of St. Bonaventure University; James Davidson, Chief Economist of the National Taxpayers' Union; and John Simpson of the *Memphis Business Journal*. I must add, however, that any errors in this book are mine alone. The views and opinions I express do not necessarily represent those of any of the individuals or institutions named above.

Technical assistance in transforming the manuscript to galley copies and, finally, to the finished copy was provided by Alex Moore. The automated manuscript (an oxymoron I use only with great reluctance) was produced by my wife, Georgine, from my virtually illegible handwritten script. Moreover, I have relied upon Georgine's constant support and encouragement throughout this entire effort, and this book could not have been completed without her.

Stephen Delos Wilson
October, 1991

Foreword

The sins of the fathers are visited upon their children. Let's hope that the visitation doesn't last until the third and fourth generations, as it says in the Bible, because the recent sins are huge. I'm referring to the gigantic buildup of debt in the last two decades without offsetting growth in productive assets.

In the 1970's, high inflation, spawned by excessive government spending on Vietnam and domestic social programs in the late 1960's, sparked speculation in farmland and other tangible assets. That required immense amounts of borrowing, which was compounded by the oil shocks as gobs and gobs of loans were poured into speculative energy and oil patch real estate, and the recycling of petrodollars. All of these excesses came to grief by the early 1980's, but did borrowers and lenders retreat to lick their wounds? No way!

By the 1980's, almost every lender or borrower who remembered firsthand the financial blood baths of the 1930's was dead or out to pasture. Consequently, fear was out and greed and glitz were in, much as they were in the 1920's. The 50 to 60 years it takes those with indelibly etched experiences to depart the scene probably also explains the similar duration of the Kondratieff wave, which continues right on schedule.

By the 1980's, then, many were willing to take on big debts, and they had many opportunities. The 1981 tax act, aided by the big defense buildup and skyrocketing costs of social programs, pushed the federal deficit and borrowing through the roof. That tax act also vastly liberalized real estate depreciation which generated tremendous but unproductive tax shelter activity and borrowing. Deregulation of the S&L's, except for federal insurance on deposits, brought in financial sharpies who borrowed mountains of money from depositors which they invested in all sorts of real estate and other flaky deals. Heads they would win, tails the deposit insurance would lose, was their game.

The virtual closing of the Anti-trust Division of the Reagan Justice Department allowed financial manipulators to turn leveraged buyouts from a tool for productive corporate reorganization into a sledgehammer for financial manipulation. They converted vast amounts of equity into debt in the process. Consumers who lost high paid but low skilled jobs in basic industries borrowed heavily to finance the good life they could no longer afford. In effect, all U.S. economic sectors borrowed heavily in the 1980's, with little prospect of repaying, and foreigners had to provide the funds, gaining them control of U.S. financial markets.

With the debt explosion of the last two decades unaccompanied by productive resources that could service it, risks skyrocketed, not only for final borrowers but for financial intermediaries as well. Banks jumped from frying pan to frying pan to frying pan – from Third World loan disasters to LBO quagmires to commercial construction catastrophes and finally to the bubbling cauldron of credit card loans. The collateral behind many of these loans – real estate, commodities, corporate earning power, and consumer incomes – range from weak to collapsed, and the trick in the years ahead is to mark down the loans to serviceable levels without upsetting the financial apple cart. Even if the current pile of debts can be unwound more smoothly than in the 1930's, it will take the bulk of the 1990's to do so.

Stephen Delos Wilson has done an excellent, often witty, job of explaining the inner workings of the U.S. economy during the 1980's and how it got to its current precarious state. He is a consummate historian who gives the reader a clear sense of how many of our basic institutions came to be and their recent changes. Understanding the past that he lays out so well is essential to anyone who hopes to survive and thrive in the treacherous and uncertain 1990's.

–A. Gary Shilling

Contents

"Modesty is more profitable to the state than dexterity with arrogance ... the more ignorant sort of men do, for the most part, better regulate a commonwealth than they that are wiser. For these love to appear wiser than the laws ... from whence most commonly proceeds the ruin of the states in which they live."

- Thucydides

THE
BANKRUPTCY
of
AMERICA

CHAPTER 1

The Harvest of Voodoo Economics

Is it possible for an economy to pave the road to hell with good intentions? Could a nation be so short-sighted and self-destructive that it kills the goose that lays the golden egg? More specifically, as the nineteen-eighties take their proper place in the perspective of history, will they tell the story of a society that became intellectually dishonest and morally bankrupt to the point of believing its own pipe dreams? Long after the basic weaknesses of America's economy were readily apparent, why was good money still being sent after bad to preserve the illusion of positive cash flow? In attempting to answer these questions, this book offers no prediction of "the coming depression" or similar economic cataclysm. The bankruptcy of America – its businesses, its consumers, and its government – was a process that was already well underway by the time this book was written. Yet, this is no apocalyptic event; though the bankruptcy reorganization of America's economy will surely be long and painful, and though it is unavoidable, this too shall pass. Thus, before the phoenix rises from its own ashes, we must learn as much as possible from the past and use it to plan for a new generation of progress and prosperity.

As the eighties drew to a close, perhaps one of the most prescient observers of the "Voodoo Economics" of that wild decade was Senator Lloyd Bentsen, running mate of the eminently forgettable Michael Dukakis in the 1988 Presidential election. Responding to the plausible Republican litany of how great things were, Senator Bentsen noted that he too was capable of creating the illusion of prosperity. Anyone with the authority to write "a trillion dollars in hot checks" could do the job equally well. Yet, even the correct official figure of three trillion dollars in federal government debt represented just a part of the burden America had accumulated – indeed just a part of what was owed by the federal government alone. During the eighties, America's households saw their net worth – assets minus liabilities – grow at a five percent annual rate, while employee compensation grew at 7.5 percent per year.

However, household debt burdens barreled ahead at a 10 percent rate to reach 83.5 percent of after-tax personal income in 1990 vs. 65.4 percent in 1980. Excluding a mountain of mortgage debt, consumer debt alone was 20.4 percent of 1990 after-tax income, well above the 18.2 percent figure for 1980. At the same time debt burdens accumulated, inflation in real estate prices and wage rates was grinding to a halt. By early 1991, the Federal Reserve reported that 14 percent of America's consumers were behind on at least one of the scheduled payments on their accumulated personal burden of $3.4 trillion in debt.

While the consumer was trying to juggle the financial obligations which loomed before him, the Congressional Budget Office was trying to keep tabs on the Resolution Trust Corporation (RTC), the thrift bailout agency that spent $7,420,000 every *hour* during 1990. Nor was the problem a purely domestic concern. The end of the Tokyo real estate boom had revealed that Japan, the economic juggernaut of the eighties, had financed its international growth and lending by a financial system that was short on capital and long on speculative real estate loans, while Japanese companies had become cheap-money junkies. Meanwhile, the Persian Gulf War, while demonstrating the superiority of American military technology over a nation that had never yet built even one tank, devastated Iraq and Kuwait, and created a huge demand for capital in a part of the world which had formerly been a net lender in the world's capital markets. Nobody was immune. Even the Vatican reported having to dip into "Peter's Pence," a worldwide collection generally reserved for the poor, to cover a projected 1991 deficit of $91.5 million. While the Vatican's problems paled against those of the RTC, the two institutions' outlooks and attitudes toward asset sales were remarkably similar. Confronted with a critic's suggestion that the Church sell some of its treasure of *objets d'art*, a spokesman responded that "the art objects have no value. The thought of selling off artistic and cultural patrimony is absurd."

As American consumers wrestled with the debt devil, American business was also confronted with the question of how to get the debt genie back into his bottle. In the nineties, it would be unrealistic to expect a boost from soaring sales and rising inflation. Since the consumer was already too deep in hock by any reasonable standard, it was becoming difficult to throw the same pie in his face again. The "Big Three" U.S. automakers were rapidly becoming the Three Little Pigs as expenses ran out of control while output of their automobiles slumped to a thirty-three year low in the spring of 1991. More than any other industry, the automakers seemed to demonstrate the incompetence of American managers, a legion which had mastered the one-minute platitude as a substitute for hands-on management. The ascendancy of graduate schools of business in the seventies and eighties seemed to have produced a generation of quantitatively inclined Whiz Kids, adept at calculating when to pull the ripcord and how to hit the drop zone in their golden parachutes after being weighed down by a career of writing off three-martini lunches. Yet, while the U.S. automakers were bleeding red ink, their Japanese competitors were increasing production levels in their U.S. assembly plants by seven percent from the year earlier.

While the automakers make a convenient paradigm for the problems confronting American industry, nothing outside the Soviet Union can match the U.S. government in the sheer magnitude of its ever more recondite approach to financial waste. The federal government allots 48 percent of its total budget – equal to one-seventh of gross national product (GNP)– to social programs. But despite spending an amount equivalent to 70 percent of the annual GNP of Germany, the gap between rich and poor continued to widen in the eighties. While nearly a quarter million Americans were homeless,[1] the City of New York – with the help of federal funds – demonstrated its own moral and intellectual state of poverty by paying up to $4,000 per month to house a family in a hotel for the homeless – one where drugs and violence were rife. This is a slice of life that can not remain forever unseen by America's 1.5 million millionaires. The top 800 highest-paid American managers received 93 times the average annual pay of industrial workers in 1989, up from 40 times in 1980.[2] Yet, in relying on government to solve the problems of crime, poverty, and an inadequate education system, America had placed burdens on its public sector for which legislators and bureaucrats were totally devoid of competence. The social problems were purely and simply due to a lack of discipline and morality. These values, which had traditionally been imparted through religion and the guidance of the family unit, had – over the years – been largely usurped by a government that perceived itself as separate and distinct from religion and moral values. The pernicious effects of this Big Brother policy were further aggravated by tax and welfare programs which clearly had the effect of weakening the family unit.

But this book is not a prescription of how to fix the problems that confronted America's economy as the nineties began. That is a problem which can only be solved by the discipline of the market. The multi-generation program of government economic management would inevitably come to an end in America in much the same way it would in Russia. The discipline of the world's capital markets makes it impossible for any nation to live perpetually beyond its means. Eventually, a reckoning comes and expenses must be brought into line with income. No further loans are forthcoming. The Ponzi scheme grinds to a halt, for the last man in line – in this case the U.S. taxpayer – finds that the entire financial edifice rests ultimately upon his willingness to pay. The Greater Fool apparatus collapses when there is no greater fool to be found. Thus, the taxpayer finally rebels, both at the ballot booth and in the marketplace. He rebels against insolent postal employees and an incompetent school system. He rebels against welfare for the rich through government support programs for agriculture and medicine. He rebels against a pay-as-you-go Social Security System which supports his own parents in relative comfort while he himself is able to support only a much smaller generation upon which the economy of the future must depend for support. And, finally, as the failure of past policy becomes evident in rising government payments to bail out its off-budget deposit insurance and mortgage insurance programs, there must inevitably be a recrudescence of traditional capitalist values. Interest will again be the reward to savers for diverting consumption from the present to the future. And in a world short of capital, where the sham of government guarantee of private debts has been exposed and defrocked, capital's highest return will be found in those hands in which it can be prudently and ethically managed. This is a quiet sort of rebellion, but no part of American society will find itself able to escape its effects. Not one worker, not one employer, not one bureaucrat.

II

As Dr. Johnson once noted, if a man knows he is to be hanged in the near future, it "concentrates the mind wonderfully." Thus, it should come as no surprise that America's financial institutions were rigorously evaluating their loan portfolios and lending policies as the nineties began. For his part, Don Dixon, the Texas real estate developer and kingpin of the failed Vernon Savings and Loan, concentrated his mind on a skillful legal defense against government charges of racketeering and "conspiracy to defraud the United States." It evidently worked well, for despite his conviction for misuse of federally guaranteed deposits (for a variety of non-banking purposes, including the services of prostitutes), Mr. Dixon received a sentence of just five years in federal prison. While the court could only pin $600,000 of the cost of Vernon's $1.2 billion bailout on Dixon, the punishment nevertheless seemed to be cut from the same bolt of cloth as Vernon's own loose lending guidelines. If it was not due to outright fraud, the 96 percent loss rate on Vernon's loan portfolio must rank as an enduring monument to incompetence. Indeed, the apparatus of government-sponsored deposit insurance is one of the greatest subsidies to incompetence yet devised. A study by the General Accounting Office indicated that the loss to taxpayers from the savings and loan bailout would amount to 10 percent of the total amount of insured deposits vs. the one percent of deposits lost during the Great Depression, before the deposit insurance system was invented to "save" the banking system.

The Dixon case is instructive not only in what it shows about what can happen to bankers who are not required to rely upon a free market for their deposits, but also for what it tells about lawmakers and government employees – in this case the presiding judge – who fail to recognize government waste as outright theft from the taxpayer. To remove the management of America's capital from the tiny minority who have demonstrated their frugality and place it in the hands of the vast majority who have not is to open a Pandora's box of financial nirvana. Even after the virtually total collapse of the thrift industry, the Bush Administration was advancing its latest Greater Fool apparatus for propping up the Federal Deposit Insurance Corporation (FDIC). Under the Bush plan, FDIC would use its $5 billion credit line from the Treasury to collateralize a further $45 billion from the Federal Financing Bank. Where could this line of reasoning lead? If the ability to borrow is used to collateralize still greater borrowing, the laws of mathematics (where infinity exists) and economics (where trees don't grow to the sky) must inevitably come into conflict. Of course, Americans had trained their eyes to glaze over at the first mention of federal finances ever since FDR's famous analogy of Lend-Lease to lending his neighbor a garden hose. This analogy might have stood muster if there was any hope of getting the hose back, but the attention span of bureaucrats – and taxpayers – did not generally extend that far. The easy part of lending is putting money out; getting it back is somewhat more difficult.

The problem with lending the FDIC more money to shore up its assets against rapidly mounting losses was the likelihood that those losses would grow even more rapidly in the future. The primary reason

FDIC's deposit insurance fund was bleeding so profusely was the rapid disappearance of capital from the balance sheets of banks as well as thrift institutions. A financial institution is no different from any other business enterprise in that its assets (loans) must be supported either by its liabilities (deposits) or the equity capital supplied by the corporation's stockholders. The equity cushion of the nation's depository institutions – the true measure of their ability to redeem their deposits, take risks, and absorb losses – had fallen dramatically during the eighties. The equity-to-assets ratio of all federally insured institutions, which stood at approximately 7.25 percent at the beginning of the decade – a time of high interest rates and tight money – had fallen to less than six percent before the onset of the 1990 recession. Yet, international agreements with America's trading partners obligated most banks to raise their capital ratios to eight percent in the early nineties. The two windows for increasing equity – selling stock to investors or retaining a portion of profits – were, however, slammed firmly shut with the 1990 recession. Banks were earning barely enough to retain any earnings, while investors were unwilling to become a junior partner to the U. S. Government in the deposit insurance pyramid – even if the profits had been high enough. Thus, in the face of an already weak economy, banks found themselves with only one road open: reduce assets to bring them in line with equity. Rather than make new loans, existing loans were called. Assets were shed in an effort to raise the capital-to-asset ratio.

With virtually every bank in the country running scared, the great financial game of musical chairs that America had played for fifty years was coming to an end as the nineties began. As banks tried to restore sanity to their balance sheets, new loan requests were given the cold shoulder. Business managers' telephone calls to formerly friendly loan officers were going unanswered with unprecedented frequency. Hardest hit were retailers – who depended on banks to finance their inventories. A small New York-based retailer, Abrahams Brothers, was advised by Manufacturers Hanover Trust Co. to obtain an audited financial statement. Rather than pay the $100,000 for the audit that would be required to get a $500,000 loan, the company simply filed for bankruptcy. A fifty year record of banking with Manufacturer's Hanover had not been enough to save the day, or even to buy a ride home on the New York Subway. Bankers were no longer interested in "relationships."

For all their tight-fistedness, America's bankers still managed to demonstrate their failure to comprehend the basic principles of prudent lending. Another retailer, Paul Harris, found banks happily offering to provide $19 million in "debtor-in-possession" financing *after* the company filed bankruptcy. The banks were using the same tired reasoning that got them into trouble with leveraged buy-out loans and, earlier in the eighties, loans to "third world" countries. Never mind that they were dealing with collateral of dubious value or a borrower who had demonstrated an inability to meet his financial obligations, the banks who provided debtor-in-possession loans comforted themselves in the knowledge that they would have an unencumbered lien on the bankrupt company's inventory. More telling was the fact that the banks were demanding and getting juicy fees – typically two percent of the loan principal – for arranging such loans. Banks had also failed to learn that bigger does not necessarily mean better. In 1991, long after the depressing economics of the banking industry should have been clearly obvious to the most casual observer, banking giant Fleet/Norstar Financial Group, Inc. was aggressively seeking to acquire failed banks, such as the defunct Bank of New England. Fleet appeared to be ignoring the problems that were already affecting its existing business. In early 1991, Fleet's own financial statements showed a return on equity of just five percent and a highly leveraged capital-to-asset ratio below seven percent.

While the problems of the thrift and banking industry were already clear as the nineties began, the recognition of the insurance industry as the next financial nightmare was only beginning. In April 1991, California's Executive Life Insurance Company was placed under the supervision of insurance regulators. Altogether the parent company, First Executive Corp. had written nearly $50 billion in potential insurance obligations. A large part of the company's obligations were to have been covered by income from its portfolio of junk bonds, which had been obtained through the efforts of Drexel Burnham Lambert's fabled Junk Bond King, Michael Milken. By 1991, Milken was in jail, Drexel had filed for bankruptcy, and Executive Life was trying to meet its obligations under the watchful eye of insurance regulators. However, the thousands of pensioners and policyholders who were dependent on Executive Life policies for retirement income could not be erased by the accountant's pencil and they would pay part of the price of the financial mania of the eighties for many years to come. Thus, as the boom of the eighties became the bust of the nineties, it was truly the passing of an era. The critical member of the Roosevelt-era economic superstructure, a government-sponsored banking system, was no longer able to deliver the stimulus to economic activity which was so sorely needed. The decline of the banking and financial system spelled the end of a time in which bankers had been induced by their federal sponsors to bid for debt in ever greater amounts from ever less creditworthy clients. Government-sponsored deposit insurance had not ceased to exist, but as its true cost became apparent, the handwriting was on the wall.

III

It would be unfair to lay the entire list of the economic woes of the nineties at the feet of America's socialized banking system. Jejune as they were, bankers were no less efficient than the insipid army of lawmakers, contractors, researchers, bureaucrats, and teachers whose vision of economic life had been distorted by their own dependence on the benevolent despot of government spending. A single industry, real estate, will serve to demonstrate how government programs can remain nearly transparent to the general public yet completely distort prices, the volume of transactions, and good business ethics.

When the hollow men of the Roosevelt Administration first got the federal government involved in the depressed real estate markets of the thirties, it was with the intent of providing liquidity to the mortgage markets by purchasing existing loans from banks and other lenders. The Federal National Mortgage Association (FNMA a/k/a "Fannie Mae") thus became the government's first finger in the real estate tar baby. The original scheme of a government-supported entity buying loans for its own portfolio took a giant philosophical leap into the future in the seventies with the Government National Mortgage Association (GNMA a/k/a "Ginnie Mae"). The innovation of GNMA was to impart the government's guarantee of timely payment of principal and interest to securities backed by mortgage loans which had already been insured by the Federal Housing Administration (FHA) or guaranteed by the Veterans Administration (VA). Private lenders would originate the loans, package them into securities known as Ginnie Maes, and service the loans as well as the securities for investors. Overnight, Joe Blow Mortgage Company with $100,000 in working capital had been granted access to America's long-term capital markets at the preferred interest rate usually reserved for the United States of America and its agencies, a better rate than that available to IBM. This was an immediate – though invisible – subsidy to every homeowner, realtor, homebuilder, and mortgage lender in America. Likewise, it was a tax in the form of increased borrowing cost on every company that was planning to issue debt to finance its plant, equipment and operations.

The opportunity cost of government mortgage programs in lost productive capacity is impossible to determine. It is certain, however, that the losses were not severe until the GNMA program of guarantees on publicly traded securities was joined by similar programs introduced by Fannie Mae and its look-alike federal cousin, the Federal Home Loan Mortgage Corporation (FHLMC a/k/a "Freddie Mac"). The dollar volume of Ginnie Mae, Fannie Mae, and Freddie Mac mortgage securities outstanding grew from $142 billion in 1980 to more than one *trillion* dollars in 1990. Of course, Americans would have borrowed a substantial amount to finance housing in any event, but no economist could estimate how many redundant jacuzzi tubs, three-car garages, and Texas-style bathrooms the nation had unconsciously substituted for lathes, presses, or subways. America had made a one trillion dollar investment of the public trust without so much as a $600 toilet seat's worth of analysis as to whether it was wanted or needed. In any event, it came in handy for Michael Sertich, owner of American Mortgage Corp. of Wisconsin. Mr. Sertich managed to sell $10.7 million in phantom loans to Freddie Mac and used the proceeds to cover his losses from speculating in the commodity futures markets.

Of course, no discussion of the real estate markets of the eighties and nineties should fail to mention that inimitable symbol of brass – Donald Trump. Mr. Trump, whose youthful countenance graced the cover of the most eminent business publications in the eighties, was to find himself more widely followed by readers of the tabloid press in the nineties. In short, Mr. Trump was a man who demonstrated that the sword of debt cuts in both directions. His heavy wheeling and dealing in New York real estate, a commuter airline, and gambling casinos during the eighties was heavily financed by debt, and his ability to muscle large loans made him a force with whom bankers and competitors were required to reckon.

As real estate prices stopped rising and banks tightened their lending standards in the nineties, Mr. Trump found himself with a great many trophies of uncertain market value. Revenues from his airline, casinos, and sundry other properties were not coming in fast enough to satisfy his many creditors. In 1990, he was able to arrange a $65 million line of credit and defer repayment on half his $2 billion in bank debt to a consortium of banks. Trump's Taj Mahal casino in Atlantic City, which had been financed by $675 million in junk bonds, failed to generate enough cash flow to make the required payments on the bonds. Meanwhile, the Trump Castle casino, financed by $300 million in junk bonds, saw its revenue drop 30 percent in early 1991. His third casino, Trump Plaza, avoided restructuring by selling $25 million in bonds secured by its parking garage.

Mr. Trump's creditors were swarming, among them his estranged wife, Ivana Trump. Mrs. Trump had entered into a pre-nuptial agreement, pursuant to whose terms she was offered $10 million by Mr. Trump in early 1991. Unfortunately, the only liquid assets which seemed to be readily available to Mr. Trump were the $18 million remaining under the terms of the $65 million bank line he had arranged the year before. Though reticent to finance Mr. Trump's divorce settlement, the banks found themselves with little choice. If the pre-nuptial agreement was not honored, Mrs. Trump could file suit and force her husband to seek bankruptcy protection. In that event, her claim might indeed be given preference to those of the banks. Mrs. Trump was, therefore, likely to walk away with more cash than anyone else involved in the Trump Empire.

IV

The problem with America's real estate markets and with many other markets as the nineties began was that an enormous gap had opened between perceived value and actual market value. By definition, no market is ever wrong in the prices it sets. However, if information or the flow of funds to a market is distorted, the market sets prices on the basis of these imperfect conditions. Unfortunately, when prices have been bid up to unrealistic levels, it takes some period of time before the market's perception reverts to the new reality, and prices may take some time to complete their downward adjustment. Sellers will continue to hold out for a time in the hope of getting what they consider a fair price. While they are waiting, their willingness to settle for a lower price generally grows. And as the willingness to sell at lower prices grows, prices drop further. Meanwhile, the expectation of lower prices develops on the part of potential buyers, who steadily lower their bids in their attempt to avoid jumping on before the decline is complete.

This, then, was the dilemma facing the American economy in the nineties. The financial system was already short of equity and was caught between the pincers of rising loan defaults and increasing

regulatory capital requirements. A vast portfolio of non-income producing assets such as automobiles and housing had been accumulated
and financed by debt. The debt payments continued to mount faster
than income and economic growth. The federal government was
unable to stimulate economic growth because it too had already
borrowed too heavily. An increasing share of tax receipts was required
to service the enormous national debt, which left precious little to
promote economic growth. Business had also borrowed heavily, often
in the junk bond market at high interest rates, to finance assets of
questionable value. As cash flow from operations declined and the
banks and capital markets became unwilling to add to their exposure,
the prices of all assets tended to fall. The value that homeowners placed
on their homes and businesses placed on their equipment was, in short,
based on the assumption that credit would be freely available and
economic growth would be rapid. These assumptions were not borne
out in reality, and anyone who had borrowed heavily in the eighties
found himself holding the bag in the nineties.

What, then would be the harvest of the Voodoo Economics of the
eighties, of the unrelenting accumulation of unproductive or
underproductive assets, of the steady growth of debt throughout the
American economy? Turn the page to the tale of how a society got more
caught up in selling the sizzle than producing the steak. Learn how form
came to be preferred over substance, prevarication over candor and,
most serious of all, debt over equity. The land of the free begot an array
of video game warriors – both on the battlefield and in the trading pits.
Meanwhile, the bread and circuses were demanded by the masses and
duly ordered up by the Peter Pan School of Finance. Economic policy
was ordained by the Five Second Photo Opportunity School of States-
manship, and – as the debts mounted – everything was cheerfully
reckoned by the See No Evil, Hear No Evil, Speak No Evil School of
Accounting. America was caught in its own form of utopian economics,
which had lost all sight of history and the basic political, economic, and
moral values on which the Republic was founded. The nation had
attempted to rise above history and was now doomed, as they say, to
repeat it. Thus, the boom-bust cycle of the post-World War II era fits
rather neatly into a long history of human foibles and folly. We turn
now to consider how America's remarkable half-century appears against
the backdrop of economic history.

CHAPTER 2

The History of Economic Cycles

American society is brave, young, and naive. As a nation, America looks more readily to the future than to the past. However, the laws which govern economic behavior, the search for wealth and success, are very little changed from the times of ancient civilization. Thus, while Americans may flatter themselves that they have risen above history, even this attitude is but an aspect of a cycle which has repeated itself through the ages. While often viewed as irrelevant, the history of economic cycles forms a basis toward understanding what was happening to the American economy as both the boom of the eighties and the bust of the nineties unfolded. A brief review of economic history will make the point that the science of economics has no more power to alter this economic aspect of the human condition than has the science of theology to change "the ways of God towards man."

A knowledge of credit, banking, and commerce can be traced back to the very origins of recorded history. The ancient Mesopotamian cultures supported large bureaucracies to direct foreign trade as well as large military establishments to defend their markets. Legal systems, dating back to the Code of Hammurabi, were refined to such a degree as to give some credibility to the legal profession's claim as the second oldest vocation. Money lending, private property, commodity trading, agriculture, and slave trading were facts of economic life which demanded a legal system to regulate them. That cycles of prosperity and depression were also a recognized part of economic life can not be disputed. The Bible contains many references which would indicate the Hebrews faced a business cycle much like the one known today, e.g. seven years of plenty followed by seven years of famine. The recognition of the 50 year Jubilee, in which debts were forgiven, testifies that money and credit were an integral aspect of these economic cycles, that cycles of varying length were recognized, and that the ability to obtain and repay debt played a crucial role in the economic process.

The ancient Romans also developed a rigorous system of laws to regulate commerce, including the permission for joint stock companies to engage in commerce and government contracting in the provinces. Julius Caesar's commentaries on the Gallic Wars demonstrate the importance of trade and trade routes as a basis for establishing relations in new lands. Money and interest were recognized both explicitly and implicitly by the Roman legal system. There was – even then – something *sub rosa* about the banking business: patricians on a level with those who served in the Roman Senate were not permitted to indulge in money lending. This prohibition has evidently been carried over into modern times. For example, banking was not considered an acceptable vocation for the British nobility during the reign of Victoria.

At the heart of Roman law in the field of commerce and business is the question of interest. Here the Romans were quite specific in their attitude and defined a usury limit as early as 357 B.C. in the Twelve Tables. The Twelve Tables stipulated the maximum permissible interest rate – 8 1/3 percent – as well as the penalty for usury: fourfold damages. By contrast, simple theft of goods could only be punished by double damages, a clear expression of Rome's aversion for what is now called "white collar" crime. Nevertheless, stiff penalties were not enough to stop creditors from taking the measure of the largely agrarian citizenry of Rome. Therefore, the usury limit was lowered in 347 B.C. to 4 1/6 percent; enslavement and imprisonment of a debtor by his creditor were forbidden in 326 B.C.[1] Roman merchants found the laws respecting commerce in the provinces far less onerous; provincial residents did not have the full rights of citizenship and, therefore, did not receive the full protection of Roman law. Thus, the economic advantages of conquest were clearly desired by the business class as well as noblemen, who participated as shareholders of trading companies.

II

While the economic cycle may be as old as man, reliable data on economic activity are not. As a result, economic theories on the business cycle are largely a development of modern times. Perhaps the first modern economist to explicitly recognize the periodicity of economic life – and develop a theory to explain it – was the Swiss historian J. C. L. Sismondi (1773-1842). Sismondi's great accomplishment was to postulate the causality in inter-temporal periods, i.e. that economic life in each time period is at once both the result of the past and the cause of the future.

A far more rigorous analysis of historical data on the economic cycle was put forth by W. S. Jevons. Jevons studied data on the price of wheat in England from 1731-1883 and compared wheat prices with the price of perpetual British bonds backed by gold, known as Consols. Jevons produced charts of these data, indicating periods of rising and falling prices. He assumed that the rise and fall of economic activity was the result of changes in the food supply, which he sought to explain via natural phenomena. His theory was that weather patterns were caused by sunspot activity, and he postulated a sunspot cycle of 10.45 years in average length. His son, H. S. Jevons, continued his father's work with research into a shorter cycle of 3½ years to better explain fluctuations in trade. The younger Jevons' findings were further refined by the American economist, Joseph Kitchin, whose 1923 analysis examined a cycle of 40 months. The Kitchin cycle continues to be a popular view of the business cycle.

The elder Jevons has been ridiculed by economists from his own time down to the present due to his attempt to link the economic cycle with natural phenomena. Throughout history, analysis of economic cycles has been conducted both on a scientific basis and on that of the occult. Numerous theories have been put forth regarding the correlation of economic cycles with sunspots, planetary activity, lunar cycles, and a host of astrological phenomena. Yet, while the causal aspects of the cycle have always been a subject of lively debate, the mere fact that the regularity of the cycle has been observed by so many diverse researchers seems to stand as testimony that the cycle is an ineluctable element of economic life.

A theory of economic cycles which has become popular in America in recent years is the "long wave" developed by the Russian economist, N. D. Kondratieff. Writing in 1925, before Stalinist repression had completely stifled academic freedom, Kondratieff acknowledged the accepted cycles of 7 and 11 years, which stem from the work of the elder Jevons, as well as the 3½ year cycle of H. S. Jevons. However, in Kondratieff's view, these were all merely components of a more encompassing cycle ranging from 48 to 60 years in length. Interest rates, wages and wholesale commodity price trends in England, France, and the United States were examined from 1780 to 1920, using modern statistical analysis to trace out alternate waves of rising and declining prices. It is noteworthy that Kondratieff's 1925 paper indicated that commodity prices had reached their last general peak in 1920, thus pointing toward declining prices in the future. We now know that the 1920's, like the 1980's, featured generally declining farm prices, which were the precursor of the general economic depression of the 1930's.[2]

III

With the variety of conflicting cycles discovered by the Jevonses, Sismondi, Kondratieff and others, it is highly instructive to review them in the light of economic history. As a beginning point, a brief summary of American history during the 100 years prior to the War Between the States indicates that the business cycle was a fact of economic life well before the age of big government. A good review of this time period can be found in the work of David Williams.[3] While Williams is no economist – he views economic cycles in conjunction with the planetary cycles of Jupiter and Saturn – one need not accept the causality of natural phenomena to appreciate how economic history appears to follow a natural rhythm.

America's existence as an economic entity pre-dates the Declaration of Independence by well over a century. However, the present review begins with the French and Indian War (1756-63). Business reached boom conditions in 1760, but then gave way to an intermittent decline extending through the Revolutionary War until finally hitting bottom in 1781. As often occurs, the final stages of the decline featured sharply lower commodity prices and a full-scale debt deflation. Farmers had borrowed heavily at high interest rates, and the newspapers of the day were full of notices announcing foreclosures and sale of real estate for a fraction of its former value. The first test of the new Republic came with Shay's Rebellion in 1786, the result of the widespread liquidation of Massachusetts' farms. The rebellion was put down, but the State of Massachusetts considered the continued threat sufficiently worrisome to declare a moratorium on foreclosures.

Throughout history, one often finds the economic cycle related to the political cycle of war and peace. While contemporary public opinion seems to oppose the use of military force for purely economic reasons—or so it would appear through the magnifying glass of network news broadcasts — this attitude is at variance with American history. The veterans of the American Revolution received large grants of land from the Continental Congress as rewards for helping to win American independence. In addition to these land grants within the area of the original thirteen colonies, the successful conclusion of the Revolution permitted settlement west of the Appalachian Mountains. This opened vast new lands for settlement, and may have been a contributing factor to the deflation which followed 1781.

Depressions were usually associated with a shortage of hard currency vs. a surplus of goods and idle productive assets. There was indeed a shortage of hard currency – gold and silver coin – in America in 1781, but there was no lack of paper currency. Due to the inflationary policy of the Continental Congress, it took nearly $20,000 in paper Continental dollars to buy one ounce of gold. There was simply no way the huge supply of paper currency could be redeemed at face value with the limited stock of gold on hand. Finally, in 1790, Congress redeemed the Continental currency at one penny of hard currency for each dollar of paper.

The vast tract of land which was to be acquired by America from Napoleon in 1803 – the Louisiana Purchase – itself presents a good study of how far paper currency prices can diverge from prices in hard currency. The land, which was almost entirely unsettled, was used as collateral by the Banque Generale of France in an eighteenth century scheme to develop a paper currency. Managed by an Englishman, John Law, the bank's scheme was to issue notes and receive deposits payable on demand, for the purpose of purchasing commercial paper. As was to be repeated many times in the settlement of the American frontier, money was lent on unprofitable projects while the collateral value of the land never rose fast enough to meet the public's wildly optimistic expectations. The Banque Generale ended in bankruptcy and took the savings of a great many Frenchmen down with it. This episode remains relevant for, with the exception of government insurance of deposits, it provides a close parallel to the experience of the thrift industry in the boom of the 1980's.

Long after Law's ill-fated experiment, the world economy had found itself in another financial panic in 1801. The Louisiana territory, despite the Banque Generale scam, remained a vast and unsettled wilderness. Commodity prices had fallen by 25 percent and Napoleon was in dire need of hard currency to prosecute his wars. Accordingly, he negotiated the sale of his American colonies to the United States for the paltry sum of $12 million in hard currency; the famous Louisiana Purchase was finalized in 1803. The Louisiana Purchase carries a lesson which appears to have been repeated in every major depression: the market value of fixed assets and real estate, when sold for cash under conditions of stress, is a small fraction of the price that can be obtained when credit is abundant.

Continuing forward in time, the next major financial panic in American history occurred in 1817. As in the 1780's, it was a reaction to the economic policy the country had pursued during wartime. Expenses for the War of 1812 and the large volume of government borrowing to finance the war led to the suspension of specie, i.e. redemption of currency in gold, payments in 1814. As often occurs in wartime, the supply of paper notes increased far above the government's actual physical gold supply. When specie payments were resumed in 1817, the money supply contracted, bank loans were sharply reduced, and commodity prices and economic activity dropped sharply.

By 1822, economic activity had recovered along with public sentiment in the "Era of Good Feeling." The economy then experienced normal cyclical expansions and contractions until another great land boom occurred in the mid-1830's. Large numbers of dispossessed Anglo-American debtors had made their way to Texas. Though slavery was prohibited by the legal government in Mexico, many brought slaves with them and agitated for legalization of the slave trade. Finally, they rebelled and were granted independence in 1836. The constitution of the new nation sanctioned slavery and put severe limits on the rights of creditors to seize property for non-payment of debts.

In the settled portion of America, economic conditions were equally euphoric. However, the boom of the 1830's ended with the Panic of 1837. The reckless expansion of credit had caused a major rise in the price of slaves, cotton, commodities, railroad shares, and real estate. As liquidity dried up, one-third of the banks in Ohio failed. Bank failures rose dramatically throughout the country and many state governments repudiated their debts. Railroad stocks and bonds fell sharply, and the assessed value of New York City real estate fell by 40 percent. The ensuing Debt Repudiation Depression was not reversed until 1845, and marks one of the severest depressions in American history.

In contrast once again to contemporary American attitudes toward the use of military force, the Mexican War provides an interesting example of war for the sake of conquest. The War occurred on the heels of a severe economic depression and can accurately be described as a land grab by America at the expense of Mexico. But this was not unique. Historically, the aggrandizement of the victor's land area and economic power have been the most common result of military hostilities. Coincidentally, economic depression has often been a harbinger of war as a depressed economy seeks to improve its position at the expense of its less powerful neighbors.

The successful conclusion of the Mexican War brought huge new territories into the United States, while the discovery of gold in California precipitated yet another land boom and an enormous expansion of money and credit as the newly discovered gold worked its way into the money supply. This culminated in the Panic of 1857, which was set off by the failure of the Ohio Life Insurance Company. Bank failures were widespread and Williams[4] reports that nearly 5000 businesses failed in 1857. Commodity prices, real estate prices, railroad stocks, and immigration all dropped sharply. Once again, hard economic times foreshadowed military conflict, which followed when the South seceded from the Union in 1861.

IV

The War Between the States was both an economic and political watershed for the United States. Politically, it established the principle that the federal government had powers well beyond those stipulated in the Constitution. As a result, the legal role that the federal government could play in the economy was to expand well beyond the role of regulating foreign trade and legal tender. The Union issued "greenback" paper dollars to finance its war effort and the dollar price of gold in New York more than doubled from 1861 to 1864. The sharp rise in the volume of greenbacks was made possible by passage of the National Banking Act, which established a system of national banks. The banks were authorized to purchase bonds issued by the Union government, and issued bank notes secured by these bonds. The greenback was a derivative currency: its value was derived from government bonds, which in turn were backed by an unsecured promise of the government. A promise backed by a promise.

Those who were enraptured by the economic possibilities of a re-unified Germany in the 1990's could find an interesting parallel in the American experience of the post-Civil War era. Due to the large volume of greenbacks which were printed to finance the war effort, a contraction of the money supply was required before the government would be in a position to resume specie payments. A partial redemption of the greenbacks caused an immediate business contraction, and in 1868 Congress again suspended the redemption of greenbacks. The battle lines were thus drawn between those who advocated sound money and those who would benefit from loose credit. In *Hepburn v. Griswold*, the Supreme Court ruled that it was unconstitutional for Congress to make greenbacks legal tender. The decision was reversed in 1871, but the government continued nevertheless to work toward resumption of specie payments. The banking Panic of 1873 was the inevitable result of this restrictive credit policy.

The United States continued to follow a policy of tight money until 1879, when the nation resumed full convertibility of its currency in gold. This was no small accomplishment. Over the twelve years from 1867 to 1879, there were five years in which the stock of money actually declined. Not until the Depression of the 1930's was this feat to be repeated. During the decade from 1869 to 1879, the population of the United States grew by slightly over 30 percent. Meanwhile, despite the severe Panic of 1873, real net national product grew at a 6.8 percent annual rate. In essence, the nation was trying to hold back the growth of its money supply while changes in population, productivity, and settlement of the West permitted output to come back into balance with the supply of dollars. Severe economic dislocations were the result: from 1869 to 1879, prices *fell* at an average rate of 3.8 percent per year.[5]

Consider the effect of these changes on a corporation which issued bonds at an interest rate of 8 percent (the going rate for railroad issues) in 1869.[6] The real interest rate, i.e. the stated rate plus the increase in the purchasing power of the dollar, would total nearly 12 percent per year. Viewed another way, the company would have paid $8,000 per year to finance an asset which cost $100,000 in 1869 but could be replaced by a new one costing $69,000 in 1879, at which time the entire $100,000 principal payment on the bonds was due. Only if the company had made highly productive use of that asset in the intervening time period would it be in a position to make payment on the bonds at maturity. On the other side of this transaction, huge profits were reaped by foreign investors, especially the British, who supplied much of the capital needed for America's westward expansion in the 1870's. The value of the dollar in British pounds grew by over 150 percent from 1864 to 1879, not counting the high interest return while investors awaited the repatriation of their funds.[7]

While the question of tight vs. loose money was debated in the 1870's, the question of which metal to use – gold or silver – also crept into the controversy. Virtually from its inception, the United States had been on a bimetallic standard, i.e. the dollar was legally defined in terms of the physical volume of gold or silver in which it could be redeemed.

However, this meant that the value of gold and silver were also defined in terms of one another, i.e. in ratio terms. The government was to find that maintaining this ratio was no more possible than it had been possible for King Canute to command the tides. Instead, the inevitable result of a bimetallic standard was Gresham's Law: the overvalued metal came into common use in trade while the undervalued metal disappeared.

As a result of an 1834 law which favored gold, silver coin was not often used in the United States until the 1870's, when large new deposits were found in the West. In a little noticed law, the so-called "Crime of 73," coinage of the silver dollar was eliminated. Since the market price of silver at the time exceeded its value for minting purposes, the law caused only a minor ripple when it was passed. However, as silver from the new mines found its way to market, the price of silver declined to a point where it would have been more profitable for producers to sell to the U.S. Mint than for commercial purposes. Naturally, this precipitated an outcry from the Western states for resumption of unlimited silver coinage at the rate stipulated by law of sixteen ounces of silver for each ounce of gold. The farmers and debtor classes who had been crushed under the burden of tight money and falling commodity prices were quick to comprehend the implications of the law and clamored for free coinage of silver – not on behalf of the mining interests but in the hope of a new era of easy money. They were not to be disappointed.

The question of currency appears to have been the major political issue during the last quarter of the nineteenth century. The Greenback party of the 1870's gave way to the Populist Party in the 1880's, whose platform was then largely pre-empted by the Democratic Party, culminating in William Jennings Bryan's campaigns in 1896 and 1900 against the "cross of gold." The Bland-Allison Act of 1878 authorized the Treasury to purchase $2 million to $4 million in silver per month. This amount was increased in 1891 by the Sherman Silver Purchase Act. To counteract these developments, the government took a variety of policy steps to inhibit the rise of silver in the Treasury's vaults, most notably through the issue of small denomination silver certificates. As often results from government policy, the effects were the opposite of those intended: the supply of money in circulation in the United States grew rapidly. From 1879 to 1897, the money stock grew 5.8 percent per year.[8] But output grew even more rapidly, with the result that prices actually declined by one percent per year over this time period.[9] Nevertheless, the fear in foreign countries that the silver interests in the United States would take the country down the road of inflation inhibited foreign investment. A law permitting free coinage of silver, passed in 1892, seems to have been the final straw. Sales of American securities by foreigners led to weakness in stock prices. By 1893 the stock market was collapsing and depositors rushed to withdraw their funds from banks. To meet the demand, the banks called their loans, which led to asset sales and deflation throughout the economy. The outflow of gold was finally brought to a halt by the government's promise to repeal the silver purchase provision of the Sherman Silver Act.[10] Thus, the politics of inflation were countered by the eventual loss of faith in the integrity of the currency, followed by bank runs, deflation and economic depression.

In the latter part of the nineteenth century, discoveries of substantial new deposits of gold in South Africa, Alaska, and elsewhere provided the monetary fuel for another great economic leap forward. The deflation which had occurred in America had lowered the price of our exports to a favorable level, and a large trade surplus was the result. From 1896 to 1900, large amounts of gold flowed into America. When the United States legally adopted the gold standard in 1900, the inflow of gold led, by definition, to a large rise in the domestic money supply. The nation fought a successful war against Spain in 1898-1899, acquired new territories, and the economy grew rapidly until the historically portentous Panic of 1907.

Early events of the Panic of 1907 resembled those of 1893. Gold flowed out of the country, banks were forced to limit redemptions by depositors, and a full-fledged financial panic was the result. Real output of the economy dropped 11 percent in one year.[11] The Knickerbocker Trust Company of New York lent its hand to several banks which were experiencing deposit outflows and soon found itself in trouble. Demands on New York Clearing House banks mounted and the U.S. Treasury came to their assistance with a large deposit. This was not sufficient to halt the panic. Money remained tight and stock prices continued to collapse. J. P. Morgan organized two large pools of money to assist troubled banks and restrictions were placed on depositors' ability to withdraw funds. The panic was eventually brought to a halt, but not before bankruptcy had become widespread throughout the nation. The experience led to a call for banking reform.

The Federal Reserve Act, passed in 1913, led to major changes in the banking system, but appears to have had little direct impact on the business cycle of the U.S. economy in its early years. Instead, the cataclysmic geo-political event of World War I, which the banking system accommodated by purchasing huge amounts of government bonds, was the primary economic force in the years 1914-1918. During the first part of the War, the United States remained neutral and was a major supplier of foodstuffs and armaments to the belligerent parties. The unprecedented scale of the conflict caused a dramatic increase in economic activity and the country was transformed from a debtor to a creditor by the large volume of orders placed by the Allies. The Federal Reserve System (the "Fed") watched passively as the money supply and prices exploded. From 1914 to 1920, the money stock grew by 13 percent per year, while wholesale prices climbed at an annual rate of 15 percent.[12] Of course, such explosive growth could not be sustained, and the Fed's policy switched abruptly to one of tight money, starting in 1919. This first major test of the Fed's ability to stabilize the currency played itself out in the severe economic contraction of 1920-21, and is worthy of study as an example of how the economy would respond to management by a central monetary authority.

The sharp economic contraction of 1920-21 demonstrates once again that the inevitable response to prosperity is a painful period of payback. Just as abruptly as economic conditions had boomed during the war effort, the economy was to crash when the circulation of credit was choked off. Benjamin Strong, a virtual founding father of the Fed, began to make the case for higher interest rates in the fall of 1919. The flagship of the Fed, the Federal Reserve Bank of New York, tightened in several steps by raising the discount rate, i.e. the rate charged member banks, from 4 percent in 1919 to 7 percent in 1920. This may not seem particularly penurious to those who have lived through the oil shocks of the seventies, but it was a level which was unprecedented at that time and was to stand as a record for the next half-century. Though the effects were not immediate, Federal Reserve credit outstanding declined sharply starting in the latter half of 1921. The economic contraction which followed was one of the sharpest on record. By June of 1921, wholesale prices were barely more than half the level of May, 1920. Real output had fallen by 18 percent.[13] Credit was simply unavailable and businesses filed for bankruptcy at a prodigious pace. The Fed had done its job with a vengeance. The economy could once again "return to normalcy." But the Fed's success in fixing the economy was even less permanent than that of the Treaty of Versailles, signed in 1919, which did not bring the peace it so earnestly sought, but rather – as Marshal Foch predicted – a twenty year armistice.

The recovery from the economy's trough in 1921 was to be abrupt and relatively long-lived. From the standpoint of the nineties, this period is especially important. The buoyant economy of the 1920's and the Great Depression which followed were to shape the thinking of an entire generation of economists. Therefore, the history of the Depression and the Keynesian economic system it spawned are worthy of closer examination. We shall return to this subject at length in the following chapter.

V

The ebb and flow of economic activity described above cries out for some explanation of underlying cause and effect. In ancient times, there was a pre-disposition to view economic events as being ordained by super-natural authority. Sacrifices were made to propitiate man to the good graces of the gods. Even in modern times, one finds the temporal relationship between the economy and natural phenomena in astronomy credible enough to seduce a scientist of the stature of Jevons. Indeed, economic history indicates a regularity in the economic cycle which has been noted by a great many scholars. Recently, Ravi Batra has summarized the pattern of depressions: a major depression occurs every third or sixth decade, and if one is avoided in the third decade, then the one which occurs in the sixth will be far worse, thus evidencing a cumulative effect.[14] And the papers of Kondratieff, who demonstrated the regularity with which the long wave repeats itself, have recently come into widespread circulation among commodity traders and economic parvenues. However, the methodology of these and most other researchers has been inductive rather than deductive. They do not propose a system which explains the economic process – whereby it would be possible to manage and, perhaps, to alter the cycle.

Prior to the Great Depression and the Keynesian system of government economic policy it spawned, a wide variety of economic systems had devolved. However, to get an idea of the range of thought involved, we need concern ourselves with only two of these, which represent the opposite poles of economic thought in the modern industrial age. At the left end of the scale is Marxism, while at the right end of the scale is classical economics. The scale has political as well as scientific implications. Indeed, one finds that, throughout history, a nation's political system is but a legal manifestation of its economy.

Most educated Americans have some passing familiarity with the works of Adam Smith, who was first to express a systematic explanation of the emerging industrial economy of the latter half of the eighteenth century. His work fit the Anglo-Saxon mindset of the young American republic as neatly as Christianity fit the declining military empire of Rome. Though it is the successor school of economists, the Neoclassicals, who expanded and fully articulated a more rigorous system of thought to explain the behavior of the free market, Adam Smith expressed the essence of the strict laissez-faire philosophy, which came to be known as classical liberalism. And classical liberalism most closely summarizes the American political consensus toward the economy in the period from the Declaration of Independence to the Great Depression.

The economics of Adam Smith, like those of Marx, had far more of the ring of religious dogma than the vapid incoherence with which so many economists of the present day are afflicted. In Smith's world, the meat we obtain from the butcher is not due to his benevolence but to his self-interest. Self-interest of consumers and producers alike became the "invisible hand" by which, in Smith's system, the optimal production and distribution of goods throughout the economy were guided. The best course of action for government was to leave the economy to its own good devices.

In the classical system, there were no barriers to full employment. Should there be a surplus of workers, wages will fall and employers will find productive use of everyone at the new wage rate. Is too little being invested to generate economic growth? Fear not, for interest rates will soon rise as the scarce supply of goods raises their prices and business profits. Production will soon begin to grow once more, until supply exceeds demand and prices fall once again. Everything was neat and orderly, as if ordained by God. Does it come as any surprise that Adam Smith was professor of moral philosophy at the University of Glasgow?

The role of government in the classical system was a limited one. Monetary policy, if it existed at all, was to be directed towards adding or withdrawing banking reserves so as to minimize the amount of fluctuation in wages and prices. Fiscal policy, i.e. conscious gearing of government spending to the economic cycle, played no role whatever. The role of government was to maintain free and open markets where self-interest could play its natural role.

The problem with classical economics is that it assumes that all men are created equal, not just spiritually, but in an economic sense as well. While one can forgive an eighteenth century Scotsman for making such an assumption, history demonstrates that, to paraphrase the pigs in *Animal Farm*, some men are more equal than others. This is certainly true as regards the propensity to save, invest, and accumulate wealth.

The Texas billionaire, H. L. Hunt, is supposed once to have said, that if all of his wealth were taken from him, he would have it back within a few years. After his death, two of his sons successfully demonstrated a type of converse corollary, i.e. that no matter how much wealth is conferred upon some people, it dissipates within a few years. In any event, it is evident that the ability to amass wealth is not evenly distributed in society as a whole, and that wealth is likely to become concentrated in the hands of the few while the great mass of society is toiling for a subsistence wage. Classical economics provided no adequate rationale or remedy for this, and so the door was open for the social engineers of the nineteenth century to propose a remedy.

A critique of classical economics and the entire capitalist system was provided by Karl Marx. For Marx, all value was created by labor. The diversion of any portion of this value as rent or interest of the capitalist class was theft. Equality was an objective rather than an assumption: "from each according to his ability to each according to his needs." In capitalism Marx saw a variety of economic cycles, all leading to the eventual breakdown of the system. He viewed the process of accumulation as central to the problem. Increases in productive capacity outpace the growth of demand and an economic crisis is required to destroy capital values, at which point the profitability of business re-emerges.

Marx was perhaps better as an economist than as a social theorist. From a theoretical standpoint, there is much to be admired in his understanding of the capitalist business cycle, and how it occurs. In fact, he went far beyond the classical economists, whose system never really adequately described the long and serious economic panics which have periodically occurred throughout history. However, Marx went too far. He saw the behavior of the capitalist class as leading to ever greater investments in new machinery and technology. One gains a temporary advantage over his competitor, who then ups the ante with investments of his own. A mad rush toward investment shoves industry toward ever greater production at ever lower costs and a falling profit rate. Eventually, there is no profit, only excess productive capacity and a massive "reserve army of the unemployed." According to the *Zusammenbruchstheorie* of Marx, it would all end in the eventual collapse of capitalist society.[15]

For many, the events leading up to the Great Depression of the 1930's seemed to be the fulfillment of the Marxist prediction. The economy had collapsed and there seemed to be no hope of its recovering. Classical liberalism was obviously flawed, and a new system was needed if capitalism was to survive. We turn now to a discussion of these events, which have done so much to shape the economic world in which we live. However, the reader may first wish to draw his own conclusions from the above review of economic history. It is obvious that the economic cycle of prosperity with booming employment and rising asset values has invariably been followed by periods of financial panic, falling prices, and widespread unemployment. What is more, the timing of the cycle occurs with a sufficient degree of regularity that numerous thinkers have employed diverse approaches to estimating the period with which the cycle repeats itself. A variety of explanations, both social and natural, have been proposed. However, one thing is clear: to rise above the economic cycle would be to rise above history.

CHAPTER 3

Of the Great Depression, FDR, and Keynes

Mark Twain once observed that, when he was eighteen, he considered his father among the most ignorant of men. However, by the time he was twenty-two, he was amazed at how much his father had learned in the past four years. In a somewhat related vein of thought, George Bernard Shaw once bemoaned the fact that youth was "wasted on the young." Each in his own fashion was acknowledging that each new generation is fairly bound to its own follies, regardless of the counsel of older and wiser heads. Each generation embarks upon a new and difficult world, but then sets out to repeat the mistakes of its forbears. Those who refuse to learn from history...

As concerns economic history, the reader has seen how the cycle of prosperity and depression has been repeated through the ages. Undoubtedly, this goes against the grain of a national consciousness which is generally unwilling to study the lessons of history. But it is impossible to understand the condition of the U.S. economy in the nineties without some reference to the events which gave birth to the managed economy of the post-World War II era. One must, therefore, approach the present only with a good understanding of the last great boom-bust cycle and the view of the economy it created. It is impossible in this short space to provide a thorough discussion of the traumatic events of the twenties and thirties, which were to shape the psyche of a generation. However, the objective is to sketch the similarity of the 1920's to the 1980's, and to recount how the Great Depression was to lead to the Keynesian rationale which was to justify 50 years of government activism.

From the experience of the 1920's, Senator Theodore Burton has noted the crisis-producing conditions, which apply equally well to the many economic booms we have noted in American history.[1]

- "An increase in prices of commodities and later of real estate.

- "Increased activity of established enterprises and the formation of many new ones, especially those which provide for increased production and improved methods, all requiring the change of circulating to fixed capital.

- "An active demand for loans at higher rates of interest.

- "The general employment of labor at increasing or well-sustained wages.

- "Increasing extravagance in private and public expenditure.

- "The development of a mania for speculation, attended by dishonest methods in business and the gullibility of investors.

- "A great expansion of discounts and loans and a resulting rise in the rate of interest; also a material increase in wages, attended by frequent strikes and by difficulty in obtaining a sufficient number of laborers to meet the demand."

The decade of the "roaring twenties" was to satisfy these conditions to perfection. We have already noted the sharp economic contraction of 1920-1921. Like the severe economic recession of 1981-1982, this contraction broke the back of inflation and was to set the stage for a protracted period during which financial assets would appreciate wildly. The price of commodities and productive assets, in contrast, was stable to declining in both the twenties and the eighties, while the federal government was to follow an economic policy of benign neglect. As Calvin Coolidge, a man of few words, was to accurately put it, "The business of America is business."

World War I had been promoted as the "war to end all wars," and the lemmings who shaped economic and foreign policy in the twenties were to behave as though they devoutly believed it. Disarmament was the unchallenged military policy of the victorious Allies – with the exception of Japan. However, the financial markets were to bolt forward in a campaign of their own. From 1921 to 1923, the money supply grew 5.4 percent per year. From 1923 to 1929, the growth rate receded to a rate of 4.0 percent per year. However, in the face of deflation – wholesale prices dropped 0.9 percent per year from 1923 to 1929 – the availability of money and credit can only be described as abundant. The monetary experience of the eighties was to be similar. From 1982 to 1989, the basic money supply (M-1) grew by 35 percent *more* than the consumer price index. Meanwhile, the inflation rate dropped from nearly nine percent in 1981 to an average rate of 3.5 percent per year from 1982 to 1989.

The parallel between the twenties and the eighties repeats in the area of fiscal policy and tax legislation. Coolidge's Secretary of the Treasury, Andrew Mellon – scion of a great banking fortune – implemented a policy of tax cuts for the upper income groups. Like the supply side economic policy of Ronald Reagan, this provided an enormous pool of funds that were to be invested in financial assets. Passive investments were the rage of the day. And the more money that flowed into the stock market, the higher share prices climbed. The higher they climbed, the more paper fortunes were created. As stories of the *nouveau riche* circulated, an ever greater number of small investors were drawn into the market. Caution and prudence were soon thrown to the wind. The heady passion for profit frothed everywhere. Pools of money were entrusted to professional "money managers."

Galbraith has noted how the advent of investment trusts satisfied the ever-rising demand by the public to participate in the investment mania of the 1920's. "The virtue of the investment trust was that it brought about an almost complete divorce of the volume of corporate securities outstanding from the volume of corporate assets in existence."[2] Like the mutual funds of the eighties, they sucked an ever greater amount of the public's capital into the stock market – and shares rose accordingly. During 1927, new trusts sold $400 million worth of securities. Two years later, during the peak year of the rally, three billion dollars of new capital flowed into the trusts.[3]

The tonic effect of an ever-growing pool of money on the stock market is evident from the rise in prices it induced. The Dow Jones industrial index rose at a compound annual rate of 19.9 percent from 1921 to 1929. From 1982 to 1989, the compound rate of return was 16.1 percent per year. The old trader's saw – "never confuse genius with a bull market" – was to be forgotten even by many whose experience extended back to the Panic of 1907. Meanwhile, a new generation of speculators was born, one whose entire investment experience was embraced by a bull market. Thus, in the mind of the vast part of the investment public, stocks could only rise; this had been the only experience they had known and, therefore, the only one possible.

Perhaps the first fly in the ointment of the bull market of the twenties was provided by that gentleman to whom we have dedicated a word of the investment lexicon – Charles Ponzi. Mr. Ponzi was but one of an entire school of enterprising financiers who were to bring the investment potential of Florida swamp land to the attention of an ever-rising number of gullible investors from the Northeast. As prices rose smartly, lots were sold in ever smaller size, and at ever greater distances from the oceanfront and existing population centers. In 1926 a hurricane caused 400 deaths, and it became apparent to all that man had not yet discovered paradise. Just as was to occur in the Texas oil bust of the eighties, prices came crashing down, and the Florida economy followed in lockstep. Galbraith records that bank clearings in Miami dropped from over $1 billion in 1925 to under $144 million in 1928. Whether they blamed Ponzi or their own greed, investors learned that their savings had been wiped out.

From a fundamental standpoint, perhaps the first frost on the blooming financial rose of the twenties, was provided by no less a personage than Winston Churchill. Sir Winston – soldier, historian, politico, and arguably the greatest statesman of the twentieth century – appears to have been something of a bungler in the area of finance, both personally and in public life. As First Lord of the Admiralty during World War I, he had masterminded the debacle known as the Dardanelles Offensive. In 1925 as Chancellor of the Exchequer, his reach was to once again exceed the grasp of Britain's declining empire when he reinstated the nation on the gold standard at the historical exchange rate of $4.86 per pound. As has frequently been the case throughout history, the return to specie payments was attempted at a rate which overvalued the vast supply of paper currency which had accumulated during the war. Gold flowed out of Britain and this imposed a crushing burden of deflation on a world-class economic power. For its part, the United States failed to monetize its inflow of gold at a high enough rate to keep commodity prices from falling. Thus, as money flowed out of Europe, it found its way to Wall Street and added fuel to the speculative fire that was burning on the New York Stock Exchange.

Gradually, the speculative excesses in America's financial markets would become a matter of concern to the Federal Reserve System. The history of money market conditions in 1929 shows the war that was waged by speculative greed on one side and the progressively tightening monetary noose on the other. The year began with broker call money – money which is lent to brokers who post securities as collateral – at six percent and the Federal Reserve discount rate at the already lofty level of five percent. In February, the Bank of England, as part of its continuing effort to stem the outflow of gold, raised its discount rate from 4.5 to 5.5 percent. The battle for international capital flows was joined and a diary of the year's events shows where it was to lead:[4]

- March - Call money hits 20 percent. Heavy gold flows into the U.S. Sugar prices hit the lowest point in 15 years.

- April - Sixteen percent call money. Heavy gold flows from Europe. W.C. Durant blasts the Federal Reserve for high interest rates. A large surplus of grain leads to a sharp break in prices.

- May - Violent break in wheat prices to below $1 for the first time in 14 years. Continued heavy flow of gold into the country, while call money eases to 7-10 percent range.

- June - Call money stable with gold flows continuing at a heavy rate. U.S. Treasury pays 5 1/8% for money – highest rate in 8 years.

- July - Violent rise in wheat and stock prices. Call money shoots up to 15%.

- August - Immense gold inflow. Call money drops to 9 percent. Sharp break in wheat prices. Gasoline price war. Record issuance of new securities. Federal Reserve raises discount rate to 6 percent.

- September - Stock market peak. Extremely heavy foreign selling. Bank of England raises discount rate from 5½ to 6½ percent. A sharp decrease in industrial production is reported.

The events of October, 1929 are imbedded in the national memory. The slide in share prices led to a sharp drop and ultimately to a full-scale avalanche. The authorities appealed for calm: President Hoover proclaimed that business was sound and his sentiments were to be echoed by John D. Rockefeller and by the foremost economist of the day, Irving Fisher. An effort to support the stock market was organized by National City Bank, Chase National Bank, Bankers Trust Company, and J. P. Morgan and Company. Meanwhile, a long list of stock speculators turned to their banks for assistance in meeting margin calls.

During November and December, money market rates fell back below 5 percent and gold began to flow out of the country. Calm eventually returned to the stock market and most major stocks managed to end the year well above their October lows. Despite the panic, however, the general public failed to understand the meaning of the warning shot which had been fired across the bow of the economy. The *New York Times* was to say in early 1930 that the big story of 1929 was Richard Byrd's trip to Antarctica.[5] However, industrial production continued its rapid decline without interruption. Humpty-Dumpty had fallen off the wall and no army was either ready or willing to put him back together.

II

The speculative excesses of the 1980's were no less spectacular than those of the 1920's. During the Reagan era, the craze for debt and financial speculation was to manifest itself in every major market. The degree to which the general investment climate of the eighties came to resemble that of the roaring twenties is truly remarkable.

Ronald Reagan took office as President in January, 1981 and immediately began implementing a policy of tax reductions and financial de-regulation. This immensely popular, even inspirational man should be given the credit he is due. He followed upon the heels of perhaps the most inept administration in memory. Jimmy Carter had led a retreat of America's interests around the globe, from Panama to Iran. The nation had been faced with military impotence and incompetence in the face of terrorism at the same time that inflation and interest rates soared to levels more typical of a banana republic than a great power.

America loves a winner and Mr. Reagan – distinguished alumnus of the fantasy world of Hollywood – knew how to play an audience. The Economic Recovery Tax Act of 1981 began a process of "supply-side" tax cuts. Supply-side economics, whose advocates included the likes of Arthur Laffer and Jude Wanniski, was to become the Doctor Feelgood prescription of the eighties, no less than was the Mellon tax policy in the twenties. Both were simply different verses of the traditional Republican song of "trickle down" economics. The trickle down theory holds that the more the tax rates of the rich are cut, the more they invest, the more jobs are created and – finally – greater tax revenues will flow into government coffers as the economic pie grows. This is a matter which is open to debate, especially as concerns the tax rates where one incurs increasing and, later, decreasing returns to federal revenues. Although the 1980's failed to provide a controlled environment to settle this issue, the rapid growth in national income was impressive indeed.

The 1981 tax cut was not aimed only at tax rates. It also provided a virtual smorgasbord of investment incentives, including individual retirement accounts, tax credits, and accelerated depreciation on capital assets. These lowered the effective tax rate, especially for higher

liquidate stocks, liquidate the farmers, liquidate real estate."[7] This concise explanation reveals more than the color of a banker's heart; it properly describes what is bound to happen when an economy which is flush with liquidity and financial leverage suddenly finds that its props have been removed. Debt can only be serviced by cash-flow, and if cash is tight, then assets must be sold at whatever price they command – often a far cry from what the owner paid.

In 1928, nearly $5 billion in mortgage loans were made on residential housing. Construction was begun on a total of 753,000 new homes. But a crack in the foundation of the real estate market was already present: 116,000 houses were taken into foreclosure. Incipient weakness in housing was to become a full-fledged disaster in the wake of the stock market crash and rising unemployment. By 1933, construction started on 93,000 new homes, while new mortgages fell to $1 billion. Mortgage lending had fallen by over 75 percent while housing construction was down by nearly 90 percent! But foreclosure auctioneers were hammering down the gavel at a record rate: over a quarter of a million homes were foreclosed in 1933. To put this into perspective, by 1950 housing starts had risen to nearly two million, new mortgage loans to over $16 billion, and foreclosures had dropped to slightly less than 22,000. Nor was the blight confined to residential housing. It would be thirty years before the market value of the Empire State Building, built in the mid-twenties, would equal the cost of building it. Small wonder that it was to remain the world's tallest building for decades. Mortgage lenders had learned a hard lesson, one which would take 50 years to forget!

The drop in real estate prices placed tight constraints on the spending of state and local governments, who depend to a greater degree than the federal government on real estate taxes for revenue. Bankruptcies of local governments were widespread during the thirties, the same pattern which seemed to be developing in the nineties. New York City unveiled plans to lay off 16,000 workers in its 1992 budget, while raising taxes on property, income, gasoline, autos, and general merchandise sales. New York State was in no better shape, as state officials pegged the 1992 deficit at $5 billion out of a total budget of $50 billion. Yet it remained a difficult task for a wastrel to mend his ways; despite declining revenues, both New York City and New York State planned to continue increasing their spending. Nor were these exceptions; hard-pressed governments in Philadelphia, California, Massachusetts and elsewhere sought to deal with declining tax revenues and their inability to borrow in a national credit crunch.

Another important aspect of the boom-bust cycle of the twenties and thirties was the concentration of wealth.[8] While the wealthiest one percent of the population controlled 31.6 percent of all wealth in 1922, their wealth had risen to 36.3 percent of the total by 1929. By 1933, the massive process of financial liquidation had reduced their share of the pie to 28.3 percent. Batra suggests the process by which the concentration of wealth helped cause the Great Depression. First, the demand for loans increases as the needs of poor and middle income groups increase. At the same time, the debtor class becomes less credit-worthy and the assets of the banking system more risky. Finally, as credit becomes less available, borrowers find it increasingly difficult to service existing indebtedness and loans end in default at an increasing rate. As banks fail, bank deposits and the money supply shrink, which leads to a further drop in production and investment. The greater the speculative excess present in the previous boom, the more painful will be the process of liquidation in the ensuing downturn.

The degree to which the process of financial liquidation occurred during the Great Depression is apparent from Federal Reserve data on the banking system. From April, 1929 to April, 1933 when bank runs were halted by government action, currency and demand deposits dropped by more than one-fourth, a decline which has never been matched, before or since.[9] The Federal Reserve seemed to be doing more to abet the panic than to stop it. In 1931, Britain departed from the gold standard. To reverse the outflow of gold from the U. S. which followed, the Federal Reserve voted to raise the discount rate from 1.5 percent to 2.5 percent. Nevertheless, the gold flow continued and rates were raised again. These actions were thought – by the greatest financial minds of America – to be necessary to preserve the soundness of the financial system.

The liquidation of the excesses of the twenties ended in the banking panic of 1933. Between December 31, 1932 and March 15, 1933, a total of 447 banks failed.[10] As panic became widespread, depositors lined up to withdraw their money and even healthy banks were threatened with failure. Immediate action was required and the new President, Franklin Roosevelt, proclaimed a nationwide bank holiday under the aegis of an obscure World War I law which was still on the books and conferred broad Presidential powers over the banking system. The Emergency Banking Act of 1933 set up a process by which the Comptroller of the Currency was empowered to take banks with impaired assets under conservatorship. As an alternative to outright liquidation, government conservators prepared plans for reorganizing troubled institutions. The Resolution Trust Corporation was to follow a similar strategy in managing failed financial institutions in the nineties. In 1933, the Reconstruction Finance Corporation (RFC) was established and authorized to purchase preferred stock of banks in need of reorganization. At the same time, the law authorized the Federal Reserve to issue bank notes for up to 90 percent of the value of financial paper acquired under the Emergency Banking Act. Over $200 million of such bank notes were issued.[11] The weakness of the banking system was also addressed by a second law, the Banking Act of 1933. This authorized the Federal Deposit Insurance Corporation, which began operations in 1934. Deposits were insured up to $5,000, and the vast majority of the nation's banks were enrolled in the program. Confidence in the banking system returned and the number of bank failures dropped sharply thereafter.

The government also took action to stem the outflow of gold. Under the Emergency Banking Act, President Roosevelt issued an executive order prohibiting gold payments in any transactions, private or official. On April 5, 1933, an executive order effectively required all owners of gold coin, bullion, or certificates to turn them in at Federal Reserve Banks. The holders were issued currency or bank deposits at the then official price of $20.67. This would prove to be a pre-meditated rip-off of the public by the Thomas Amendment to the Agricultural Adjustment Act, which passed on May 12, 1933. The Thomas Amendment authorized the President to reduce the gold content of the dollar by as much as half. This immediately became the conscious objective of U.S. monetary policy as the Reconstruction Finance Corporation undertook open market purchases of gold at steadily rising prices. This manipulated bull market in gold prices culminated in the Gold Reserve Act, passed January 30, 1934, which authorized a new fixed price for government transactions in gold at $35 per ounce. The price rise from $20.67 to $35 per ounce had effectively confiscated (through the invisible tax of inflation) 40 percent of the value of the nation's private gold hoard, which had been surrendered at the lower price.

Conversely, the rise in the price of gold created an immense paper profit for the government. Friedman and Schwartz have estimated that the Treasury received a $3 billion windfall.[12] However, this was not the intent of the Thomas Amendment nor that of the Gold Reserve Act. By setting the gold price at an artificially high level and prohibiting private ownership of gold, the U.S. effectively removed itself from the gold standard. As a result, the government had the power to increase the money supply, thus raising commodity prices and stimulating industrial output – which quickly occurred. The artificially high price of gold led to further increases in the amount of gold in government vaults; the supply of official gold reserves more than tripled from 1934 to 1940. In effect, the policy permitted the government to increase the amount of money in circulation as gold purchases were funded by paper dollars of the new fiat currency.

A similar policy of reflation was followed with respect to silver. The Silver Purchase Act of 1934 authorized the purchase of silver by the government at a price of $1.2929... per ounce, roughly five times the prevailing market price of silver during 1932. Production of silver rose accordingly and huge amounts were redeemed for paper currency, which found its way into a rapidly recovering economy. Industrial production rose by over 50 percent from 1934 to 1937, when a severe secondary depression set in. From the low point in April, 1933, to the onset of renewed monetary contraction in March, 1937, the basic money supply increased by over 60 percent. The government policy of monetizing gold and silver supplies was obviously effective in reversing the effects of the financial panic as the money stock climbed above 1929 levels, but it would not be until the onset of World War II that the government would fully utilize its new powers over the economy.

IV

The Depression led the federal government into a brave new world of economic policy. The Glass-Steagall Act regulated banking activities as never before, while the Securities Act of 1933 established the Securities and Exchange Commission to oversee capital markets. The National Labor Relations Act set up a board to mediate labor disputes and regulate union activities. The tentacles of government found their way increasingly into the private domain by sponsoring a variety of economic recovery programs. The Tennessee Valley Authority (1933) and the Rural Electrification Administration (1935) were involved in power generation, while the Home Owners Loan Corporation (1933) and Federal Farm Mortgage Corporation (1934) sought to support mortgage lending. Meanwhile, the Social Security Act and new provisions for employer-supported unemployment compensation created a social safety net to be funded largely by employers. New Deal legislation intruded upon previously sacrosanct rights to private ownership of property and the means of production. While the Supreme Court was to interpret the Constitution in a strange new light to support these laws, an economic rationale for the aggressive role government had elected to play was provided in the person of Britain's Lord John Maynard Keynes.

What can be said of Mr. Keynes that would properly demonstrate the perverse role of his thinking on the science of economics? If, in its purest form, economics can properly be described as the elevation of cynicism to science, then Keynes' role must stand as the consummate historical case of one-upmanship. He was able to mold an entire generation of cynics into his gullible disciples. The son of intellectual and social activist parents, Mr. Keynes burst upon the international scene with his 1919 treatise, *Economic Consequences of the Peace*. As representative of the British Treasury at the Versailles peace conference, he correctly foresaw that the punitive reparations imposed upon Germany would do more harm to the victors than to the vanquished. In fact, his expertise in the practical aspects of international economics extended well beyond the ivory towers of Cambridge. It is estimated that he accumulated a personal fortune of half a million pounds by speculating in foreign currencies, while the investments of King's College of Cambridge grew at a spectacular rate under his guidance.[13] This was peculiar behavior indeed for the so-called "dismal science" of economics.

The bias of Keynes is clear from his book, *The End of Laissez-Faire*, published in 1926.[14] In Keynes' view, classical economics paid insufficient attention to the ruthless process which brings the most rapacious profit-makers to the top of the economic ladder by bankrupting the more passive and less acquisitive classes. Nothing better described his sentiments, for which all his later works were nothing but a scientific rationale, than the following passage:

> "Yet the cure lies outside the operations of individuals; it may even be to the interest of individuals to aggravate the disease. I believe that the cure for these things is partly to be sought in the deliberate control of the currency and of credit by a central institution, and partly in the collection and dissemination on a great scale of data relating to the business situation...These measures would involve Society in exercising directive intelligence through some appropriate organ of action over many of the inner intricacies of private business, yet it would leave private initiative and enterprise unhindered...

> "Devotees of Capitalism are often unduly conservative,
> and reject reforms in its technique, which might really
> strengthen and preserve it, for fear that they may prove
> to be first steps away from Capitalism itself...For my
> part, I think that Capitalism, wisely managed, can
> probably be made more efficient for attaining eco-
> nomic ends than any alternative system yet in sight, but
> that in itself it is in many ways extremely objectionable.
> Our problem is to work out a social organization which
> shall be as efficient as possible without offending our
> notions of a satisfactory way of life."[15]

Keynes' masterpiece, *The General Theory of Employment, Interest, and Money*[16] was to provide a scientific description of how the economy operates. Two tenets were central. First, the national economy in aggregate tends to save and spend stable proportions of income. Second, the pool of investable capital could be divided into transaction, precautionary, and speculative balances. These are independent vari- ables and – if economic prospects were poor enough – there was no national tendency for the rate of interest to fall to a level which would bring about a sufficient rise in investment to resuscitate the economy. Thus, the so-called "liquidity trap" was a state of economic stagnation which could persist forever if the government took no action to stimulate economic activity. And, for Keynes, there was nothing particularly novel in his view of the world:

> "Ancient Egypt was doubly fortunate, and doubtless
> owed to this its fabled wealth, in that it possessed two
> activities, namely, pyramid-building as well as the search
> for the precious metals, the fruits of which, since they
> could not serve the needs of man by being consumed,
> did not stale with abundance. The Middle Ages built
> cathedrals and sang dirges. Two pyramids, two masses
> for the dead, are twice as good as one; but not so two
> railways from London to York."[17]

As a result of Keynes, the emphasis of government policy was to shift from monetary policy, i.e. regulating the amount of money and credit, to fiscal policy – government spending to stimulate economic activity. If the private sector failed to invest sufficiently to promote economic growth, then the government could, in effect, supplant the investment deficit by running a deficit of its own. Thus, private savings were to be appropriated by the government through bond sales, the proceeds of which would finance an increased level of spending and national output. The federal government was to play the role of economic watchdog: by increasing or decreasing government spending relative to tax revenues, the economy could be "managed," i.e. depressions could be averted and the speculative mania of an economic boom could be subdued.

The Keynesian system of economics owed more to its political appeal than to any special scientific ingenuity. In fact, a major ingredient of the success of Keynes was the simplicity of his system. Complex economic relations were reduced to a few simple aggregate equations. And the economic process was not described as a dynamic, evolving one but as a static set-piece engagement of vast armies of economic agents. Moreover, as an iconoclast, Keynes was to draw a broad array of avant-garde malcontents who were more than willing to swallow his dogma hook, line, and sinker. The Calvinist virtue of saving – which Adam Smith extolled – was considered a harmful impediment to full employment. An entire school of disaffected economic radicals — much like the "politically correct" Visigoths of the nineties — rallied to the cause of re-shaping the economy in their own image and likeness – rather than to the whim of a capitalist class solely in pursuit of maximizing the rate of profit.

V

The Keynesian orthodoxy was to be virtually inscribed in stone by the Employment Act of 1946. The essence of this law was to impel the government to take whatever action might be necessary to keep the economy on track toward the goal of full employment. Presumably, the newly discovered prescriptions of Keynes would be used to do so. Yet this was a very peculiar law indeed for a nation whose three highest ideals had always been life, liberty, and property. Nowhere in the Mayflower Compact did it specify that the Pilgrims would be guaranteed employment without regard to the profitability of their endeavors. Nowhere in the Declaration of Independence did it hold this "truth" to be self-evident: that every man has the right to gainful employment. Nowhere in the *Federalist Papers* did Madison and Hamilton assert the obligation or even the prerogative of the federal government to create public works. Nowhere in the Constitution of the United States does there appear an article to promote the general welfare via legislation to engage the services of the private economy. Nor does the Bill of Rights guarantee the right to perpetual employment regardless of productivity or competence. Should the present generation have the right to consume production of the future? Is the government bound to care for those who are too reckless to care for themselves? Prior to FDR – and Keynes – such questions were beyond the scope of mainstream politics.

In fact, the entire modern conception of democracy would have been anathema to America's founding fathers. As George Washington had written in the wake of Shay's Rebellion "Who besides a Tory could have foreseen, or a Briton predicted (these disorders)?...I am mortified beyond expression, when I view the clouds that have spread over the brightest morn that ever dawned in any country... What a triumph for the advocates of despotism, to find that we are incapable of governing ourselves, and that systems founded on the basis of equal liberty, are merely ideal and fallacious."[18] More succinctly stated by Jefferson, that government governed best which governed least.

The anarchy which would proceed from vesting too great a power in the interest of labor rather than the interest of property-owners had found a case in point in the French Revolution. But at no time in American history before the administration of Franklin D. Roosevelt was it commonly assumed that the beneficence of government was to be preferred to the self-interest of private citizens. This entirely new view of things emerged during the thirties and stands today as an outmoded and unwanted monument to the legacy of the Great Depression, the economic advocacy of John Maynard Keynes, and the political pragmatism of FDR. And once this Frankenstein escaped from the laboratory, it was impossible to get him back without a violent confrontation indeed. But this confrontation was put off to some distant time in the future, a time which would not be ripe for over fifty years.

CHAPTER 4

Capital Rules the World

Vince Lombardi once said – with reference to football – that winning was "the only thing." Similarly in business, capital is the only thing. The question of capital cuts to the quick. Capital is, always and everywhere, a necessary condition for economic progress. Without capital, America is – by definition – bankrupt. And so it is impossible to discuss the bankruptcy of America without a discussion of capital. But, one must first purge the mind of any concept of what is fair, equitable, or – in the context of the nineties – "politically correct." Capital has no ethics, no heart, no emotion, and no values save one: the rate of profit.

Capital appears to have played an important role in the well-being of society from the earliest of recorded history. For example, Julius Caesar related the following custom of the barbarian Gallic tribes:

> "The men, after making due reckoning, take from their own goods a sum of money equal to the dowry they have received from their wives and place it with their dowry. Of each such sum account is kept between them and the profits saved; whichever of the two survives receives the portion of both together with the profits of past years."[1]

Arguably, these uncivilized pagans had a better appreciation for capital than does our own society as America enters the twenty-first century. For example, note that the responsibility of marriage was not taken so lightly that either party would enter the contract before having some material wealth to sustain the union. Apparently, the barbarians understood the importance of saving, and did not confine the rewards of abstinence to financial matters alone. Elsewhere, Caesar instructs us that the Germanic tribes deemed it a disgraceful thing for the young to indulge in sexual intercourse before the age of twenty, and honored those who remained celibate beyond that age.[2] Abstinence, which later came to be viewed as an important aspect of capital formation, was clearly understood as a virtue by the barbarians.

It is also evident that the Gauls understood the role of profit as the reward of capital. Is it beyond reason to assert that they had some understanding of the power of compound interest? Perhaps it was only at an intuitive level that they expected the accumulated profits of a modest sum to grow large enough over the course of a generation to sustain the surviving member in old age.

It was to be a long time – about 1900 years – before the science of economics would provide an acceptable explanation of what the barbarian tribes seem to have implicitly understood. But, alas, it is the plight of economists – like theologians – to develop obtuse explanations of man's primordial instincts. Thus, the Austrian School of economics (known more precisely as the Marginalists), especially Eugen von Böhm-Bawerk (1851-1914), postulated that the product of a given quantity of labor increases with every increase in the amount of investment capital, though productivity increases at a declining rate.[3] Böhm-Bawerk extended his explanation of capital in terms of a "round-about production" process to include the dimension of time and, with refinements by others, this came to constitute the riposte of "bourgeois economics" to the Marxist assault on capitalism. Capital is the product of abstinence and, as congealed labor, can speed up the process of production. Like labor, land, and entrepreneurial talent, capital is, in its own right, a factor of production deserving of its own return – interest. So much for economic theory.

The high standing of capital in economic theory would be quite a shock to the Internal Revenue Service (IRS). According to IRS, "earned income does not include such items as interest, dividends..."[4] This official instance of discrimination against the owners of capital is not an isolated exception. A misunderstanding of the importance and role of capital extends to almost every level of American society. Worse, in many instances, government policy is directed toward the mis-allocation of capital, which must ultimately result in its destruction. And this is the most insidious form of discrimination possible, for capital is the source of all economic activity in our society. Without it, there can be no wages, no rent, no profit, and no advancement. This we shall see.

Capital is amorphous, fungible, and mobile, and it will always tend to seek the highest rate of profit, or – more precisely – interest. This natural tendency for capital to seek the highest return lies at the heart of America's capital deficiency in the nineties. The thirst of capital for interest will admit of some qualifications, but no exceptions. For example, illegal activities such as drug-running will not attract capital from most investors due to moral or legal restraints. However, at an aggregate level, this merely indicates that these activities are fraught with hidden costs or risks which must be compensated by a higher rate of interest. But if the return is great enough – and apparently it is – investment funds will be forthcoming from some source. The less stringent are the penalties that society places on the illegal activity, the lower the interest rate, an implicit recognition of the reduced level of risk.

At the opposite end of the spectrum one finds the recent trend toward "socially responsible investing." Here we have another qualification to the power that the rate of return holds over capital. But social consciousness is simply profit in a psychic form. The bleating fringe elements of society are not generally possessed of much in the way of financial resources – is it due to insufficient abstinence? – but those who are may be willing to sacrifice some or all of it to satisfy non-economic objectives. As Jeremy Bentham – the founder of the Utilitarian School of philosophy – would have explained it, charity is merely one means by which we satisfy our own self-interest. Have you a moral objection to investing in gold mining firms which operate under apartheid in South Africa? Then perhaps you would forego a 10 percent return and take an eight percent return on a comparable firm in North America. Then, if we ignore the possibility that the premium is the result of some other form of risk, we can infer that the South African company is paying a two percent premium for capital to compensate for the investment public's moral qualms. The point is that, once returns are adjusted for various forms of risk (which may include one's concept of morality or religious values), the objective of investing is to maximize the rate of return. Capital seeks interest; interest is the *sine qua non* of capital.

Modern society has often found itself in conflict with capital. Do we flatter ourselves that we can shape the world according to a whimsical view of progress and happiness? Capital will likely sneer at our values, and – in the end – will triumph. Perhaps nothing better illustrates the power of capital than the fact that so many tyrants throughout history have tried to abrogate its free movement:

> "As I listened to Gottfried Feder's first lecture about the breaking of 'interest slavery' I knew at once that this was a theoretical truth which would inevitably be of immense importance for the future of the German people. The sharp separation of stock exchange capital from the national economy offered the possibility

of opposing the internationalization of the German economy without at the same time menacing the foundations of an independent national self-maintenance by a struggle against all capital. The development of Germany was much too clear in my eyes for me not to know that the hardest battle would have to be fought, not against hostile nations, but against international capital."[5]

These are the words of the twentieth century's most egregious despot, Adolf Hitler. But draw up your own list of the ten most repressive regimes in the world today and ask yourself, do they have free capital markets? No. Capital – or those who own it – has its own objective – and it is not to suit the whim of a tyrannical government. And if the motives of the government should be inimical to personal freedom – as Hitler's clearly were – capital will very quickly seek a safe haven where its preservation can be more certain.

Thus is capital the master of the free world. To own it is to dictate what activities, what industries, and what countries will prosper. Is the government of Japan stable and the work force efficient while the government of Zimbabwe is unstable and the work force untrained? Then the profit rate in Zimbabwe must be high indeed if it is to attract international capital. Similarly, if the State of New York pursues a confiscatory tax policy and produces high school graduates who are illiterate, will it attract new capital from Texas where taxes are low and the work force efficient? Thus does capital impose its yoke of efficiency on the free world. And those who prove to be its most reliable servants will find that their services are well-bid, while those who prove unwilling to subjugate their needs to those of capital, will find that their opportunities are limited indeed.

If capital is indeed the master of the world economy, it must follow that those who have want of it are its servants. Worse off yet are those who have no capital but only debts. Consider the hierarchy: the capitalist can send his capital out wherever he deems its return greatest; the laborer can go where he believes his wages can be maximized; but the debtor owns not even his wages for he has mortgaged his future labor to the account of the capitalist. Does this differ from slavery? A slave is required to toil for the slaveowner at the slaveowner's direction. The slaveowner has purchased the future earnings of the enslaved. A debtor is required to toil for his creditor at the direction of the employer of the debtor's "choice." *Quelle différence!*

Finally, as concerns both capitalist and debtor, the power of compound interest is the most insidiously powerful force in our economy. As interest is reinvested at a rate of 10 percent per year – with no other additions to principal – it virtually doubles in seven years. On the other side of the transaction, if the debtor does not reduce his consumption enough to retire loan principal, he will find himself continually paying interest – but always in debt. But this is a lesson that one won't find in any school curriculum. Instead, Americans are bombarded by television commercials that profess the availability of credit and the distorted sense of status it imparts. Our mailboxes are filled with offers of personal loans and home equity credit lines. The cashless society uses plastic to pay for anything over $10 and the queue at the supermarket is delayed by the many who rarely carry even enough cash to pay their weekly grocery bills. And playing the float with one's checking account is the order of the day; society makes it far easier to spend and borrow than to save and invest. Consciously or otherwise, America has taken the decision that it prefers credit to cash, debt to equity, indentured servitude to financial independence.

II

America is confused. Everywhere the focus has been on income rather than on capital. When the business owner concerns himself more with his income than with his liquidity, net worth, and income-producing assets, he is placing his faith on a tenuous lifeline in preference to capital, which is the long-term measure of his well-being. The tendency is to take on an ever-increasing burden of debt under the assumption that income will grow fast enough to continue to service it. But, eventually, if debt is substituted for equity capital, a point is reached when even a brief interruption in income will result in default. And – if income does not soon resume or if it declines – the debtor finds himself in bankruptcy.

The problem of debt vs. equity can be better understood if we consider an example of a single firm, Hills Department Stores. Hills, like so many American retailers, has demonstrated what happens to debtors when the economy fails to meet their expectations; the company found itself in financial jeopardy even though its sales were steadily increasing. Hills was taken private during the leveraged buy-out (LBO) boom of the eighties. In a transaction of this type, a small group of investors obtains bank financing to acquire a controlling interest in the firm. After obtaining ownership, the company pledges its assets to borrow enough money (either via the bond market or from banks) to allow the new owners enough cash to repay their personal debts. Now what has occurred? A previously healthy company remains unchanged to the public eye, but a large amount of the corporation's equity has been replaced by debt. Where formerly the corporation had no obligation to make fixed payments to its shareholders, it now has a contractual obligation to make payments to its creditors. But the company's owners won't spend much time fretting over this. Generally, their objective is to take the company public or sell its most marketable assets, thus realizing a quick gain. They are then off the hook, but the company and its employees are not.

In the case of Hills, like so many of the LBO's of the eighties, the corporation's post-buyout balance sheet was so heavily laden with debt that a steady and rapid rise in revenues was needed to meet the newly incurred debt service obligations. The company was thus left struggling under a burden of $640 million in debt – which comes to nearly $3 million for each of Hills' retail outlets. By January, 1991 – six years after the firm was taken private – the company was beginning to miss interest payments. The liquidity squeeze came despite the fact that the company had recorded a sales gain in 1990 of 2.2 percent over the prior year! And how did the company propose to solve its problems? First, by increasing its credit lines with its banks – which presumably would result in increased interest costs. Second, by closing over 10 percent of its stores – which presumably would result in a reduction in the company's ability to capitalize on an improving economy.

Now let us consider what would have happened if Hills had never acquired this burden of $640 million of debt. First, there would be no interest payments. The $640 million would simply be the shareholders' equity in the corporation. After paying its salaries and suppliers, the company would be profitable. However, the return to shareholders might be too low for the company to attract new equity capital, and the company could have well decided to close some of its less profitable stores. But these decisions would be internally driven – not imposed by external forces – and the company would remain viable until improvements in profitability allowed it to capitalize on new opportunities. Instead, the company was faced with the prospect of bankruptcy and its creditors would then coerce liquidation of the company's assets – perhaps for a mere fraction of the amounts they were owed.

Hills was not a unique case. Moody's Investor Services, Inc., a bond-rating agency, noted that seven retailers defaulted on a total of $3.1 billion in 1990. And these were generally names which had viable operations and were held in good repute by the public. But in each case, cash flow failed to grow fast enough to meet the owners' projections. So this, then, is the heart of the debt vs. equity question, whether it be at the level of the consumer, business, or government: *the decision to take on new debt is driven by an optimistic view of one's future prospects.* The debt can only be serviced and repaid if the amount borrowed is invested at a greater rate of return than the interest rate paid, and this requires an optimistic – and often unrealistic – view of the future.

The alternative to debt, equity capital, is far more conservative. It requires the business manager to wait patiently while earnings accumulate from existing operations. Only after the cash is in the till can funds be committed to new projects. Or, if a company's prospects are bright enough, it may be able to sell additional shares by convincing investors that it is capable of providing them an acceptable return on the capital they commit. Frequently, the decision to take on debt is the result of a process in which the borrower is unable to convince the hard-headed owners of equity capital that his prospects are as bright as he believes. Failing to take the best advice the market has to offer him, he plunges forward by financing his spending via debt and commences a process of gradual financial strangulation.

A look at selected aggregate data on the U.S. economy provides an insight of how far America's starry-eyed view of the future has progressed. Back in 1965 – before a lost war was to wreak its terrible consequences on the national will – the total debt in the U.S. economy was less than 1.30 times gross national product. In terms of the money available to service this debt, M-3 (the broadest measure of the domestic money supply) was over 45 percent of total debt. These relationships have an intuitive appeal as measures of our profligacy. On the one hand, debt/GNP measures our capacity to produce goods (GNP) and repay our debts. More immediately, the money supply, M-3, measures how liquid the economy is and, therefore, how much trouble we encounter finding the cash to make regular payment on our debts.

After 1965, both the debt ratio and the liquidity ratio showed a steady deterioration. By 1990, the debt/GNP ratio had risen to 2.35, an increase of over 80 percent! Meanwhile, the liquidity ratio, M-3/debt had fallen below 32 percent. Thus, in general, America had taken on far more debt in relation to its ability to repay and was less liquid in terms of the funds available to make scheduled debt service payments.

Aggregate data on the economy like those above ignore important qualitative aspects of the changes in debt, which would seem to indicate that the increased burden has been concentrated in specific sectors of the economy. For example, the federal government has demonstrated a disturbing inability to live within its means. The government's total debt of over $3 trillion in 1990 was 2.9 times its annual receipts. And the size of the federal debt has consistently grown at a greater rate than GNP, which means that it is outpacing the economy's capacity to generate tax revenues.

Ominously, as America entered the nineties the federal interest burden was approaching $200 billion per year, and this would have dire consequences for the government's ability to stimulate economic activity. Over 85 percent of the present federal debt remains in the hands of Americans, which means that the government is simply transferring cash from the broad mass of taxpayers to the narrow class of government bondholders. From an economic policy standpoint, a deficit of $200 billion is simply the amount of transfer payment necessary to make coupon payments to government bond holders – who are unlikely to spend much of this income. Moreover, the inability of a government to finance its programs from equity capital, i.e. increased taxation, is indicative of a lack of public support for that government's policies. It is a road that took the *ancien régime* of France as well as Czar Nicholas of Russia to a bloody destination. The bill must eventually be paid. Will the taxpayers be willing, or will they repudiate?

If the United States of America intends to honor its debts, it might start by adopting a simple policy of honesty. Instead, the federal government has inured the American public to a continual policy of "see no evil, hear no evil, speak no evil" with regard to its inability to balance its books. In January, 1980, the government released a fiscal 1981 budget predicting a *surplus* of $24.5 billion in fiscal 1983. The actual figure? A deficit of $195.4 billion. The pattern of overestimating revenues and/or underestimating spending continued for so long that, in 1986, it was thought necessary to pass a law – Gramm-Rudman – which would require a balanced budget by fiscal 1991. Law or no, by January 1991 the Congressional Budget Office was predicting that the red ink would exceed $300 billion for that fiscal year. To accomplish even this monumental failure required President Bush to eat his famous words from the 1988 campaign: "Read my lips, no new taxes." Incidentally, the Bush pledge was not to be the only thing eaten in the historic budget compromise: budget summit negotiators, in typical profligacy, consumed some $60,000 in food and drink during the 10 days they were holed up at Andrews Air Force Base.

Of course, the framers of Gramm-Rudman were far-sighted enough to provide for exceptions in the case of war or recession. As it turned out, 1991 was to see both. Just like the deadbeats of the private economy, the federal government is always able to cite good excuses for failing to meet its obligations. But in the world of finance and credit, there are *no* good excuses. A good credit is someone who foresees all possible setbacks and husbands an adequate cash reserve to meet them. Instead we have a government – which, after all, represents our society – that has neither the foresight to accurately forecast, nor the discipline to cut expenses. The road we tread is parlous indeed.

The hedonist ethic of "spend now, pay later" shows up in the behavior of consumers as well. From 1953 to 1983, American households generally saved between six percent and eight percent of their disposable personal income. However, a steady decline began in the mid-seventies, and by 1987 the savings rate had dropped below three percent, barely enough to cover interest on credit cards and installment loans. By 1990, the saving rate was creeping back toward normal levels, though still below five percent. It appears that first, inflation, and later the decline in home prices have been important factors. *The New York Times* reported that, by 1983, 22 percent of homeowners had over $75,000 equity in their homes, while in 1970 the figure was a mere 10 percent. In addition, the huge increases in stock prices and other financial assets prior to 1987 were probably also looked upon as a substitute for the pain of saving via reduction of current consumption. Thus, it was possible to rationalize that we were "saving" by the appreciation in our assets. In the late seventies and early eighties, appreciation in house prices and the "good deals" some had gotten on "low" fixed rate mortgages of 9-11 percent were common topics of discussion at cocktail parties. The nerd who consistently saved 10-20 percent of his income and paid cash for his house would receive precious little shrift in the age of trophy cars, trophy wives and trophy homes.

III

If America's consumers became inebriated by their steadily improving lifestyle during the eighties, they could not hold a candle to the "rocket scientists" of Wall Street who were to invent ever more creative means for the business of America to indulge itself in an ever more deadly game of financial self-delusion. The menu included such morsels of financial esoterica as original issue discount (OID) bonds, equity and debt with payment-in-kind (PIK) provisions, junk corporates, junk municipals, and zero coupon bonds; bonds based on automobile and credit card receivables, as well as boat loans; and a mind-numbing array of derivative mortgage securities to include stripped coupon securities, accrual bonds (Z-tranches), "Jump-Z" tranches, and – only in America – "stick Jump-Z" tranches. But underneath it all was always the same thing – someone who needed money for a project or purpose which, without the financial legerdemain, would find the funds only at a higher price, if at all.

The amount of paper pumped out by Wall Street was enormous. The dollar volume of all publicly registered securities issued in 1988 was over $400 billion, more than five times the 1980 level. And until then it seemed as if Wall Street was operating under some modern version of the maxim of the nineteenth century French economist, Jean-Baptiste Say, i.e. that the supply of a product tends to create its own demand. And, as the inevitable by-product of increased volume, a host of unsavory operators were to victimize the public in a wide variety of scams and misleading practices. Nor were the practices restricted to "bucket shops" and "boiler rooms." Some of the most respected names on Wall Street have been assessed fines by the self-regulating arm of the National Association of Securities Dealers.

When Wall Street's party came to an end after 1988, America was left with an embarrassing residue from the days of hot check capitalism. Moody's downgraded a record $345 billion of U.S. corporate debt in 1990. The number of companies downgraded exceeded the number upgraded by a ratio of 4.4 to 1, and for financial institutions the ratio exceeded eight to one. The weakness of financial institutions was partly due to the so-called highly leveraged transactions (HLT) for which they provided financing. Large banks were left with $50 billion of such HLT loans on their books at the end of 1990, and some found that the only prospect for disposing of them was to pool their loans and sell them at a discount (read "loss") in the form of securities.

At the same time many of the nation's best banking names were to be snake-bitten by HLT's, some of the biggest insurance companies were to be wounded by their investments in junk bonds. One of those was USF&G. One insurance analyst expected a writedown (reduction in book value for accounting purposes) of as much as $300 million on this one portfolio alone. And this kind of money could no longer be easily replaced; by cutting 900 jobs and other expenses the company hoped to reduce its annual expenses by just $42 million.

As it liquidates the offenders, society often finds that it must pay a high price for misdeeds of the past. LTV Corporation, which filed for protection under Chapter 11 of the U.S. Bankruptcy Code in 1986, was still undergoing reorganization five years later. And running a bankrupt company has its compensations: David Hoag was named chairman in February, 1991 at an annual base salary of $550,000 with a performance-based bonus that could double his pay. Meanwhile, his predecessor, who had presided over the firm at the time it filed for Chapter 11 protection, was granted a consulting contract of $375,000 per year plus $82,500 a year towards his insurance policy.

But if there is money to be made – at the expense of bondholders – in presiding over a bankrupt institution, it pales against the income of the clever arbitrageur in trading junk bonds. One such lucky trader was Lawrence Hillebrand, who was paid $23 million by Salomon Brothers in 1990 for his ability to find profits in price discrepancies between various issues in the bond market. If this seems like a lot of money, at least it was earned honestly by his ability to develop complicated mathematical relationships from historical data. Compare this to the $550 million compensation paid Drexel Burnham Lambert's junk bond king, Michael Milken, in 1987. But this is getting ahead of our story.

IV

Those who are uninitiated in the arcane methods of Wall Street are frequently inclined to think that it takes great genius to amass great wealth in the hallowed corridors of American capitalism. Wall Street's greatest investment houses themselves perpetuate this myth by employing "economists" to issue frequent forecasts on the economy, interest rates, and stock prices. "Where we stand...we're bullish on America." The Street's advertising cleverly implies that, like the investor, the great trading houses are taking positions to profit from an ever-rising market. Bunk!

The securities business is no different from any other retailing business. It has customers (the public), a product (stocks, bonds, and other financial instruments), and a source of supply (public exchanges and dealer-to-dealer markets). To make a profit in this business, it is necessary to do two things: 1) buy low; and 2) sell high. Better still is not to buy at all but merely tack on a commission for facilitating a transaction through a floor broker on a major exchange.

If an investment house does take ownership of securities which are not available on a public exchange, it makes its profits by "making markets." Making markets in a security means bidding for a security at one price and offering for resale at a higher price. The bid-offer spread is the firm's mark-up, its profit. The firm employs traders to decide where to set bid and offer prices in relation to market conditions and to keep the size of the firm's "position" in the security at manageable levels. Meanwhile, a vast array of salesmen hit the phones and try to find buyers and sellers. They are paid a percentage of the firm's mark-up, in roughly the same fashion as the encyclopedia and vacuum cleaner salesmen who peddle their wares door-to-door. And whether the market for a security subsequently goes up or down is not their problem.

In the environment of Wall Street, economists exist for the sole purpose of adding to their employers' sales and profits. A good economist is one who – whether for the right reasons or the wrong ones – is able to induce investors to buy or sell – and on a fairly frequent basis. In practice, this means that most Wall Street economists nearly always recommend an almost fully-invested position. If they are truly "bearish," i.e. they expect prices to fall, they recommend that investors consider "defensive" issues such as utility stocks or government bonds. Why? Perhaps because these sales generate commissions. Cash in the bank does not.

Another great profit center for Wall Street is "underwriting," which means sponsoring a firm's issuance of securities under the procedures established by the Securities and Exchange Commission. Investment bankers shepherd new issues of stocks and bonds through a "registration" process by which the issuer reports its financial condition, operations, and use of security proceeds to the Commission. Large casts of securities lawyers are assembled to write, review, and render opinions on mountains of documents which stipulate how the security is to operate and the relations between and among the issuer, the investment banker, and banks which may serve as custodians, trustees, transfer agents, or paying agents. A great deal of money is made by all, especially the investment banker, when the security finally goes public, i.e. is ready for sale to the public.

The more money in the banking system, the higher the prices of financial assets and, accordingly, the greater the volume of new issues going public. We have already seen how the great money-printing binge of the eighties led to boom conditions, with the volume of new securities reaching its peak in the late eighties. However, from 1987 onward, the Federal Reserve failed to provide enough liquidity to keep the Wall Street gravy train rolling along. For example, the basic money supply, M-1, grew at an annual rate of barely more than three percent over the four years starting in January, 1987. This is in contrast to money growth at double digit rates during the mid-eighties. By 1989, Wall Street was to learn it had had its oxygen supply cut off, as volume and profits dropped sharply.

The reduced demand on the part of the public for financial instruments at the end of the eighties translated into a reduced demand by security dealers for employees. The Securities Industry Association reports that the number of employees at New York Stock Exchange (NYSE) member firms declined from over 250,000 in 1987 to 200,000 by 1990. And the hemorrhage was still continuing! One firm estimated that an additional 60,000 would eventually receive their pink slips. Additional cost-cutting steps were also taken through the closing of branch offices, distribution centers and the curtailment of employee bonuses. However, revenues were shrinking even faster than expenses. Underwriting fees, for example, dropped from nearly $5 billion in 1986 to less than $2 billion in 1990. The number of member firms in the National Association of Securities Dealers dropped from 6500 in 1987 to 5500 in 1990. Meanwhile, profit margins of NYSE member firms as a group fell from over 10 percent in 1986 to negative rates in 1990.

And so the cuts on Wall Street would continue until investors increased the volume of securities they purchased. Merrill Lynch and Co. and Goldman-Sachs and Co. both planned to continue cutting payrolls in 1991. In Goldman's case, this was a good indication of the sharp drop in investment banking fees, as the firm had been a star performer in the weak market of 1990. But the depression mentality was finally setting in. A senior executive of the firm indicated the firm would be run on "the assumption of adverse conditions, even though we are doing well...surprises will be on the upside, not the downside." As to Merrill Lynch, one analyst estimated that, even when planned cuts were complete, the firm would only be earning slightly over five percent on stockholders' equity. This was well below the firm's objective of a 15 percent profit on their equity capital.

So we see that the lever which capital provides the economy as a whole is no less important in governing the role of Wall Street itself. In the American economy the role of capital is, in fact, central to every business activity. Do you enjoy the comedy of Bill Cosby? Only because of the profits he provides his producers. Do you enjoy professional football? Only because it is profitable. Do you enjoy your work? Only because it is profitable for your employer. Thus is capital – and the rate of profit – the impetus to all activity and – ultimately – all advancement in the private economy.

V

If capital is the lifeblood of the economy, government borrowing is its leech. As the federal government runs ever larger deficits, it takes an ever greater share of the limited capital available for industry. Worse yet, it forces those businesses which are viable to pay an ever higher premium vs. the *trillions* of dollars of investments which carry the full or implied guarantee of "risk-free" government debt. If the 1980's is to stand for any great achievements in the evolution of capitalism, it will probably not be for the creation of ways for America's capital to develop new and creative technologies. Instead, the decade is likely to stand as the final step in a sixty year process of destroying the economic hegemony of private American capital.

The degree to which government was pre-empting private capital formation as the nineties began is apparent from a "quick and dirty" analysis of the distribution of debt outstanding. As of June, 1990 a total of $12.8 trillion in credit market debt was outstanding. Of this amount, federal government, federal agencies, and state and local governments accounted for over $4.5 trillion. However, mortgage pools or trusts having the full or implied guarantee of the U.S.A. accounted for an additional trillion dollars. Thus, government was on the hook for over $5.5 trillion and this constituted over 43 percent of all debt outstanding. And the trend was worsening: from 1985 to 1990 federal government debt grew at an annual rate of 10.75 percent, while total debt grew at an annual rate of 9.2 percent.

As America increasingly substitutes debt for equity financing, it is becoming increasingly difficult to foot the bill. For example, if one assumes an average annual interest rate of 10 percent, the $12.8 trillion of debt outstanding requires nearly $1.3 trillion per year to carry the debt. This amounts to nearly 30 percent of total national income in 1990. Purists will say that this figure includes double-counting, i.e. most households both pay and receive interest. Nevertheless, Commerce

Department data indicate that the share of *net* interest income in GNP grew by nearly 18 percent from 1987 to the first half of 1990, which indicates that a rising percentage of GNP merely represents the re-cycling of interest on debts.

Is American society immune to the laws of economics? If debt is allowed to continually outpace income growth and if we allow our liquid assets to continually dwindle, can the day of reckoning be far in the future? Is our society as a whole any different from the wishful thinkers who generated the LBO boom of the eighties? Isn't America just a jumbo size version of Hills Department stores? Our interest burden mounts continually and we must work ever harder to fight the wolf at the door. As the standard of living from current income continually falls short of our expectations, we increasingly find ourselves, hat in hand, at our banker's doorstep. And as the banker, ever more grudgingly, accedes to our request for a cash infusion, we find it ever more difficult to repay him. And, as we do, we progressively lose our ability to make it through the tough times. Increasingly, the tendency is to mail the banker the keys to the house. He owns it, but nobody can afford to buy it at his price. And so we go homeless while our house stands vacant. "Loan oft loses both itself and friend."

CHAPTER 5

America's Socialized Banking System

During Paul Volcker's tenure as Chairman of the Federal Reserve, one of the major weekly news magazines featured him in a cover story as the "Second Most Powerful Man in America." The article was remarkable for, among other things, it vastly overestimated the power and influence of the President, who was presumably the one to whom the Fed Chairman played second fiddle. The President's powers are derived from the electorate and subject to political consensus: if he is elected and if he has the support of the Congress and if his policies are popular, then he can serve as a catalyst for change. The Chairman of the Federal Reserve, on the other hand, has no constituency to serve. His actions are largely taken in secret. But with the other members of the Federal Open Market Committee and the Board of Governors, he can directly influence the lives, not only of Americans, but of virtually everyone in the industrialized nations of the world. The Chairman of the Federal Reserve Board is the banker of the United States of America.

How our arcane central bank came into existence is itself a story fraught with intrigue. We have already noted the severe financial panic of 1907 and the cries it evoked for banking reform. Congress responded and President Theodore Roosevelt executed a 1908 bill which authorized a National Monetary Commission under the chairmanship of Senator Nelson Aldrich. Hence, with blinds drawn, a sealed railway car carrying Senator Aldrich and his commission departed Hoboken, New Jersey around Thanksgiving in 1910 for a "duck hunting" trip to Jekyll Island off the coast of Georgia.[1]

The outing to Jekyll Island had far more important issues than duck hunting on the agenda. As *The New York Times* later noted, "one-sixth of the total wealth of the world was represented by the members of the Jekyll Island Club."[2] Besides Aldrich and his secretary, the group included Henry P. Davison (a partner of J. P. Morgan), Paul Warburg (a partner of the powerful investment bank of Kuhn, Loeb, and Company), Frank Vanderlip (president of the National City Bank of New York), Charles Norton (president of the First National Bank of New York), and A. Piatt Andrew (Assistant Secretary of the Treasury). What this small group did was to draft "The Aldrich Plan," which would constitute the basis for The Federal Reserve Act of 1913.

That the interlocutors of Jekyll Island found it necessary to shroud themselves in secrecy is consistent with America's populist monetary history. The establishment of a "central bank" had been – for good reason – opposed by American lawmakers from the earliest days of the Republic. The battles fought by Thomas Jefferson and, later, Andrew Jackson against early versions of a central bank illustrate the struggle between a largely agrarian country and the feared "money trusts," which might be subject to the influence of their counterparts in Europe. Thus, for the first one hundred thirty-seven years of its existence, the United States government operated an independent Treasury, which successfully maintained the autonomy of the government's financial transactions. The National Banking Act, rammed through during the truancy of the South at the time of the War Between the States, had established a national banking system to assist the federal treasury in financing the Union war effort, but stopped short of establishing a central mechanism for controlling the nation's money supply.

The Federal Reserve Act was designed to provide the banking system with the additional powers needed to control monetary policy, while remaining independent of the federal government. To preserve the myth that America had no central bank, the country would be divided into districts, each of which was to have its own Federal Reserve Bank. All national banks were automatically incorporated into the system and became stockholders in their respective district banks in proportion to their share of deposits outstanding.

The division of the nation into Federal Reserve districts satisfied Congressional opponents of a central bank. In theory, each district bank would have control over the discounting of loans and the trading of government securities from banks within its district. In practice, however, New York was the center of the nation's financial markets and foreign trade, and the New York Fed quickly gained primacy over the other banks and, under Benjamin Strong, was successful in dominating open market policy in the early years of the system. Indeed, a case may be made that Mr. Strong's untimely death in 1928 helped precipitate the Great Depression, for his passing led to a vacuum of both power and expertise as the economy slipped irretrievably into the vortex of economic decline.

II

As the experience of the Great Depression would prove, the power to control the Federal Reserve's open market policy is virtually the power to control monetary policy itself. In more recent years, the Federal Open Market Committee, which consists of the Fed's Board of Governors and selected Fed district bank presidents (on a rotating basis) has met twice each calendar quarter to consider the condition of the economy and a suitable posture in the Fed's money market and foreign exchange operations. In effect, the decisions taken by the Federal Open Market Committee have determined whether reserves of the banking system should be made more or less abundant by the Fed's money market desk. In turn, the availability of reserves has influenced the federal funds rate – a key interest rate to which all other money market interest rates are closely related.

The proceedings of the Federal Open Market Committee have not been made immediately available to the public, and this policy of suppressing information has been upheld by the Supreme Court. However, six weeks after each meeting – by which time the Committee is due to meet again – a summary of the previous meeting is released to the press. The System has thereby managed to conduct its operations under a veil of secrecy. Nor is the decision-making process much less enigmatic to some of the Fed's own governors. One mystified participant was Fed Governor Martha Seger, who was continually at odds with her peers during her tenure in her efforts to loosen the monetary reins. Before resigning from her position on the Board in 1991, she related to the *American Banker* that she received agendae no more than 48 hours before scheduled meetings. Nevertheless, she was expected to cast her vote – aye or nay – as soon as the meeting convened. The governors themselves had very little discussion or input in the process. Having come to the Fed from a career in business, she found this a most extraordinary manner of formulating policy. Corporate America is far more accustomed to developing a group consensus before making important policy decisions. To borrow Ms. Seger's analogy, the president of an auto company isn't exposed to the new models the day he goes down to the auto show.

Secret or not, professional money managers and bankers are generally able to surmise the decisions of the Federal Open Market Committee long before they get the Fed's sanitized news release. At the Committee's direction, the Fed's money market desk conducts its operations with major banks and securities dealers on a daily basis. If the decision has been made to ease reserve pressures, i.e. move toward lower interest rates, the Fed will be visible to dealers as an active purchaser of government securities in the open market. As the Fed buys securities, it credits its member banks with new reserves as *quid pro quo* in the transaction. The banks' reserves with the Fed thus become more plentiful, and they quickly learn that they need no longer bid so aggressively for reserves in the interbank market – and they may in fact find themselves in a position to offer reserve credits for sale to other banks instead. Inevitably, the greater availability of funds will lead to a lower federal funds rate – the interest rate charged between banks for short-term loans of their reserve accounts with the Fed. Hence, a move by the Fed to become a net buyer of government securities will immediately add liquidity to the banking system and lead to lower interest rates.

As banks find themselves with a surplus of reserves with the Fed, they are also faced with the question of how these funds should be employed. The nature of banking being what it is, the Fed's member banks will eventually be forced to lend these funds directly to their customers or, indirectly, to other borrowers via their purchases of commercial paper and corporate securities. Conversely, if the Federal Open Market Committee were to decide to exert greater pressure on reserves, i.e. move toward higher interest rates, it would sell government securities from the Fed's own large portfolio, thus draining reserves from the banking system and forcing its member banks to bid more aggressively for funds.

Now all of this may appear to be somewhat more complex than it really is. William McChesney Martin, who was Chairman of the Federal Reserve during the 1960's, once provided a concise description of monetary policy when he said that his job was to "take the punch bowl away just when the party is getting good." This metaphor is apt. A small group meets behind closed doors in Washington and decides what type of drink we're going to be imbibing. We know we're going to a party and will probably be taking a few drinks, but we don't know how potent the host will make his brew. But, if we get too carried away tonight, we probably won't fully realize it until tomorrow morning. Thus, the Fed spikes the cocktail to meet its own particular view of our taste.

Without the cooperation of the Fed's open market desk, the federal government can do very little to influence economic activity. If the Fed does not wish to abet the government's policy of deficit spending, it simply allows private investors to purchase new government bond issues with their own funds. The federal government can and will pay whatever rate the market requires. Without support from the Fed, government bond sales will result in higher interest rates and the inability of many private borrowers to afford the limited supply of funds remaining to them. Therefore, the Federal Open Market Committee has it within its power to decide whether business will find credit conditions favorable or unfavorable. As has been noted, the Fed seems not to have clearly understood the importance of this power in its early years. Benjamin Strong had been governor of the Federal Reserve Bank of New York from its inception until his death in 1928. The forceful and widely respected Strong clearly understood that, if the Fed's powers were used effectively, they could "stop any panic which might confront us."[3] Eventually, the Great Depression was to demonstrate just how powerful the Fed was. Unfortunately, the experiment was conducted in the opposite fashion from what Strong had in mind, i.e. the draining of bank reserves from a weak economy exacerbated the economic decline that was already in progress.

Perhaps the best independent measure of how the Great Depression was to shape the Fed's view of its own powers is the behavior of prices, both before and since. Before the advent of the Federal Reserve System, monetary growth occurred in a free market; credit booms were inevitably followed by debt deflation and depression. As a result, prices tended to be more stable over long periods of time, e.g. prices actually fell slightly over the long period from 1800-1913. From the inception of the Fed in 1913 to 1922, wholesale prices reversed course and rose slightly over one percent per year. After the deflationary phase of the twenties and the Great Depression ended in 1933, prices rose at an accelerating rate of over three percent per year through 1970. Finally, from 1970 to 1990, with the dollar free from its "barbaric" link to gold, modern economic science was able to freely work its wonders, and inflation exceeded six percent per year. Is it any coincidence that the federal share of GNP rose from less than two percent in 1913 to over 20 percent in 1990? In the Federal Reserve, the federal government had found an understanding banker while by mysterious coincidence politicians had found a pork barrel with no apparent bottom. The federal government appeared to have perfected its control over the nation's private economic affairs.

III

The powers the Fed exerts over the U.S. economy are indeed a mystery to most Americans. However, it is easier to appreciate the power of the Fed's monetary policy if we understand the role the Fed's individual member banks play in circulating liquidity throughout the economy. Once again, just like any other business, successful banking is based on the uncomplicated principles of buying low, selling high, and prudently using financial leverage. However, banking is dependent upon the public's confidence in the soundness of the bank, far more than, say, the corner deli. Like the flimflam man, the banker relies upon our trust to work his miracles. If we have faith, we will not demand immediate payment, and thus our funds can be employed at higher interest. But contrary to the likes of Mr. Ponzi, of whose skill in building financial pyramids we have earlier taken note, the local banker has a rich uncle to help him out – the Fed. Which brings us to the miracle of fractional reserve banking.

The mysterious art of fractional reserve banking is more potent than any form of black magic yet devised. In essence, it depends on the proven experience – the magic of statistics – that only a small percentage of a bank's deposits will be redeemed on a given day. Hence, it is necessary to reserve but a small portion of the bank's liabilities to satisfy its liquidity requirements. This is not so difficult to understand if we consider the analogy of the household that carries tens of thousands in financial liabilities while maintaining but a few hundred dollars in liquid assets. Banks operate under the same principle, but with the leverage rules set by the Fed, which may vary its guidelines from time to time. For example, in 1991 the Federal Reserve required that its member banks hold reserves of three percent of the first $41.1 million in checking deposits and 12 percent of the balance above that. As a result, the enterprising banker had as much as 97 percent of his deposits available for loans and other approved investments. Your $100 deposit becomes my $97 loan and – Poof! – money has been created. If deposits cost seven percent and reasonably safe loans yield 11 percent, the bank has successfully applied its objective of buying low and selling high – and without breaking a sweat. Ah, a business made in heaven!

But a souring economy can quickly turn banking's heaven to hell, and this turn of the financial screw has been the root cause of every major financial panic in American history. In a weakening economy, the banking system will see a rising percentage of its loans going into default. As the situation deteriorates, banks will begin to set aside an increasing portion of their net worth as reserves against the losses which are sure to result from the liquidation of bad loans. But banking is a leveraged business, and if losses are incurred, lending must be reduced by some multiple of those losses, lest the bank allow its equity to slip below the minimum set by regulators. At the same time, should depositors become concerned about the safety of their deposits, the bank will find that it must pay more to attract funds and that prudent management dictates that it remain more liquid to meet depositors' requests for funds. This is the worst of both worlds: at the same time that deposits – the bank's liabilities – are becoming scarce, the volume of solid income-producing assets they can support is declining. As a result, the bank will eschew new lending – no matter how safe the credit – and will step up its efforts to recover funds from borrowers who may already find themselves squeezed by poor business conditions. We have, then, the financial equivalent of a small pox epidemic – a *credit crunch.*

Tight money conditions can wreak havoc with banks that are highly leveraged and have low quality assets. Typically, banking institutions' equity capital is less than 10 percent of total assets. The vast majority of a bank's assets are funded by borrowed money, i.e. the money from the bank's deposits or money borrowed from other banks. Hence, like any highly leveraged business, the bank's entire equity can be wiped out by the loss of even a relatively small percentage of its assets. Therefore, bank examiners pay careful attention to the bank's lending guidelines to insure that depositors' funds are not subject to imprudent risk.

For regulators to keep abreast of the soundness of the banking system, the manner of accounting for bank assets is an important issue. Like any business dependent on credit, the bank will find it to its benefit to put on a happy face when presenting itself to its creditors – the public. For example, banks generally report the value of their investment accounts, such as bonds, at cost. This manner of accounting puts the banker on a one-way street to mischief: if their price goes up the bonds can be sold at a profit, while if the price declines the bank will continue to report them on its books at cost. Should the Financial Accounting Standards Board (FASB) require the banks to report their investments at market value, as was proposed in 1990, a sizeable portion of the banking system's purported net worth could be erased.

The manner of accounting for loans – which are the banking system's biggest asset category – was an important factor in the credit crunch which began in 1990. Evaluating assets of national banks falls within the purview of the Comptroller of the Currency, whose auditors review loan files and render opinions as to the appropriateness and soundness of the banks' loans as well as the adequacy of reserves set aside for loan losses. However, the quality of information that is made available to the public has generally been quite low, and with rising credit losses the loss of confidence on the part of the investing public was so great in 1990 that many investors became unwilling to buy bank stocks at any price. Therefore, the Comptroller of the Currency began moving in 1991 to correct the problem. Under proposed revisions to regulations, banks would break their weak loans down into three tiers, based on just how poorly the loans were performing. Depositors and investors would then be in a better position to monitor whether a bank's asset quality was improving or deteriorating. Nevertheless, uncertainty from past experience with audits by the Comptroller of the Currency in the continually deteriorating market of the late eighties and early nineties developed the "waiting for Godot" syndrome in the financial industry.

Besides worrying about audits from the Comptroller of the Currency, bankers must contend with a host of legal restrictions. Most of these were inspired by commercial banks in the stock manipulation schemes of the twenties. For example, the McFadden Act of 1927 essentially forbade interstate banking while the 1933 Glass-Steagall Act forbade banks from operating non-banking businesses, including the underwriting of securities. But in the eighties, these restrictions were greatly relaxed as regulators allowed the lines between banks and non-banks to blur. This was partly the result of the increasing competition banks were getting from non-bank competitors, whose holdings of debt nearly equalled those of banks by 1990. These non-bank lenders – which include finance companies, insurance companies, pension funds, even the likes of Ford, Sears, and ATT – held 48 percent of the nation's debt in 1990, up from 35 percent in 1981. The non-bank lenders generally had few restraints on their powers. Nor were they required – as were banks – to place non-interest bearing reserves with the Fed, which resulted in a loss of bank income estimated at over $2.5 billion per year.[4]

Another burden on the profitability of the banking system has been the recent regulatory trend toward "socially responsible" lending. The Community Reinvestment Act (CRA), which was further enhanced by the S&L bailout law (FIRREA) of 1989, is the government's latest effort to let the fox into the chicken coop. Contrary to government aspirations, banking is an inherently discriminatory business: it requires the banker to decide who is a good credit risk and who is not. Nor should it come as any great surprise that good credits tend to concentrate in certain professions, businesses, and neighborhoods. The intent of CRA was to negate this process by requiring banks to demonstrate that they have distributed their loans about the community in a non-discriminatory fashion. The irony of this type of legislation is that it ignores the fact that only conservative, profitable institutions can survive and be in a position to do anything for their communities. At least this appears to be the lesson of Freedom National Bank, a model CRA-type institution, whose Harlem and Bedford-Stuyvesant customers were cast adrift by the bank's failure in the fall of 1990.

During the latter part of the 1980's, the banking system found itself assailed by the slings and arrows of outrageous fortune on virtually every front. The deteriorating quality of loans from years of progressively worsening asset inflation and financial leveraging throughout the economy resulted in an ever-rising tide of loan defaults. Meanwhile, the Comptroller of the Currency became increasingly difficult to please, and an ever-rising percentage of loans was required to be reserved. Inevitably, the rise in bank failures led to a flight of equity capital at the same time that deposit insurance premiums were being raised to meet the ever-rising cost of bank failures. Yet, even as the equity of many banks was disappearing, the Federal Deposit Insurance Corporation (FDIC) was pressing banks to cut dividends and raise equity capital. Investors could not be enticed to buy new bank stocks while existing equity was being decimated by loan losses. The only avenue open to banks wishing to meet their minimum capital requirements was to sell assets. Just when borrowers most needed the funds, and the traditional buyers of such assets had become net sellers, the banks were trying to sell assets and shrink their balance sheets. The credit crunch was in full swing!

IV

The deteriorating quality of assets painted the banking system into a tight corner as the recession of 1990 began. However, were it not for the artifice of deposit insurance, there would have been widespread panic. Yet the role in which the federal government found itself as the implied guarantor of the deposit insurance fund was unwanted. The founding father of government interventionism himself, Franklin D. Roosevelt, had – at the inception of deposit insurance – taken this position: "As to guaranteeing of bank deposits, the minute the government starts to do that...[it] runs into a probable loss. We do not wish to make the United States Government liable for mistakes and errors of individual banks, and put a premium on unsound banking in the future." Of course, this is the same President who promised that his proposed social security system would never lead to a national system of identification. How many times were you required to use your social security number in the past week?

Regardless of FDR's intentions, his foray into deposit insurance left America with two more of his alphabet menu of quasi-public agencies: the Federal Deposit Insurance Corporation (FDIC) to insure bank deposits, and the Federal Savings & Loan Insurance Corporation (FSLIC) to insure thrift institutions. And what deposit insurance came to mean to America was this: virtually all of the deposits of the financial system were guaranteed by the U.S. taxpayer in the event of failure of an institution with the FDIC or FSLIC seal on the door. The system was designed to maintain the public's confidence in the financial system, and it was to soon find that, if this goal was to be achieved, certain financial institutions were "too big to fail." This became clear with the failure of Continental Illinois National Bank – one of the nation's largest – in 1984. Every dollar of deposits of Continental Illinois, regardless of how big the account or its owner, was eventually made whole by the insurance fund. Thus, the insurance system became a woman of uncertain virtue to an eager public of male callers. In the view of most money managers, big banks were seen as safe havens for large blocks of funds no matter how fragile their financial condition.

The "too big to fail" doctrine was to prove an unkind cut indeed for some depositors. For example, several charitable and religious organizations found themselves holding the bag when Harlem's Freedom National Bank failed in 1990. With but $91 million in deposits, the FDIC evidently felt free to more strictly interpret its statutory insurance limit of $100,000 per deposit. Some of those "big depositors" caught with losses included the Hale House Center, which cares for poor children, and the Harlem Churches for Community Improvement. Not unreasonably, in their suit against FDIC, these depositors alleged that the corporation often insured 100 percent of deposits exceeding the $100,000 limit in other banks. Nor did they have long to wait for a case in point. Two months later, in January 1991, the FDIC closed the $23 billion Bank of New England and – at enormous cost – redeemed every penny of its deposits.

Obviously, the "too big to fail" doctrine had led FDIC into troubled waters, and a more explicit policy limiting insurance was needed. The

Bush Administration moved to limit each person to an aggregate amount of insurance of $100,000. This was in contrast to the existing system in which any one individual could establish separate accounts in multiple institutions – each insured up to the $100,000 limit. But the degree to which government insurance of bank deposits had come to be viewed as one of America's God-given rights is attested by the opposition to the Bush program from the politically potent Independent Bankers Association. The 6200 member banks of this organization, which represents smaller "community banks," feared the proposed limit on insurance would induce large depositors to keep all their funds in larger banks. But the lady doth protest too much! If these banks are unable to attract deposits on their own merits, then we have their own admission that they would not exist in a free market, i.e. without the implied government subsidy of deposit insurance.

Regardless of what reforms were to be imposed on the deposit insurance system, the huge demands placed on the fund's limited supply of bailout money was placing severe liquidity constraints on activities by 1991. It became clear that FDIC would soon need a bailout of its own – either directly from the taxpayer or from the 13,000 member banks. The FDIC's fiscal 1992 budget forecast that the Bank Insurance Fund would run out of money that year, and would show a deficit of $22 billion by 1996. One obvious prescription was higher insurance premiums, and FDIC Chairman William Seidman responded by proposing a special one percent assessment on the $2.2 trillion in insured deposits to shore up the fund. By proposing an invisible tax which banks would pass through in the form of lower interest rates for depositors, the FDIC was following a time-honored political formula: "Don't tax thee and don't tax me; tax the man behind that tree." Politicians would be less amusing if they were less predictable.

Any FDIC rescue plan which relied upon the member banks themselves was sure to aggravate the already severe liquidity squeeze facing the banking system. This was made clear by the position of the American Bankers Association, which noted that the nation's 13,000 banks were concentrated at the healthy end of the spectrum. The 11,000 healthy banks accounted for one-half of all deposits, had equity of more than six percent of assets, were making money, and could be expected to survive even a sharp recession. At the other extreme, the 600 banks in fragile health controlled but one-tenth of the nation's deposits and were likely to fail by 1993. Thus, an infusion of $22 billion from the banks' own resources would merely be a tax for the benefit of the errant at the expense of the healthy members. But the weak were doomed to failure anyway. The draining of $22 billion from the banking system could not possibly save the comatose, but was sure to place further liquidity strains on those marginal banks that were struggling to remain profitable. And, incontrovertibly, any increase in the cost of deposit insurance must be covered by reducing the interest rates paid depositors or increasing the rates paid by borrowers. Thus, by increasing insurance rates, the effect would be for funds to flow out of the banking system and to make credit less abundant for borrowers, which would merely worsen an already serious credit crunch. A direct subsidy from the U.S. Treasury seemed to be the only feasible solution.

If anyone had any doubt how critical the role of government had become to insuring the soundness of the financial system in 1991, a good example of the alternative was provided by the bank holiday in Rhode Island. Some 1400 small banks and credit unions in the United States – with over $20 billion in total assets – were insured under individual state laws by a variety of privately sponsored insurers. Rhode Island Share & Deposit Indemnity Corporation insured some 45 of these small institutions in the amount of $1.7 billion.

If you had wanted the truth about Rhode Island Share & Deposit, you wouldn't have gotten it from the audit by Ernst & Young. Ernst & Young took over as auditor for the corporation in 1982 even though the rival accounting firm of KPMG Peat Marwick had earlier qualified its opinion of the firm's finances. The last audit done by Ernst & Young, which covered 1989, gave the firm a clean bill of health. But as Harry Schult, managing partner of Ernst & Young was to later say, "We don't have a crystal ball." The auditors had factored in the insurer's capacity to handle some financial turmoil, but "What hit us here in 1990 wasn't turmoil; it was a typhoon."

The typhoon got started when the president of one of the Rhode Island institutions, Heritage Loan & Investment Co., decided to stick his hand squarely into the cookie jar. The guilty party then disappeared along with several million dollars of his institution's deposits, and it soon became apparent that the Rhode Island indemnity fund's $14 million loss would leave it with insufficient reserves. As a result, the state's newly inaugurated governor, Bruce G. Sundlun, in a bit of *déjà vu* for depositors old enough to remember FDR, ordered the insured institutions closed for a "bank holiday."

Incidents similar to the Rhode Island crisis had occurred in Maryland and Ohio in 1985. In each case, depositors found that their plight was to depend on a combination of factors, including government largesse and the strength of each individual institution. About half of those closed in Rhode Island were immediately accepted for insurance by the National Credit Union Administration and soon re-opened. However, FDIC denied insurance to five institutions citing "undue risk to the federal insurance fund" and the State of Rhode Island was left to sort out the problem.

As an economics professor at Bryant College put it, "the state can't pay everyone their money immediately because, unfortunately, the State of Rhode Island is broke." Thus, with a potential expense of $150 million staring him in the face, Governor Sundlun had little alternative but to propose half-measures for Rhode Island's depositors. Those with less than $10,000 in their checking accounts and those with less than $2,500 in savings received the full amount of their deposits within three weeks of the bank holiday. Amounts in excess of these limits would be covered by non-interest bearing certificates of indebtedness of a new state agency called Depositors Economic Protection Corporation, which took the job of liquidating the assets of the closed institutions. The governor expected that it could take as long as four years for the liquidation process to be completed. However, waiting four years was better than the fate of some depositors: those accounts of $100,000 or more would not be reimbursed for the excess above $100,000.

The Rhode Island experience demonstrates the critical role government plays in the viability of America's financial system. Without it, depositors will be faced with outright financial losses as well as the loss of liquidity. A lack of confidence in the system leads to panic and bank runs. The contagion was further demonstrated by what happened at a healthy Rhode Island bank, Old Stone Corp., which had the misfortune of having one of its branches shown on TV in a CNN Headline News story on the Rhode Island crisis. The airing of file footage by CNN was enough to set off a panic which resulted in withdrawal of $20 million from Old Stone in one day. Only a statement from FDIC's Boston office that Old Stone Bank was sound and well-run could stop the panic. So, like it or not, nearly six decades of deposit insurance had led to the nationalization of America's banking system. No less enlightened an observer than William Issac, former chairman of FDIC, summed it up: "It's not the size of the fund that comforts the public, but the commitment of the government to put the full faith and credit of the U.S. Treasury behind the fund." Without the support of the federal government, the banking system was subject to panic, bank runs, and certain collapse. In effect, America had socialized its banking system.

V

Middle America's great gift to posterity, Harry S. Truman, once observed that the only new thing in the world is the history you don't know. Nevertheless, every generation provides yet another covey of airhead social scientists who presume that their pet nostrums will empower society to rise above the immutable human passions of greed and fear. Thus was the specter of bank runs in the early nineties to mock the accelerating decline of a sixty year experiment with government - sponsored deposit insurance. But America's banking system has a second and equally important support mechanism, its "lender of last resort," the Federal Reserve System. And the transmogrifying manner in which Fed policy has engineered the economy through the harrowing cycle of boom / inflation / panic / reflation since World War II demonstrates how – like deposit insurance – Fed policy has also become a brittle pillar.

We have already seen how the Fed exercises its open market power to pump reserves into the economy and propitiate economic recovery. For a quarter-century after World War II, the Fed found itself able to exercise these powers in a virtual financial vacuum. America produced over one-half of world output in the immediate postwar years and – in the U.S. dollar – controlled the world's reserve currency. External imbalances, which were small, were handled by accommodating a gradual drain in the nation's gold reserve. More important, fiscal discipline was maintained to a sufficient degree that deficits remained small. In fact, government debt – which had exploded to meet the crisis of World War II – declined in relation to national income during this era of low inflation and high economic growth. In the 1950's – the last decade to have the distinction of at least one year with a federal budget surplus – money supply (M-2) grew at an annual rate of just 3.4 percent. The Fed was behaving responsibly and the federal government had taken the attitude that what was good for General Motors was good for the U.S.A.

Under Eisenhower, social change hadn't happened fast enough to suit some, and so the 1960's brought forth a "new generation that would pay any price, bear any burden, etc." One member of this generation was Lyndon B. Johnson, who thought the nation capable of waging war on Vietnam and poverty at the same time. America was to wage two un-winnable wars.

To mix metaphors, the buck that once stopped on Harry Truman's desk was passed by LBJ to Richard Nixon, who promptly fumbled the ball. In January 1969, when Nixon was inauguated, inflation was already on the rise, as were interest rates. The Fed had begun tightening the monetary noose and growth in the basic money supply (M-1) dropped from 7.5 percent in 1968 to slightly more than three percent in 1969. A brief recession developed, during which the failure of Commodore Vanderbilt's legacy – the Penn Central railroad – was a notable event. The enormity of this financial shock was not acceptable to an America that thought itself master of its own destiny. In response, the Fed immediately began to ease monetary policy in early 1970 and money growth accelerated for three successive years. In hindsight, this appears to be the point of departure from the monetary discipline of the immediate post-World War II era. Consumer prices rose by a still high 5.5 percent in 1970, but the Fed was already hard at work at the printing presses. By January 1973, growth in the real money supply (M-1), i.e. the inflation-adjusted supply of transaction dollars, hit a post-World War II peak and inflation was also on the rise.

The severe economic recession of 1973-74 was an economic watershed. For the first time, the dollar's direct link to gold had been severed, the supply of dollars worldwide had greatly expanded, and the United States was an importer of many commodities, including oil. The Chairman of the Fed was Arthur Burns, who had accommodated his old pal – Richard Nixon – by rapid money growth during his 1972 re-election campaign. By 1973, inflation was rising toward nine percent, Nixon was on the way out, recession was on the way in, and Mr. Burns was still proclaiming that no recession was in view. But the Fed had turned off the monetary spigot with its traditional punch bowl-snatching *savoir faire* just as abruptly as it had opened the floodgates a few years earlier. Three-month Treasury bills shot up from 3.2 percent in February 1972 to 8.7 percent in August 1973, while the nation tuned in to the Watergate hearings and the Arab countries prepared themselves for military war against Israel and economic war against America. In October 1973, the Arab nations embargoed oil; America had obviously gotten into a predicament of rather severe economic imbalances and the situation was becoming increasingly intractable. By 1975, Mr. Burns was letting the money supply expand once again, White House staffers wore WIN buttons – Whip Inflation Now – and someone named Alan Greenspan was advising President Ford on economic policy matters. However, the trick of goosing the money supply didn't work its economic miracle in 1976 and a disaffected public elected a man who was trained in nuclear engineering but couldn't pronounce it – Jimmy Carter.

Mr. Carter was to be swamped by events – both political and economic – which were beyond his aptitude to control. His nominee to chair the Federal Reserve Board – William Miller – was even more inscrutable than the President in his qualifications for national leadership. As chairman of a defense contractor – Textron – he had surely commanded greater moral influence over his colleagues than he evinced from his fellow governors at the Fed – who consistently ignored his "Thank you for not smoking" sign during meetings. In any event, America was off to the monetary sweepstakes, as the Fed sought to accommodate rising commodity prices rather than to combat them. Money growth accelerated for three successive years, with its peak growth of nearly eight percent coming in 1978. At the same time, the maturation of the post-War baby boom had prodigious effects on the housing market, and house prices were rising rapidly. Tangibles and housing came to be viewed as "investments," the demand for credit was great, and inflation was assumed as an immutable fact of economic life by consumers and business alike. Borrow money and buy now, for the price will surely be higher tomorrow.

President Carter's appointment of Paul Volcker to replace Chairman Miller in late 1979 was to mark the beginning of a prolonged period of monetary restraint and two recessions over the next three years. The 1980 election of a new President, Ronald Reagan, occurred largely as a result of the Carter Administration's dubious economic hat trick of double digit unemployment, double digit inflation, and double digit Treasury bill rates. The recession which accompanied Mr. Reagan's first year in office was to be a severe one, but the monetary spigot would not be opened until August 1982, when the strain of recession was leading Latin American nations to consider defaulting on their U.S. bank loans. Thus was 1982 to mark the beginning of a final *dénouement* in monetary discipline: money was pumped into the banking system in ever increasing amounts, not simply to revive the economy, but to save the banking system itself. Ironically, Mr. Volcker, who would be remembered as an inflation fighter, was actually the most profligate of reflationists ever to preside over the Fed. From mid-1982 to mid-1986 the inflation-adjusted money supply (M-1) grew at an annual rate of 7.4 percent, a post-World War II record.

What had happened during the Volcker era – and was to endure during the subsequent tenure of Chairman Greenspan – was a change in the Fed's ability to manage aggregate economic activity. The relationship known as velocity (GNP divided by the money supply) had tended to grow at a stable rate until 1982. Indeed, this was the basis for the monetarist prescription for a hands-off monetary policy: assuming velocity is stable, stable money growth results in stable growth in GNP. But from 1982 to 1987, velocity dropped rapidly and the Fed initially found itself having to compensate via increased money growth. In 1987, velocity reversed course and began growing. For example, velocity fell by over 12 percent from 1982 to 1986 but was nearly back to its 1982 level by the middle of 1990. Thus, the Greenspan Fed found itself having to restrain money growth to keep the economy and inflation under control. Inevitably, the tightening of reserves led to further pressures on an already illiquid and highly leveraged financial system.

Given the fragile nature of the banking system as the 1990's began, economic policymakers were faced with a Hobson's choice. A vast financial edifice had been maintained for nearly sixty years on the twin pillars of deposit insurance and an activist monetary/fiscal policy accommodated by an all-powerful Federal Reserve and a strong currency. However, an increasing share of the federal debt was going not for economic stimulus but for interest on the national debt and the liquidation of the bad debts owed the thrift and banking system. *Good money was being sent after bad.* Increasingly, the Fed found that its efforts to stimulate monetary growth were increasing currency in circulation but not demand deposits. Was the money going into mattresses? A silent systemic run on the banking system appeared to be underway. Like the emperors of the latter days of the Roman Empire doing battle against the Vandals, the monetary authorities – though not yet powerless – were in a reduced condition to combat the menace. The first order of business was to get the bad money off the national balance sheet – and thus was the Great Bailout of the nineties born.

CHAPTER 6

The Great Bailout

By the time it is complete, the bailout of America's financial system may prove to be the greatest rip-off in history. In sheer dollar terms, the Great Bailout will rank as one of the greatest financial undertakings ever. For comparison, consider the experience of World War II. In that mammoth effort, America developed the technologies of computer science and nuclear weapons, put over 10 million men under arms, dispatched its forces to every corner of the earth, and became the arsenal of the victorious Allies. To finance this Promethean effort, from 1941 through 1945 the U.S.A. borrowed $180 billion and spent nearly twice that amount.[1] The outcome was to be the *Pax Americana* – a half-century of American hegemony and relative peace and stability. Yet, the total cost of World War II may well be less than what America will spend on the bailout of its financial system – an effort that will not increase national output by one widget, repair one bridge, or train one worker.

When the government first stuck its pinky finger into the tar baby of deposit insurance during the Great Depression, it was to restore confidence in an industry which had been decimated by bankruptcy and bank runs. For commercial banks, FDIC proved to be the magic elixir which soothed the public fear. Therefore, the system was quickly extended to the nitwit stepchild of the financial system – the savings and loan industry. Thrift institutions sprouted like mushrooms in response to the new subsidy. At the time the Federal Savings and Loan Insurance Corporation (FSLIC) was introduced in 1934, total deposits in thrift institutions were less than $5 billion, and they rose moderately to just $7 billion at the conclusion of World War II.[2] However, in the post-War era, total assets of thrifts grew at an explosive rate to over $600 billion in 1980, at which level they nearly equalled those of the commercial banking system.

As to the question of what the thrift industry was doing with its newly discovered wealth, the role of the thrift operator was aptly played by Jimmy Stewart in the classic movie "It's a Wonderful Life." Thrifts took deposits and usually reinvested the money in their local communities as mortgage loans on residential properties. Somewhere along the line, America had developed the consensus that every household's aspiration for a suburban single family home with a white picket fence was a desirable social goal, even worthy of taxpayer support. For a while, it seemed to work. By 1980, the thrift industry had amassed over $33 billion in net worth. But during the inflation of the seventies, the rates thrifts paid to attract deposits had soared to double digits, while their assets were mainly fixed rate mortgages at low rates. Expenses were growing faster than revenues. As profits fell, the industry's net worth stopped growing and it became increasingly burdensome to support the large and still growing asset base.

As the 1980's began, the industry was already bankrupt by any reasonable set of accounting standards. But rather than admit to this, the regulators decided to kill the messenger. Thus, the rape of the U.S. taxpayer gathered momentum with the introduction of "regulatory accounting principles" (RAP) which allowed thrifts to sell their unprofitable loans – at prices which were often as low as 60 cents on the dollar – and amortize the loss over the *expected remaining life* of the loans. From the standpoint of the more conservative generally accepted accounting principles (GAAP), the loss should have been recognized immediately. But the net worth of many institutions would thereby be wiped out and this pill was too bitter to swallow. Instead, a deadly game of financial self-delusion was underway; the thrift industry was no more solvent in 1981 than would be the man who dies with $60,000 in the bank and $100,000 in liabilities. His heirs can continue making interest payments to his creditors for a while, but by doing so they only increase the deficit. The power of the accountant's pen is great; it cannot, however, change reality.

By 1990, the truth was out. Even under its own ludicrous accounting methods, the regulatory Office of Thrift Supervision was responsible for insured institutions with aggregate net worth of but $28 billion, a mere 2.5 percent of total assets. Even with liberal accounting methods and dangerously high use of financial leverage, the assets of the thrift industry had declined to barely one-third of those in FDIC-insured banking institutions. The growth of the industry had slowed significantly due to lack of investment capital. And, unless equity capital could somehow be induced into the thrift industry, some $700 billion of thrift assets would need to be sold to bring the industry's assets down to a more reasonable – but still highly leveraged – regulatory goal of $16 in assets for each dollar in equity capital.

The predicament of the savings and loan industry is illustrated by Glenfed, Inc., parent of the nation's fourth-largest thrift. With loans defaulting at an accelerating rate, the company had over $600 million in non-performing assets vs. tangible capital of approximately $500 million at the end of 1990. In addition, the thrift listed $486 million in "good will"; tangible capital, the true worth of the corporation, was only slightly over two percent of total assets. And this is the essence of The Great Bailout: the thrift industry was faced with the prospect of trying to raise capital in a tight market or selling assets to meet its required capital objective. However, most assets on the books of thrift institutions could not fetch the book values recognized by the thrifts' accounting methods. And with a deficient capital base it is out of the question to sell at a loss, for this would wipe out yet more equity capital. Nor was the pinch in which Glenfed found itself an exceptional case: of the 15 largest thrifts operating in California in 1987, all but four were reporting big losses or had already failed by 1990.

One of the California institutions which did show a profit in 1990 was H. F. Ahmanson & Co., parent of America's largest thrift. However, year-over-year earnings were down 99 percent in the final quarter of the year, as non-performing assets soared by 60 percent. Was the company learning from experience? A spokeswoman attributed Ahmanson's poor performance to the record volume of loan originations in recent years. In her view, "When you add a lot of loans, in the course of time deliquencies naturally go up." Naturally?

While the problems of the thrift industry were old hat by 1990, the problems of the banking industry were just emerging as the general economy began to weaken. The problem most often cited was declining real estate values, and in areas like New England where real estate had boomed, the recession was especially painful. One New England bank that still had a good chance of surviving was Bank of Boston, which was nevertheless planning to cut its work force to 16,000 by the end of 1991, down 21 percent from four years earlier. For 1990, the bank reported a loss of nearly $400 million – about 20 percent of its capital. And, in an oft-repeated tale, non-performing loans of $1.8 billion exceeded the bank's net worth.

Even geographic areas that were less hard hit by weakening real estate were caught in the undertow. NCNB Corp., parent of North Carolina National Bank, reported declining earnings in 1990 as loan charge-offs for the year rose to $185 million from less than $70 million in 1989. The NCNB results were remarkable in view of the company's large interest in NCNB Texas, which enjoyed the benefit of a real estate market which seemed to be in an upswing.

Texas was an exception, both domestically and internationally. The weakness in real estate markets was beginning to spread across national borders. During the eighties, foreign depository institutions had greatly increased their presence in the U.S. banking industry. For example, problems at New York's Marine Midland banks were being felt across the Pacific at the parent Hongkong & Shanghai Banking Corp. Marine Midland's 1990 loss of nearly $300 million required the Hongkong parent to increase the amount of capital it held in Marine Midland, at the same time it was cutting the American subsidiary's assets by $7 billion.

In a nutshell, the problem facing America's financial system as the nineties began was the poor quality of its assets. Loans had often been made without regard to the liquidity of the borrower or the true economic value of the collateral. The financial system as a whole found itself in the same condition as a number of potentially bankrupt companies: large fixed rate liabilities vs. illiquid assets with uncertain cash flow, and all supported by a thin capital base. Inflation was assumed. An improving economy was assumed. The continued insouciance of regulators was assumed. Murphy's Law was not assumed.

II

As President George Bush took charge of a "kinder, gentler" nation in 1989, the savings and loan mess was just beginning to rear its ugly head. Of course, the enormity of the problem was not yet fully appreciated – early government estimates fell below $50 billion – but it was nevertheless clear that FSLIC did not possess the financial resources to deal with the problem. And the wisdom of getting the required funds from the bankrupt thrift industry itself would have been about the same as imprisoning debtors until their debts were paid. An imaginative solution was clearly needed. The problem was caused by a government agency subsidizing an unnecessary and inefficient industry and then refusing to recognize reality through reasonable accounting guidelines. The solution would be the same: create a new government agency subsidizing an unnecessary and inefficient industry and refuse to require strict accounting guidelines to identify the magnitude of the problem. And so the Resolution Trust Corporation (RTC) was born, and it would soon be staffed by a pin-striped army of former employees of banks, thrifts, and brokerage firms – who had not exactly covered themselves in glory in private industry.

A little background on the financial aspects of thrift liquidation will aid the reader's understanding of the problem facing the taxpayer. In 1990, the typical thrift institution had approximately 75 percent of its assets in mortgages and mortgage-backed securities. About seven percent of assets were commercial, consumer, and other non-mortgage loans, while approximately 13 percent of assets were in the form of cash and investment securities. The remaining five percent was real estate, stock in the Federal Home Loan Bank, and other miscellaneous assets. When an institution having, say, $100 million in assets and no equity is seized by FSLIC and transferred to RTC, the depositors must be paid 100¢ on the dollar. However, assets do not fetch 100¢ but must be sold for the best price available – thus generating a loss on sale.

Now try to imagine how the RTC works its way through a sample transaction. The preferred course of action was usually to find some "healthy" bank or thrift to take over the existing institution lock, stock, and barrel. But, of course, potential bidders would soon learn – through their own due diligence investigation – that a large part of the failed institution's assets should be avoided. In addition to those loans already in default, a great many more would be found to have been underwritten under lax guidelines or to be lacking required legal documentation. These so-called "junk loans" the bidders would wisely eschew, either by bidding a very low price or by requesting the option to "put" the loans to RTC, i.e. to re-sell them to RTC at book value within a prescribed time period. As a result, the price the failed institution's assets commanded would be dependent on the yield of the portfolio and how strictly the failed institution had enforced quality control guidelines in its lending operations. But, alas, thrift institutions had never been noted for their strict adherence to quality control guidelines.

Often, RTC was able to find an institution to take over the bankrupt institution's deposits, but perhaps only half its assets. In the present example, assume that RTC was left with $50 million in mortgage-related assets. The objective at this point would be twofold: first, to provide interim financing for the entire $50 million and, second, to dispose of these assets at the highest price obtainable. The first objective – the $50 million funding requirement – results from the transfer of all of the institution's deposits to the successful bidder. In essence, RTC would find itself having paid off all of the failed institution's liabilities, but able to dispose of just half of the assets.

If RTC had known how many institutions would fail and how much it could recoup from sale of their assets, it could have estimated the cost of the bailout with some degree of accuracy. But neither of these variables was known when the bailout began. It became obvious that RTC was not having much success in the early years of its existence. For example, during 1990 the agency drew down $50 billion in "temporary" working capital, but managed to recover only $9.8 billion through asset sales and loan pay-offs. In any event, the bailout funds required exceeded all forecasts and the only way they could be obtained at a reasonable cost was for RTC to issue bonds with the full or implied guarantee of the federal government. Eventually, most of the funds were borrowed directly from the U.S. Treasury. For example, in early 1991, the Bush Administration requested $77 billion in emergency funds to be spent on the crisis for a period of just seven months! Of this amount, it was estimated that $30 billion would be unrecoverable, while the balance would be repaid in the future via asset sales.

The cost of RTC is only part of the bill for the Great Bailout. When RTC assumed the obligations of the bankrupt FSLIC in 1989, the bank insurance fund of FDIC was still operating on its own resources, though they were declining rapidly. But an even more immediate economic cost than FDIC's dwindling bank insurance fund was already being paid by stock and bondholders of the failed institutions as the liquidation of America's banking system gathered steam.

An example of how FDIC was handling its share of the bailout was provided by its 1991 seizure of Bank of New England. When FDIC took control of Bank of New England's assets, it was acting in its role as the bank's senior creditor to protect its interests. And though the $2.3 billion loss FDIC was projecting was large (and would later grow larger), it was by no means the entire extent of the problem. The seizure of Bank of New England led to the immediate filing under Chapter 7 of the federal Bankruptcy Code by the bank's parent, Bank of New England Corporation. In its court filing, the parent company declared $50 million in assets, of which but $20 million was cash. On the other side of the ledger were $181 million in senior debt, $525 million in junior bonds and, of course, the company's common stock, which only three years before had an aggregate market value of $2.1 billion. In effect, nearly three billion dollars of wealth was destroyed by the bankruptcy, and this was in addition to the cost ultimately borne by the taxpayer through FDIC. These were not merely paper losses. They were real, immediate, and their impact on economic activity could only be negative. In the case of one of the bank's vice-presidents, who saw 20 years of savings wiped out, "...that stock was to support me in my retirement, which looks like it will be forced on me a little earlier than expected."

The crux of the problem of evaluating the true cost of the Great Bailout was this: America was not simply spending money, it was destroying wealth. Every time an institution was seized, the entire value of its stock and bond issues was immediately wiped out. As the assets of failed institutions were seized, the bad debts of the private economy were, in effect, to be made good by the taxpayer. Thus, the capital market was tapped by the U.S. Treasury and RTC, but the funds were used, not to build aircraft carriers or highways, but simply as an accounting entry to substitute for the bad debts of the banking system. This type of government spending would not stimulate economic activity *à la* John Maynard Keynes; it was simply withdrawing funds from productive uses in the nation's capital markets and replacing them with, well, nothing.

III

Perhaps the cost of the Great Bailout was not entirely wasted. One sector of the economy that was to see the operation as a boon was the legal profession. It seems that, rather than follow King Richard's admonition to "kill all the lawyers," the regulators intended to line the pockets of the legal profession with gold. During 1990, FDIC alone paid nearly $300 million in fees to private law firms for work related to failed thrifts and banks. An equal amount was spent by banks and thrifts which were operating under government conservatorship. Often, FDIC found itself stuck with the legal bill for work on behalf of healthy banks – such as NCNB Corp. – which negotiated government assistance as part of the price for taking over failed banks in Texas. At any rate, the legal gravy train was to continue rolling; FDIC estimated total legal fees of $750 million in 1991.

The Financial Institutions Reform, Recovery and Enforcement Act of 1989 (FIRREA) was largely to blame for the rising legal fees. Under provisions of FIRREA, the number of lawsuits filed by FDIC quintupled from 1988 to 1990. Frequently, these suits were not against just the officers and directors of failed institutions, but also against their real estate appraisers, law firms, and accountants.

One accounting firm which was feeling the heat from the government's legal storm troopers was Ernst & Young, including the predecessor firm of Arthur Young & Co. Arthur Young & Co. had been the auditor for Republic Bank Corporation of Texas. Arthur Young rendered favorable audits prior to Republic Bank's 1987 merger with another teetering Texas bank, InterFirst Corporation. In 1988, the combined entity, RepublicBank, earned the dubious honor of becoming America's second-largest bank failure, at a cost of $3 billion to FDIC. In sifting through the wreckage, the agency's legal eagles found that several of Arthur Young's partners had received real estate loans from the failed bank, and some were apparently used as a means of assisting the partners' investments in commercial properties.

Ernst & Young was taking flak in other parts of the country as well. As auditor for American Continental Corporation, the parent of Lincoln Savings & Loan, Arthur Young was accused of "gross negligence" by the California Board of Accountancy. In the Senate Ethics Committee's probe into the thrift's relations with five U.S. Senators, a letter from an Arthur Young partner surfaced as evidence that thrift regulators took "unusually antagonistic positions" against Lincoln and that examiners "did not have the requisite experience or knowledge to evaluate the types of transactions entered into by Lincoln." The letter's author, Jack D. Atchison, later went to work for Lincoln at a cool $1 million per year. The Resolution Trust Corporation was surely not amused by the irony of this as it scrambled to fund an estimated $2.5 billion loss on the failure of Lincoln. To appease the regulatory powers, Ernst & Young subsequently agreed to pay $41 million in cash plus several million dollars of future work for the government.

While RTC had many thrift directors and consultants living in fear of lawsuits, the agency's own employees were to find that they were operating on a much longer legal leash. In the case of Franklin Savings and Loan, a solvent and well-managed institution seemed to have been arbitrarily seized, wiping out millions in stockholder equity for no other reason than the apparent failure of regulators to understand the institution's sophisticated arbitrage operations. A federal court was later to cite M. Danny Wall, head of the Office of Thrift Supervision, for contempt due to his refusal to answer questions about how this particular decision was made. However, an appeals court overturned the ruling, citing a 1941 Supreme Court decision that upheld the "sanctity" of the government decision-making process. In other words, regulators could decide an institution was insolvent, but they need not justify their decisions to its stockholders or to the public. This prospect was not particularly encouraging for stockholders of insured institutions.

One Washington law firm, Steptoe & Johnson, was able to enhance its income via its four-volume report to the Bush Administration on how federal regulators had mishandled the 1988 bailout of 87 failed Texas thrift institutions – the so-called Southwest Plan. This deal, which resulted in an estimated loss of $69 billion to taxpayers, appeared to provide special treatment for the successful bidders. Eight of the 14 successful bidders were provided information in special meetings long before disclosures were made to the general public. Furthermore, the report noted that "in at least two instances, groupings of thrifts appear to have been specifically created for and negotiated with only a single bidder, with no notice of these new groupings to other bidders."

The Steptoe & Johnson report, which indicated that regulators were operating a "good old boy" bailout, seems to have thrown an added degree of caution into the operations of RTC. For example, one idea – advanced, no doubt, by Wall Street's eager investment bankers – was to pool some of RTC's $146 billion in assets in the form of securities for sale to the public. It was claimed that many of these assets, such as the $5 billion of junk bond holdings, could be more readily marketed in this fashion. The fact that most junk bond funds were then trading at a discount to book value seemed to belie this assertion, but Wall Street has never been known to let such facts interfere with its pursuit of a fee. In any event, RTC officers were concerned that they could be held personally liable for losses stemming from the "securitization" of such assets, and requested a special Congressional exemption in early 1991. To his credit, House Banking Committee Chairman, Henry Gonzalez, told RTC to get on with its business to "fulfill its statutory mandate of selling assets."

While RTC was not showing much alacrity in selling assets, it was conducting a record-setting performance in acquiring them. About $4 billion of the taxpayers' rapidly growing junk bond portfolio was acquired from one deal – Columbia S&L. In happier days, Columbia had been the eager client of the King of Junk – Drexel's Michael Milken. But by 1990, the institution found itself sinking under the weight of a falling junk bond market and attempted to negotiate sale of $3 billion of the portfolio. It offered favorable financing and a "put" feature to a group of Canadian investors led by Gordon Investment Corp., but the deal was vetoed by nervous regulators. Later, when Columbia was seized in 1991, the value of the portfolio had dropped by an additional $700 million. The failure of RTC to approve the sale earlier had been costly, and it demonstrated the folly of confronting a government bureaucracy with the prospect of making a business decision.

While Gordon Investment Corp. was blessing its good fortune at not being permitted to "take advantage" of the U.S. taxpayer, another group of Canadian investors – the Belzberg family – was licking its wounds from having been a little too eager in its foray into the thrift bailout. The Belzbergs obtained control of Far West Financial Corp., the parent of California's Far West Savings and Loan, and quickly lost $25 million in their hope that the institution could be revived. But that was not to be. Far West might well have been called "Far Out," with its portfolio of $3.8 billion, mainly in junk bonds and risky commercial real estate loans. By the end of 1990, net worth was in the minus column by $110 million, a quarter-billion less than the regulatory target of three percent of assets in equity capital. When regulators offered the chance for the Belzbergs to keep the thrift operating by coming up with an additional capital infusion of $200 million, the Canadians showed themselves smart enough to avoid the trap of sending good money after bad. They were also astute enough to understand the perils of dealing with regulatory agencies. As their spokesman said, there was "no guarantee that the rules wouldn't change again."

IV

Change had certainly become the operative word in the financial system in the wake of the Great Bailout, and what was changing faster than anything was the public's attitude toward deposit insurance and those who had abused it. One of the first casualties of the public backlash was the system of brokered certificates of deposit (CD's). Brokered deposits were yet another element of the Wall Street financial boondoggle of the eighties. When the deposit insurance limit was raised to $100,000 per account, it immediately became attractive for investment bankers to break up larger blocks of money into $100,000 and disseminate them around the country in search of the highest yield. And, of course, the highest yields were usually paid by the riskiest institutions. One study in 1991 found that, of the 54 largest thrift failures, one-third of their deposits were over $80,000 – the size most commonly brokered.

But Wall Street is never keen to see a cash cow go to its slaughter. During 1990, the brokering of CD's was estimated to have placed some

$90 billion of this hot money. Merrill Lynch Money Markets, Inc. – which captured about one-third of the market – was one of the beneficiaries of this no-risk business, in which brokers charge a percentage fee simply for placing investors' funds with the right institutions. Given the lack of incentive for seeking out safe institutions, the market for brokered CD's virtually guaranteed that no insured institution would ever lack the funds it needed for even its most ambitious projects. However, in early 1991, the Treasury Department recommended that brokered deposits be phased out over a two-year period.

Without brokered deposits, Paul Cheng and Simon Heath could never have worked their financial mischief at Texas' $2 billion Guaranty Federal Savings and Loan. As owners of the thrift, the two directed millions in loans to their closely held company, Pacific Realty Corp. As federal Judge Robert Maloney later put it in handing down their stiff fines and long sentences, "These two young men stole almost $6 million just as surely as if they had stuck it in a bag... and gone off to shoot craps in Las Vegas."

Shooting craps was indeed a good analogy for what was happening at another Texas institution, which had already been bailed out once – First City Bank. Banker A. Robert Abboud and his group of investors had persuaded FDIC to give them ownership of First City in 1988 – at a cost of $920 million to the insurance fund. Under the new management a new portfolio of junk loans was soon generated – such as a fourth-lien on an aging Las Vegas hotel, or the $140 million credit – which wasn't current in early 1991 – secured by art work and real estate located in Spain. True to form, the bank paid consulting fees quite liberally, e.g. one million dollars went to one consultant for selling off the bank's foreign debt. What all this added up to was a net loss for First City for 1989 and 1990, the first two complete years of operation under the Abboud regime. The good old boy banking system that led to the first bailout was raising the possibility of a second one. It seemed that only the faces had changed.

The tendency for bankers to provide favorable treatment to their friends and associates was a common refrain as the story of the bailout unfolded. At the same time Bank of New England was taken over, federal authorities were arresting Lewis Shattuck, a former vice-president of the bank. Mr. Shattuck was charged with fraud, embezzlement, and solicitation of kickbacks from real estate developers. His 1991 indictment estimated that the alleged violations resulted in $1.1 million in losses for the bank, while another $18 million in losses were still under investigation.

The system of deposit insurance was slowly destroying the confidence of its supposed beneficiary – the small depositor. In early 1991 at Bank of New England's Dedham, Mass. branch, Marybeth Agostinelli demanded payment of her $3475 savings in full – and in cash. When the teller offered her a check, she replied that she had no way of knowing whether it was good. All over New England, the run was on. Eastland Bank of Woonsocket, R.I. needed two truckloads of cash to meet the demand. And after they got their money, much of the public may have been thinking the same as Ms. Agostinelli: "Now, where do I go from here? Is there a safe bank left in New England?" Throughout the economy, the idea was gradually sinking in. The banking system had a problem, and if the folly of a government-subsidized deposit insurance system was to be preserved, it might cost as much as $500 billion to fix. An obvious question which hadn't yet been asked was this: if the cure would cost $500 billion, could the disease possibly be any worse?

V

At the time the Persian Gulf War was getting underway, pundits noted that the alliance between America and Kuwait was a marriage made in heaven: while Kuwait was a banking system without a country, America was a country without a banking system. But, if America lacked a banking system, there was certainly no shortage of bricks and mortar which purported to be banks. And the problem of overcapacity – largely the result of federal deposit insurance – was clearly not on the government agenda as it continued to pour money into the bailout.

Perhaps the best case study for what to expect from the Great Bailout was the experience of Texas, which had gotten a five-year headstart on the business of financial liquidation. But as it progressed, everyone seemed to be pretending nothing had happened: during 1988 and 1989, FDIC seized 246 Texas banks, but closed the doors of only 36. The overcapacity which seemed to exempt banks from the discipline of the market economy was to be an abiding problem. On every corner, a bank was still offering FDIC insurance, bidding for depositors' funds, and ready to lend money, regardless of whether it could find a worthy project. So Texas was left with the same number of banks and the same deposit base, but a great deal less in equity capital to support this magnificent financial edifice.

Nor had the FDIC shown any inclination to modify its approach as the financial disease spread to New England. In early 1991, as Standard and Poor's was downgrading the quality of bonds issued by Fleet/Norstar Financial Group, Inc., citing "continued increases in problem loans," the FDIC was honoring the Rhode Island bank holding company with the $1.3 billion in assets of the defunct Maine Savings Bank. Fleet, with nearly $1.4 billion in non-performing assets of its own and nearly 20 percent of its loan portfolio in so-called HLT's (highly leveraged transactions), was clearly not daunted by the nearly $50 million loss it had just reported for the previous quarter.

One small step towards eliminating the excessive infrastructure of the banking system was made by the Bush Administration's proposal to allow interstate banking. Banks which had successfully circumvented the previous restrictions had done so by setting up independent banking companies in each state. As a result, millions were spent in duplicating operations which could be efficiently centralized in a multi-state operation. For example, BankAmerica Corporation estimated that it could save $50 million per year under the Bush reform plan.

Regardless of how efficiently the banking system was to operate its excessive number of branches, interstate banking would never solve the problem which afflicted some of America's greatest banking concerns, i.e. a shortage of equity capital. Citicorp, America's largest bank holding company, was a good example of the problem as it struggled to cut costs by $1.5 billion per year and boost its equity capital by 50 percent. Moody's downgraded the company's preferred stock in January, 1991 to Ba-1, which is considered a non-investment grade or "junk" category. While the downgrades were occurring, Citicorp found itself opting to redeem $500 million of its "auction-rate" preferred stock rather than pay the higher rates investors were demanding. The company also found itself reducing its dependence on its increasingly costly commercial paper, which declined to $3.2 billion at the end of 1990 vs. $10 billion a year earlier.

The end result of declining bank profitability was declining bank capital and reduced lending. Citicorp reduced its assets by $13 billion in 1990 in an attempt to get footings in better balance with its capital base. But with declining profitability, investors were avoiding the stock: Citicorp Chairman John Reed estimated that the bank's stock lost $5.4 billion in market value during the year. Since the domestic market had put a premium interest rate on any funds advanced to the banking system, Mr. Reed found himself trotting the globe in his search for equity capital for the bank. And, apropos the symbiotic relationship between America and Kuwait, it was rumored that one of the parties he visited was the financial manager for the then-exiled government of Kuwait.

Citicorp's problem was that it was too big for anyone to buy – $217 billion in total assets. Smaller banks, such as California's Wells Fargo could consider other options, including merger with other banks. Wells Fargo, the nation's twelfth-largest bank, though highly profitable, was beginning to feel a bit apprehensive about the one billion dollars of commercial real estate loans on its books, whose collateral properties featured vacancy rates in excess of 25 percent. In a weak market, all lenders found themselves painted with the same brush. While the bank had been a conservative lender, it had, nevertheless, a large share of its loans in the vulnerable California real estate market. On the other hand, the nation's fifth-largest bank, Security Pacific, might provide both the portfolio distribution and cost savings for a strong merger candidate. Egos were cited as an inhibiting factor, but misery acquaints a man with strange bedfellows.

Despite the depressed economy, the banking system was still building castles on foundations of sand. Regardless of mergers, the major obstacle to improving bank profitability – poor asset quality – was present and growing. Salomon Brothers estimated that the largest New York and Chicago banks held over 10 percent of their loans in commercial real estate and seven percent in HLT's. Moody's estimated that 25 percent of all HLT loans would eventually default and that banks would lose 25-40 percent of the principal on the defaulted loans. And there was no friendly secondary market in these loans for banks who wished to trim their exposure. Loans on one such HLT – Revco – were valued by traders at 60 cents on the dollar in 1990, while Federated Department Store loans were estimated by Salomon Brothers as a "45 cent piece of paper." As HLT's such as these defaulted at increasing rates, bankers were to learn that, as one investor put it, "Bankruptcies are the Bataan death march. Collateral just keeps dropping off the side while lawyers' fees pile up month after month and revenues slide."

The greed which had led banks into the commercial real estate and HLT business would alight on yet another form of financial self-delusion even as bankruptcies rose: debtor-in-possession (DIP) financing. As companies such as Pan Am Corp. and Best Products Co. filed for protection under Chapter 11 of the federal bankruptcy code, bankers eagerly lined up to grant new loans. DIP financing is granted after Chapter 11 proceedings are initiated and provides the lender with a senior claim on certain assets in return for financing the company's continuing operations while the business is being reorganized. The twin enticements for bankers in these transactions are the high interest rates and juicy up-front fees for arranging the loans. For example, Pan Am paid a four percent fee for its $150 million loan from Bankers Trust and UAL Corp., while Chemical Bank and Manufacturers Hanover Trust received a two percent fee for the $250 million DIP loan to Best Products. As the 1990-1991 recession worsened, one eager banker predicted a busy year in DIP financing as the former subjects of the leveraged buy-out craze of the eighties defaulted at increasing rates. And so the same banks which had plunged into the LBO boom of the eighties found themselves diving into the DIP boom of the nineties.

As the Great Bailout proceeded, the Bush Administration demonstrated a partial understanding of its root cause when it unveiled its plan for banking reform. Each depositor's insurance would be limited to $100,000 per institution. Well-capitalized banks would be permitted to offer other financial services, such as securities brokerage. Deposit insurance premiums would be higher for institutions with lower capital levels. Well-capitalized institutions would be less regulated. The restrictions on interstate banking would be removed. This was an odd mixture of economics and politics for it implied that poorly capitalized banks and unlimited deposit insurance created the problem, but it failed to eliminate government support while opening up new horizons for malfeasance.

America had a problem that was not going to be solved by locking the barn door after the horse had already been stolen. The country had far too many banks and their depositors had too little risk. The financial system's proclivity for providing funds for unprofitable ventures led to loan losses and poor profitability. The record was clear: America's banks earned less than $20 billion in after-tax profits in 1990, which translated to a fair market value (at a 12% annual return) of about $165 billion. In theory, this is the amount of equity capital rational investors should be willing to pay to purchase the entire banking industry. But, if the system was to keep a conservative cushion of 7.5 percent of assets in capital, the fair market value of the industry's capital could support only about $2.2 trillion in assets. Yet, by its own method of accounting, the system had over $3.3 trillion in assets. From the standpoint of the free market, America's banking system was thus faced with the prospect of divesting $1.1 trillion of assets before it could be considered healthy. And this led to the same rub which had killed the thrift industry: the $1.1 trillion in excess assets might fetch only $800 billion if they were sold.

Thus the dilemma: while the limited capital base was overleveraged, divestiture of assets was no feasible solution in that it would result in losses which would wipe out equity entirely. And so, like Adlai Stevenson – "too hurt to laugh and too old to cry" – the walking wounded continued to operate and the Great Bailout went full steam ahead.

CHAPTER 7

Real Estate:
Death of a Sacred Cow

Real estate is the sacred cow of the American economy. During colonial times and in the early years of the Republic, land ownership was the primary motivating force behind European immigration to the New World. In fact, the push to settle beyond the Appalachian frontier was a contributing factor to the American Revolution. Real estate has always been the measure of a man in the New World. Under the laws of the various states, land ownership was generally a necessary condition for voting. From *Poor Richard's Almanac* to the end of the twentieth century, the American attitude continues to be that "a rolling stone gathers no moss."

Given Americans' already strong pre-disposition toward property ownership, a variety of factors – especially inflation – greatly enhanced the investment aspects of real estate during the 1970's. The wide availability of long-term fixed rate mortgage loans, favorable tax treatment, and a rapid increase in household formations produced a quick price rise and large capital gains for most homeowners. Owners of farmland and commercial real estate were also to benefit from the run-up in prices, and America soon came to regard its real estate as a foolproof investment. The view was widely held that, as long as you could stand the cash flow to service your debts for a short holding period, "you just can't go wrong in real estate." In other words, real estate investments traded on the Greater Fool Theory: they did not make economic sense, but government tax policy and a willing buyer would make everything right in the end.

Despite a rapid rise in interest rates, house prices were rising at double digit rates from 1978 until the onset of the severe recession of 1981. Since most homeowners were either free of debt or had fixed rate loans at single digit rates, the appreciation in home prices during the seventies produced large capital gains which, even though they may not yet have been realized, came to be regarded the same as money in the bank and were thus considered a substitute for saving. However, every winner in this game also produced a loser: homeowners were the beneficiaries of the loss suffered by thrift institutions, who found themselves holding a depreciating asset as rising interest rates reduced the value of their loan portfolios. Like the capital gains of most homeowners, the full extent of the losses the thrifts suffered had not yet been realized, since loan portfolios were not written down to their true market values. Yet the rising tide of losses profoundly troubled lenders as well as their regulators.

The eighties were to be less exuberant than the seventies, but favorable tax policy created a generally friendly environment for real estate. However, as the decade progressed, appreciation in house prices proceeded at an ever slackening rate. Until 1987 the gains continued to be impressive nevertheless. The ten year period ending in 1987 witnessed a compound annual increase of eight percent in prices of existing homes. Notable exceptions were visible, however, e.g. the average house price in Houston dropped by 18 percent from 1983 to 1987. But such cases were generally regarded as aberrations. Certainly, homebuyers in New England gave no indication in 1987 that they were worried that the real estate slump might soon affect them as well.

While Texas and the other "oil patch" states did have their own unique problems due to the mid-decade collapse in commodity prices, nationwide real estate prices had indeed reversed the trend of the seventies and were growing at a slower rate than personal income. The inflation of the previous decade had pushed prices relative to income to a level which was difficult to sustain. For example, by 1980 the income of the average adult American had fallen below 18 percent of the average house price. This was far below the rule-of-thumb used by many mortgage lenders to qualify homebuyers: gross family income should exceed 40 percent of the price of the house. Even families with two wage-earners found themselves being pushed out of the housing market. The more measured rate of inflation during the eighties improved the affordability situation somewhat. By 1989, average adult income was approaching 20 percent of the average price of a home. Despite a price increase of over 60 percent during the eighties, housing had become more affordable in terms of the typical family's income.

Though home prices were coming within reach of a greater share of American families during the eighties, there was no headlong rush toward the tasks of house-cleaning and lawn-mowing. Existing home sales approached 3.6 million in 1986, declined in 1987, regained the lost ground in 1988, but then began a steady decline. Indeed, if one examines data on housing starts, the boom of the mid-1980's never reached the same physical volume of homebuilding as was achieved in earlier booms. For example, in the early seventies, housing starts exceeded two million per year, while the peak year of the eighties – 1986 – saw construction begin on only 1.8 million new houses. The demographic impetus for housing demand was no longer as great and, inevitably, this had translated into a less exuberant market for housing and a less dramatic appreciation in home prices.

As the 1990's began, the temperature of the real estate markets had definitely cooled. By December 1990, an index of construction activity compiled by F. W. Dodge, a unit of McGraw-Hill, Inc. had fallen to a seven-year low. For the year as a whole, the index plummeted by 26 percent, while the actual dollar value of new construction projects was down by 11 percent. A 1990 study of the Manhattan co-op market indicated that the average bid by prospective buyers was 29.5 percent below the asking price, a steep drop from 1989. Commercial property owners were also suffering from slack demand. Cushman Realty Corp., a large commercial property leasing concern, reported aggressive use of inducements by landlords to lure new tenants. Decorator allowances and free rent for as long as one year on a five-year lease were not uncommon. And commercial property prices were dropping sharply. Security Pacific Corp. sold New York's Crown Building for $93.6 million at foreclosure in 1991, far less than the $120 million one prospective buyer had offered a year before.

Perhaps a harbinger of what lay ahead for the real estate market was to be seen in the sharp drop in apartment construction. Apartment developers had benefited from the Reagan Administration's initial stab at tax reform in 1981. Actually, the word "benefit" fails to describe the exuberance with which developers responded. The Roman soldier's implementation of the Rape of the Sabine Women was no more happily executed than was the construction industry's response to the Economic Recovery and Tax Act of 1981. While income tax rates remained relatively high, liberal breaks were given for business expenses such as depreciation and interest. Despite high mortgage rates, building activity soon boomed. Projects were syndicated to farm out the tax benefits of ownership to high-income investors in the upper tax brackets, who could write off losses against their current income, thus cutting their tax bills. With inflation, it was often assumed that these losses would eventually be made good by capital gains, which would be taxed at a lower rate. To more aggressively market these partnerships,

many investors were provided financing for their "equity" contributions. As a result, on a cash-flow basis, many investors found that they
were able to cut their tax bills by more than the amount of their initial
cash contribution to the project. For example, a $50,000 investment
might require an initial down payment of only $5,000 from the investor,
who might then reduce his tax bill by $15,000 in the same year.
Apartment starts zoomed upward from 380,000 in 1981 to nearly
670,000 in 1985. Nobody seemed interested in demographic tables
which showed a shrinking pool of young adults to occupy these new
structures.

An investment that relies upon government tax policy rather than
its own inherent profitability is no better than the roulette wheel. The
tax breaks of 1981 were reversed by the 1986 Tax Reform Act, and –
worst of all – the changes were applied *retroactively*. This meant that
owners of unprofitable projects could no longer use the losses from
their passive investments to reduce the tax liability on non-passive
income such as wages and salaries. New apartment projects sponsored
by such partnerships immediately became unattractive investments,
and many investors in existing projects found it convenient to default
on their previous commitments. Yet, the glut of apartments from the
boom years hung over the market like the sword above Damocles. In
many cities, such as Phoenix and Denver, rents declined by as much as
15 percent. Adding to the hardships of investors was the fact that many
projects built in the mid-1980's were financed with seven-year
balloon-payment mortgages, which would come due in the early 1990's
– when the availability of funds was highly doubtful. The National
Apartment Association, reflecting the industry's state of depression,
estimated that only 250,000 new units would be started in 1991.

Homeowners were also soon feeling the pinch of the slackening
demand for real estate. While home prices were dropping in much of
the country in the early 1990's, sellers often found that the 1986 tax act
had made it more difficult to swallow the pill of trading down. After
1986, the Internal Revenue Service taxed capital gains at the same rate
as ordinary income, and any gains from sale of a home not reinvested
in a more expensive house were subject to the tax. Often, homeowners
who had withdrawn some of their capital gains via second mortgages
found that the tax due was greater than the net cash proceeds from sale.
And those who had bought at the peak in house prices discovered a
painful anomaly in the tax code: losses on sale of a home were not
tax-deductible. In many cases, homeowners found themselves stuck
with oppressive mortgage payments and falling home prices, but they

could not afford to sell. The tax code was biased against trading down. In the civilian equivalent of imprisonment in quarters, America was doomed to remain the most over-housed nation on earth.

II

The cooling housing market of the latter part of eighties was to lead to an environment of rising loan defaults and tight financing conditions in the early nineties. Often, the troubled loans were linked to the thrift industry's push to provide loans on marginal real estate projects. The failure to require developers to provide substantial amounts of equity financing enticed many borrowers with a one-way proposition: if the project succeeded, an enormous gain on a modest investment was likely. However, if the project could not be sold at the right price and sold quickly, the lender would soon find himself faced with the prospect of foreclosure.

The already weakened real estate market received what proved to be a knockout punch from the Financial Institutions Reform, Recovery and Enforcement Act (FIRREA) of 1989. This baby step toward more prudent lending guidelines limited loans to one borrower by insured institutions to no more than 15 percent of the lending institution's capital. For example, a thrift with $10 million in equity capital – which would typically have a $200 million loan portfolio – could lend no more than $1.5 million to one borrower. Overnight, most thrifts found they lacked the capital to finance the type loans to which their borrowers had become accustomed. Lenders were required to assemble groups of institutions to participate, i.e. share ownership of their loans. As a result, it became increasingly difficult for developers to find financing.

The optimistic attitude of lenders in the eighties also played an important role in the new era of tight money. Expenses often ran over budget, while sales lagged. An example of the result could be seen at Port Liberte, a luxury waterfront development in New Jersey within view of the Statue of Liberty. City Federal Savings Bank provided 100 percent financing on a revolving construction loan in return for a 50 percent equity stake in the project. As the real estate market eroded, so did the value of the proposed project: a 1989 appraisal estimated value at $90 million vs. $156 million a year earlier. Eventually, City Federal was seized by regulators and RTC found it necessary to foreclose on the project. The best offer RTC received was $35 million vs. its $170 million in secured debt on the project. Thus, while real estate appraisers were lowering their estimates, they were still far from the actual cash value of properties which changed hands under distressed conditions. A sudden awareness of this fact was to color the attitude of bankers and regulators as well. In the new environment, the customarily optimistic assumptions of developers were given little credence and appraised values were viewed with an ever more skeptical eye.

Texas' Cullen/Frost Bankers, a conservative and well-managed institution, demonstrated that few financial institutions would be left untouched by the real estate malaise. The demand for real estate financing in the distressed Texas economy led increasing numbers of developers to Cullen/Frost as other Texas institutions found it necessary to cut their lending. As a result, real estate loans rose from five percent of the Cullen/Frost portfolio in 1985 to over 25 percent in 1990. But, despite tight controls on lending, the bank's profits in the first half of the eighties turned to a steady stream of weak earnings or outright losses in the latter half of the decade.

To counter the losses from non-performing loans, banks had no alternative but to cut lending and sell assets. Cullen/Frost cut its portfolio by 30 percent. Bank of New York shrank its assets by nearly seven percent in 1990; Continental Bank Corp. of Chicago trimmed its portfolio by over eight percent. Meanwhile, as loan loss reserves mounted, investors waited for the other shoe to drop. Many bank stocks plunged 50-70 percent from 1988 to 1990. The volume of real estate lending was sure to suffer. As the nineties began, commercial real estate lending dropped to the lowest level since 1983.

The stress in the real estate markets inevitably led to a search for new sources of financing. The Federal National Mortgage Association – Fannie Mae – introduced a pilot program to fund up to half of the principal amount of qualifying construction loans originated by thrifts and commercial banks. However, the government-sponsored agency wasn't exactly diving in head-first: the $50 million it initially allocated to the program was no more than a hiccup for the $100 billion-a-year market for home construction. Nor were the previously ubiquitous Japanese taking up much of the slack. Japanese real estate investment peaked at $14.8 billion in 1989, fell in 1990, and was pegged to fall further in 1991, according to a survey of Japanese companies.

A port in the storm for some real estate operators was provided by so-called "vulture funds." These funds, which were originally set up to buy distressed properties at bargain prices, soon found a lucrative niche in providing financing for cash-starved projects. Many investors found the vulture funds their only source of money to re-finance balloon payments. Other owners of distressed properties with negative cash flow found it to their benefit to surrender their majority control of properties in return for the immediate liquidity the funds offered. The help did not come cheap; one advisory service estimated that vulture funds were reaping returns as high as 30 percent for taking on the risks everyone else was trying to avoid. In a credit crunch, cash is king. The vultures were strutting like peacocks.

III

A major source of support for the American real estate market in its fifty year boom was the crazy-quilt of government programs. Starting in the 1930's with the Federal Housing Administration's (FHA) program for granting government insurance on mortgage loans, the federal government had long been directly involved in the business of residential mortgage lending. Less obvious to the general public but equally important, was government support of the secondary mortgage market through such agencies as Fannie Mae, the Federal Home Loan Mortgage Corp. – Freddie Mac – and the Government National Mortgage Association – Ginnie Mae.

The FHA home mortgage insurance program and the Veterans Administration (VA) home loan guaranty programs were designed to provide home ownership to qualifying borrowers who lacked the down payments generally required on conventional mortgage loans. By insuring against lenders' credit loss on approved loans with little or no down payment, the FHA and VA home loan programs induce otherwise reticent lenders to provide financing for borrowers who have not demonstrated the ability and/or willingness to accumulate the funds needed. Despite this inherent economic flaw, the government loan programs were intended to be self-supporting; borrowers pay an insurance premium to defray losses suffered in the event of default. FHA insures 100 percent of losses suffered by lenders through foreclosure, while the VA guaranty covers no more than 25 percent of the reasonable value of the house at the time the loan was originated. During most of the post-World War II era, the programs appeared to function smoothly at little cost to the taxpayer. However, like the deposit insurance system, these FHA and VA programs required a modicum of inflation in real estate prices if they were to be kept on a self-funding basis. Instead, the slackening appreciation in home prices and rising defaults in the latter part of the eighties led to a 1989 audit of the FHA insurance fund by the Price Waterhouse accounting firm which indicated that the fund was technically bankrupt. The VA program, despite a 1989 increase in "funding fees" paid by borrowers, also found itself relying on Treasury funds to meet its cash requirements. Adding insult to injury, many lenders were no longer offering VA loans due to their experience in Texas: the 25 percent VA guaranty was often insufficient to cover lenders' losses upon foreclosure sale.

The FHA home loan program, no longer subsidized by home price inflation, moved in 1989 and then again in 1991 to stem the flow of red ink. The 1989 reform virtually eliminated the availability of mortgage financing for investors, and greatly reduced the ability of non-qualifying homebuyers to assume existing loans. The 1991 reform supplemented the initial mortgage insurance premium of 3.8 percent of the principal on the most common 30-year loan (a premium which borrowers usually financed as part of their mortgage loans) with the requirement for borrowers to pay a monthly insurance premium as well. By increasing the monthly mortgage payment, this change effectively reduced the loan amount for which the borrower could qualify. More important, however, was FHA's move to limit the amount of settlement costs which were eligible to be financed. For example, on a $70,000 house the homebuyer's required cash contribution rose by about $525 – an increase of over 15 percent. While this may not sound particularly onerous, it was a significant sum for the illiquid FHA clientele. The entire system was based on the buyer with little or no cash in the bank.

Even with the 1991 "reforms" in the FHA loan program, the typical loan amount still exceeded the purchase price of the home. This was due to the fact that FHA permitted most of the closing costs and mortgage insurance premiums to be financed via additions to the original loan principal. Thus, as it increased premiums and cash requirements, the FHA insurance fund found itself approaching the financial point-of-no-return. On one hand, higher premiums were needed to defray losses. On the other hand, the increases in insurance premiums were raising the true cost of financing a home. Responsible borrowers who could make a 10 percent down payment found that the effective interest rates on conventional loans were lower. Further attempts to remove the government subsidy by raising the price of credit to its true cost would, therefore, tend to discourage those borrowers with the best credit and further increase the overall default rates in the future. It was simply not possible to make money lending to marginal borrowers without charging an interest rate premium.

Far worse than the Department of Housing and Urban Development (HUD) mortgage insurance program was the HUD program of subsidized housing for the poor. In this program, HUD made no pretense of being self-supporting. Subsidized housing projects were clearly and plainly an attempt by government to put the poor in a kind of cold storage, i.e. in such fashion and in such a place that they would not inhibit the functioning of the private economy. By the standard of any rational person, the program had been a dismal failure. The typical high-rise Gehenna was a hotbed of drugs, violence, and teen pregnancy. It would require the determination of a god for a child to rise above this cultural and moral wasteland. And the economic cost of this abysmal performance was enormous: in 1991 the Philadelphia Housing Authority – which housed 10 percent of the population of the City of Brotherly Love – estimated the cost of repairing the typical high rise unit at roughly $90,000. The only consolation America's taxpayers could possibly derive from this subsidy of crime and poverty was that, with the meltdown of the Iron Curtain, it provided America with an enduring example of the folly of social engineering.

Government-supported mortgage programs which are geared more toward the middle and upper-middle classes were provided by Fannie Mae and Freddie Mac. Of course, the officers of these quasi-government agencies would loudly protest that they were private corporations. In truth, they would survive no longer as truly private enterprises than Mikhail Gorbachev would survive a truly free election. Each of these agencies had a direct credit line from the U.S. Treasury, had a government-appointed director, and operated under a charter which was approved via Congressional oversight. And, as with government-sponsored deposit insurance, the capital markets generally assumed that the federal government would not permit Fannie Mae or Freddie Mac to fail, any more than FSLIC was allowed to fail.

In essence, Fannie Mae and Freddie Mac were a pork barrel for every homebuilder, realtor, and mortgage banker in America. With the implied government guarantee of their debts – a guarantee for which they paid nothing – the mortgage agencies imparted their own agency guarantee to investors in pools of mortgages originated by approved lenders. Approved mortgage bankers thus gained ready access to the long-term capital markets; they could originate and sell an unlimited dollar volume of home mortgages, as long as they met the agencies' modest capital requirements. They need merely pay a small guaranty fee – less than one-half percent of outstanding principal per year – to Fannie Mae or Freddie Mac. This mortgage agency trough nourished many a mortgage lending sow: in 1990 Fannie Mae guaranteed $96.7 billion in mortgage securities while Freddie Mac gave its blessing to $73.8 billion. Approximately two million mortgage loans thus found funding in America's secondary mortgage markets. In addition, the Ginnie Mae program, which imparted the "full faith" government guarantee for securities backed by FHA and VA mortgage loans, guaranteed over $20 billion of new securities in 1990.

The profusion of government-sponsored mortgage securities had adverse consequences for capital formation in America. In essence, Harry Homeowner was able to tap the market for nearly $200 billion in long-term fixed rate financing each year. At the same time, all but the most highly-rated private corporations found these markets unreceptive and were required to rely instead on the increasingly fragile banking system for liquidity. Even with the sharp rise in single-parent households, sixty-four percent of U.S. households owned their own homes in 1990, largely as a result of the generous subsidy of homeownership which the government-sponsored agencies provided.

Naturally, government-sponsored mortgage programs provide a tough competitor even to other government-subsidized lenders in the mortgage markets. Portfolio lenders – such as thrifts and insurance companies – have found it difficult to profitably offer mortgage loans at the rates which typically prevail in local housing markets. As a consequence, in the 1980's many lenders eschewed price competition and adopted a strategy of relaxing underwriting guidelines as an inducement to borrowers. Most commonly used were the low documentation or "low doc" loans which promised minimal verification of borrower credit data in return for a down payment of 20 percent or more. Some lenders decided to take borrowers at their word in return for the safety of a higher equity cushion. But these low doc lenders, whose rates were typically one-half percent higher than those charged by Fannie Mae and Freddie Mac lenders, failed to ask themselves an obvious question: why would anyone pay a higher interest rate than necessary? Whether the answer be stupidity, laziness, or outright fraud, none of these is the attribute of a sound credit risk. As a result, the failure of home price appreciation to meet the public's expectation in the early nineties led to a rising tide of defaults on low doc loans.

Equally disastrous as low docs, were the "teaser rate ARM's" offered by many banks and thrift institutions. If ever an example was needed of the flaccid perception of a subsidized banking system, teaser rate ARM's were the perfect choice. Mortgage lenders began offering adjustable rate mortgages (ARM's) in the early eighties in an attempt to reduce the interest rate risk of owning a fixed rate mortgage loan portfolio. The most commonly used ARM permitted the interest rate to be reset annually to the yield of the one-year U.S. Treasury bill plus a margin of, say, 2.75 percent to provide a profit for the lender. However, due to the subsidy of fixed rate mortgages provided by the government agencies, which artificially depressed rates on this type of loan, the "fully indexed" yield on an ARM, i.e. one year T-Bill rate plus 2.75 percent, was often higher than prevailing fixed rate offerings. To compete with fixed rate loans, portfolio lenders offered artificially low teaser rates and annual limits or caps on rate changes such that the ARM rate would remain lower than fixed rates in the early years.

Teaser rate ARM's tended to attract two types of customers, both of whom were unprofitable customers for the lender. One type was the rational and creditworthy borrower who computed the interest saving and opted for the ARM with the intent of selling the home or refinancing in a few years. This left the lender with an unprofitable loan during the teaser period and nothing thereafter. The other type of borrower was the one who could not qualify for the size loan requested at prevailing rates for fixed rate loans. However, at a teaser rate of three percent or more below the fully indexed rate, payments were kept low enough that the borrower appeared to pass standard payment-to-income criteria. Obviously, any lender who closed a loan of this type was taking a bet on interest rates. If rates fell over the life of the loan, the borrower could reasonably be expected to faithfully make the payments. If rates remained constant or rose, the probability of default was great.

The heavy use of government guarantees and easy access to the secondary mortgage markets created a wrong-headed approach to mortgage lending throughout the mortgage industry. Prudent lending implied the rationing of a limited supply of funds to the safest credits at the highest obtainable interest rate. But when loans can be originated for a fee and sold in the secondary market, the focus of the business changes to maximizing *volume* rather than quality. Mortgage lenders aggravated this tendency by paying loan officers on a commission basis. Commissions were seldom predicated on loan quality; the greater dollar volume of loans closed, the greater the loan officer's remuneration. Furthermore, most loan officers had difficulty recognizing who their customer was. They did not often look upon the borrower – who would buy his house and never again be heard from – as a source of future business. And, as to the investors in the secondary mortgage market, they were never seen and little understood. Instead, the loan officer's customer could only be the builder or realtor who referred the borrower and would refer many more in the future if everything "went smoothly."

Unfortunately, from a realtor's viewpoint, for a home closing to "go smoothly" was often inimical to the traditional interests of the mortgage lender. Going smoothly might include using the real estate appraiser, closing attorney, title insurer, and termite inspector of the realtor's choice. Going smoothly might include not excessively bothering the borrower for "silly" or "useless" loan documents. Going smoothly might require the lender to withhold some information regarding truth-in-lending disclosures or real estate settlement procedures as required by law. But, most of all, going smoothly required that the borrower's loan be approved so the builder or realtor could close the sale and be paid for his efforts. Under these circumstances, the incentive for relaxing or fraudulently circumventing the lender's underwriting guidelines was often too great to overcome. The results were a deterioration in overall loan quality and a rising default rate on home mortgage loans.

An example of the penalties for fraud, in the rare cases where the perpetrators were prosecuted, was provided by Freedlander, Inc., "the Mortgage People." The family-controlled Virginia mortgage banker packaged and sold more than $500 million of mortgage-backed securities to Fannie Mae and private investors during the eighties. Eric Freedlander was later indicted by a federal grand jury on 83 counts relating to fraudulently inflating values and misrepresenting payment histories. The maximum possible sentence of 425 years and $20 million in fines would certainly give other lenders pause, and the fallout from cases like Freedlander's was to be far-reaching. As the credit crunch of the nineties began, many realtors found that their pet loan officers were becoming more conscientious in enforcing their employers' quality control guidelines. The approval rate on mortgage applications dropped and so did home sales. From the standpoint of the economic policy-maker, one of the traditional tools for stimulating economic activity had been lost. Interest rates could fall, but home sales would not necessarily increase. As the 1990-91 recession dragged on, few economists realized the degree to which the housing industry depended upon loose underwriting standards to support the high level of volume which had been associated with every previous economic recovery in the post-World War II era.

IV

The declining influence which economic policy-makers held over the real estate markets in the early nineties was due – at least in part – to the glut of mortgage securities produced during the eighties. For example, as 1980 began, total mortgage pools or trusts outstanding – including Ginnie Mae, Freddie Mac and the Farmers Home Administration – came to a total of less than $120 billion. However, the warm market acceptance of mortgage-backed securities, which had been pioneered in the seventies by Ginnie Mae, led to rapid growth in the market. Fannie Mae soon jumped on the bandwagon and expanded the scope of the program to include "seasoned," i.e. previously originated loans from the portfolios of thrifts and banks. Coincident with the re-liquification of the banking system beginning in 1982, mortgage-backed securities were issued at an astonishing pace. By the end of 1989, an aggregate principal amount of over $940 billion in these securities was outstanding – a compound annual growth rate of nearly 23 percent!

While the American public became justifiably concerned by the rapid growth in the federal deficit during the eighties, the growth rate of the official federal debt (13.3% per year) paled against that of off-budget obligations such as mortgage-backed securities. Despite the public outcry against "the deficit," little was generally heard or known about this voracious amoeba which hung over the credit markets as the 1990 recession began and threatened to overwhelm any attempt to revive the real estate markets.

At first glimpse, mortgage-backed securities appear to be an entirely self-supporting government enterprise and, were it not for the diversion of capital from more productive purposes, might justify but little public concern. Mortgage originators approved by Ginnie Mae, Fannie Mae, and Freddie Mac were authorized to issue securities in principal amounts of at least $1 million and backed by qualifying home mortgage loans closed in the course of the mortgage company's ongoing operations. The transaction was invisible to the homeowner, who continued to make monthly payments to the mortgage company. After originating the loan, the mortgage company recouped the loan principal through sale of the security and then performed a dual role as intermediary: mortgage servicer for the borrower and security servicer for the investor. The individual homeowner's payment was aggregated with others in the same pool, the mortgage company deducted a "service fee" (typically about one-half percent of the loan principal per year) as well as a guaranty fee for the government agency and passed the balance through to investors in the mortgage pool. In addition to its service fee, the mortgage company controlled the borrowers' tax and insurance escrow accounts and received additional cash flow benefits due to the time lag between receipt of borrower payments and pass-through of investor payments. As purely a cash flow and clerical operation, mortgage servicing soon came to be regarded as a lucrative activity by depository institutions, and a resale or secondary market for "servicing rights" soon developed.

So far, so good. Now deregulate the thrift industry and give them plenty of deposits to invest in diversification of their basic business lines. Add an avaricious community of brokers and investment bankers and one will soon find the development of an inflated market in mortgage servicing rights as was visited upon the mortgage industry during the eighties. Valuation of servicing requires a highly complex model to which several macroeconomic assumptions are critical. What will be the future level of interest rates and – ergo – the prepayment experience of mortgages in the pool? What will be the cost of servicing loans in the future? What will be the default rate – which greatly influences expected life, as well as labor and capital requirements of servicing? What will be the course of future legislation governing the payment of interest on escrows and guaranty fees charged by the guarantor, e.g. Ginnie Mae? Who could possibly know?

None of these concerns dissuaded financial institutions from bidding the price of mortgage servicing rights continually higher during the financial boom of the eighties. And this introduced two evils which had not previously been present. First, it developed an entirely new market for mortgage brokers, who originated loans for immediate sale of servicing rights. Obviously, these brokers had little further interest in the loan after it was closed, and were operating with the sole objective of maximizing volume. Second, it led to the capitalization of servicing rights at increasingly inflated prices, where previously it had been common accounting treatment to merely mention the potential benefit of servicing rights as a footnote on the servicer's balance sheet.

Now consider the impact of the proliferation of mortgage-backed securities on the economy. Homeowners, builders, and realtors found a bonanza as capital was misallocated to their use by lenders and brokers who paid little heed to the borrower's credit history or the vulnerability of the loan to falling real estate prices. Mortgage servicers, many of whom already had highly leveraged balance sheets, paid hard dollars for an asset of dubious value, which could disappear quickly under certain conditions. And, finally, the federally-sponsored guarantors, i.e. Ginnie Mae, Fannie Mae, and Freddie Mac, faced not only the prospect of having to make good the losses of investors due to loan defaults, but also of finding new servicing agents to replace those lost in the ongoing liquidation of the financial industry.

Given the weak foundations of the mortgage-backed securities markets, as noted above, the rocket scientists of Wall Street took it upon themselves to further confuse mortgage investors by developing a Rube Goldberg apparatus of derivative securities. The first breakthrough in this area was the collateralized mortgage obligation (CMO), the partitioning of a mortgage-backed security into various classes. Wall Street's bond salesmen had found that many investors were avoiding mortgage securities due to their long life – usually thirty years – and the uncertain timing of cash flows. The borrower's option to prepay his loan in full at any time made it difficult for fixed income investors to know at what point they would have their funds available for re-investment. The development of CMO's enabled salesmen to pitch their investor prospects with greater certainty as to the life and yield of the security. As a result, a new class of investors was cultivated and the market grew far beyond its traditional limits. Ominously, the new class of mortgage investors included such neophytes as the hapless Japanese financial institutions, whose aptitude for being the last in the proverbial chain of "greater fools" had been frequently demonstrated in the financial mania of the eighties.

Mortgage-related esoterica were not confined to CMO's. Goldman Sachs sold Fannie Mae on the idea of developing real estate mortgage investment conduits (REMIC's) that would divide mortgage pools into one class owning principal payments and one owning interest payments. In effect, this development would permit one class, the interest class, to benefit from rising interest rates while the principal class could benefit from falling rates. Mortgage securities were no longer simply portfolio investments; they took on an entirely different aspect as hedging vehicles and – for some institutions – a means to speculate on interest rates. And this was just the beginning. Subsequent developments included such nirvana as I-TRAINs – Inverse-Total Return Adjustable Index Notes. This was not exactly the stuff with which Jimmy Stewart could kindle public sympathy had he attempted a sequel to "It's a Wonderful Life."

To summarize the condition of the real estate markets during the eighties would be to write another chapter in the great feeding frenzies which have occurred throughout financial history. Just as occurred in the tulipomania of seventeenth century Holland, non-income produc-ing assets had captured the public imagination and had come to be regarded as a substitute for income-producing investments. As in John Law's role in financing the eighteenth century Mississippi land boom, the manipulation of bank credit with the imprimatur of semi-official government agencies abetted the process. And, finally, as occurred in the stock market crash of 1929, the central bank's attempt to restrain the rising tide of speculation reversed the leveraging process and was to lead to the liquidation of inflated real estate and the widespread repudiation of debts as the nineties unfolded.

CHAPTER 8

Currency Markets:
The Lubricant of International Capital

"**W**ar is not so much war of arms as war of money by means whereof arms are useful." Such, according to Thucydides, were the sentiments of Sparta's King Archidamus as, in the fifth century B.C., the city debated whether to make war on Athens.[1] Little has changed. Above all other things, the strength of a nation in geopolitical and military matters depends upon its financial strength, the ability to attract capital investment from foreign lands and to keep domestic capital from seeking greener pastures abroad. Indeed, with the possible exception of the two undeclared wars of the post-World War II era – Korea and Vietnam – America's idealism rarely overcame its economic sense of *Realpolitik*; most wars in American history – and world history – have been the result of a quarrel related to international trade and commerce. The attractiveness of America's capital markets is reflected, therefore, in the value of the dollar. As the dollar goes, so goes the nation.

The deterioration of America's position in the world marketplace which occurred during the eighties is difficult to measure, but the evidence is abundant that a decline in America's external position did in fact occur. As to the basic gauge of accumulated wealth, the international capital position, it is clear that America behaved like a dowager who was forced to consume her capital rather than meeting expenses from current income. For example, in 1980 – when America ran a surplus in its foreign payments – the nation's earnings on its foreign investments (net of payments to foreigners) amounted to the huge sum of $32.7 billion. By 1989, the interest surplus had evaporated and become a deficit of nearly one billion dollars. The fruits of economic hegemony which the nation had accumulated during the generation following World War II had been entirely dissipated in a ten-year orgy of consumption. In the nineties, America would have no capital to finance a continuation of this spending spree. Our trade accounts would be on a "pay as you go" basis unless we could somehow convince the international capital markets that we were deserving of further credit.

As to current consumption, the nation's trade accounts showed that – by the end of the decade – the condition was no longer deteriorating, though it was still a long way from healthy. The 1989 trade deficit of $109.4 billion was 2.1 percent of GNP, far above the $24.2 billion deficit in 1980 (0.9% of GNP), but well below the record $152 billion deficit posted in 1987. Moreover, there was no panic selling or "run" on the dollar. Official reserves of the Federal Reserve System against foreign claims were nearly one-quarter the size of official foreign claims against the U.S., up from roughly 16 percent in 1980. And the Federal Reserve System's reserves of foreign currencies quadrupled from 1987 to 1990 – indicating that the Fed was generally doing more to suppress the dollar's exchange value than intervening to support the dollar.

Such is the privilege – and the curse – of the dollar as the world's reserve currency that the effects of American monetary policy can not be restrained to the domestic economy alone. No longer are currencies backed by gold; they are backed by dollars. When foreign central banks reserve funds against claims on their own economies, they often reserve them in the form of dollar-denominated assets, such as debt obligations of the U.S. Treasury. Purely for purposes of international exchange, foreigners therefore demand a certain amount of dollars over and above those needed to settle their transactions with America. As a result, America is able to consume somewhat more than it produces. Such is the patrimony of holding the world's reserve currency.

As arbiter of the world's capital markets, America bears great responsibility as well as great privilege. In the 1920's, a large influx of dollars from foreigners led to an increase in America's purchasing power vastly exceeding the increase in output, and these dollars were not recirculated in world trade. This led to an immense rise in the price of financial assets in America, culminating in tight money and a stock market crash. The eighties were to see a similar sequence of events.

Recognizing the importance of the exchange value of the dollar, and wishing to better monitor its attempts to stabilize world currency markets, the Federal Reserve has developed an index of the exchange value of the dollar in terms of the currencies of our ten major trading partners – the U.S. dollar index, USDX. In computing USDX, each currency is weighted by its share of America's trade accounts, from 20.8

percent for the deutschemark to 3.6 percent for the Swiss franc. The result is an index number beginning with the base of 100 as the dollar's value after it was devalued in the so-called Smithsonian Accord of March 1973.

During the 1970's, due to high inflation and low real interest rates, the dollar generally weakened. However, as the eighties began, the tight money policy of the Volcker Fed made the dollar attractive to foreigners and USDX embarked upon a dramatic rise from 85.5 in January 1980 to 158.4 in February 1985. Without considering differences in inflation rates, the purchasing power of the dollar had risen by over 85 percent in five years! From America's standpoint, everything in the world was on sale at "blue light special" prices. Conversely, from the viewpoint of foreigners, everything made in America became prohibitively expensive. While foreign investment capital was pouring into the United States in search of bonds and financial assets, so were foreign goods. As in the twenties, America once again became the land of rising financial assets. Great fortunes were made. In terms of the world marketplace, however, American goods were being undersold by the products of Germany, Japan, and the newly industrialized countries.

Recognizing that the country was suffering serious long-term damage in its international capital account, the U.S. Treasury and the Federal Reserve undertook an active policy of dollar depreciation starting in 1985. To accommodate the demand for dollars, the Fed expanded bank reserves at a furious rate. Total reserves of the banking system jumped by 17.8 percent in 1985 and by a further 23.4 percent in 1986. With the increased supply of dollars, USDX dropped sharply – to 106.6 at the end of 1986.

By 1987, the opposite problem of a too-rapid depreciation of the dollar seemed to be threatening world capital markets. Dollar-denominated assets acquired by foreigners in early 1985 had lost one-third of their value due to the dollar's drop in the currency markets. To reduce the momentum of the decline, the Fed abruptly tightened domestic money market conditions. Interest rates rose sharply and total reserves of the U.S. banking system grew by just 3.7 percent in 1987. The financial markets were suddenly hit by the worst of all possible worlds. Bond prices plummeted. At the same time, the stampede by foreigners to dump U.S. bonds further aggravated the drop and led to a continued decline in the dollar. Interest rates were rising and money was tightening while the momentum of a rising stock market continued for a while longer and carried valuation in the stock market to ridiculous levels. A crash in the stock market was both necessary and inevitable, and when it occurred in October 1987, it propelled the dollar even lower. By December 1987, USDX had dropped to 88.6, and foreign central banks were actively cooperating with the Fed to avert a panic run on the dollar in world currency markets. The Fed's holdings of foreign currencies dropped to a mere 5.4 percent of claims of foreign central banks against the U.S. Yet, the nation's trade deficit continued to post new records month by month. America was no longer the kingpin of world trade, but America's loss was also the world's loss for there was no obvious replacement who could exert both the power and the will to impose order on the world's capital markets.

The debt binge of the eighties had not been confined to America. Germany's huge $75 billion trade surplus was overwhelmed by the cost of its 1990 reunification with the former German Democratic Republic. The rebuilding of East Germany would require hundreds of billions of dollars, which converted the Germans overnight from international lenders to borrowers. Government budget deficits of DM 100 billion, about four percent of GNP, were as serious as those of the United States.[2] And the traditional German attitude of a "social contract" between government and the people would make Germany's federal debt every bit as intractable as America's.

Third World nations were even worse off. A total of $1.3 trillion was owed by such financial basket cases as Argentina, Brazil, and Nigeria. And the banks who had taken the attitude that "you can't go wrong lending to countries" were now paying the price for their foolishness. An index of the resale value of loans made to third world countries was developed by Lehman Brothers and indicated that these loans were worth but 33½ cents on the dollar in early 1990. Meanwhile, Sub-Saharan Africa had accumulated $135 billion of debt with no visible means of repaying it, while Eastern Europe and the Soviet Union were $150 billion "in the red" financially, if no longer politically.[3]

What about the vaunted economic success story of the eighties: Japan, Incorporated? The Japanese were never so careful in financial affairs as they were in building automobiles. Japanese corporations relied upon their partnership with a generous banking system to borrow approximately 70 percent of the book value of their assets during the eighties. But the value of many of these assets was highly suspect. Japanese real estate prices – a large part of corporate assets – had jumped by over 200 percent in the latter half of the eighties. Japan's 12 largest commercial banks were sitting on $365 billion of real estate loans – nearly a quarter of their assets.[4] Meanwhile, Japan's banks held vast amounts of stock in Japanese industry – and this had been marked up under regulatory guidelines to reflect 45 percent of the paper profits from Nippon's stock market boom. The drop in Japanese share prices in 1990 wiped out well over one trillion dollars in value, much of it owned by the banks. Meanwhile, a sharp rise in Japanese interest rates was increasingly putting the pinch on companies which had benefitted from the cheap credit environment of the eighties.

America's financial problems were by no means unique. The problem of excessive leveraging of corporate balance sheets and high government debts was a world problem. Indeed, with a statutory federal debt somewhat over 50 percent of annual GNP, the United States was in far better shape than most nations. Were it not for the tremendous burden of its off-budget obligations and the weakness of its banking system, the United States would not have been in bad shape at all. But this was not the case, not in America, nor anywhere else in the world. Virtually every nation had added significantly and unsustainably to its debt burden during the eighties. Especially in the wake of the Crash of 1987, the common problem of excessive and poor quality debt brought the need for closer cooperation and coordination of economic policy into sharp focus.

II

From the time Richard Nixon severed the dollar's central role in the international gold payments standard in 1971, coordination of monetary policy among the free nations of the world has evolved more as a response to economic conditions than as the result of a coherent plan for managing the world economy. Indeed, during Ronald Reagan's first term (1981-1984), it can accurately be said that America's policy toward the currency markets was no policy at all. The free market bias of the Reagan era had led to a new era of benign neglect of the dollar. Nothing was done to brake the sharp rise of the dollar until, as noted above, the overvaluation of the dollar began to exert an overwhelming handicap on America's competitive position in foreign markets.

The Plaza Accord of September 1985 was to augur in a new era of coordination, not only in the exchange markets, but in monetary and fiscal policy as well. While the Plaza Accord was concerned mainly with depreciating the dollar, the Tokyo Summit of May 1986 extended the coordination to include a wider array of policy tools, and listed a set of indicators to gauge and monitor progress toward common goals.

The developments of 1987 – and their outcome in the worldwide stock market crash in October – were to show that the economic policies of the major industrial nations were inextricably related. The Louvre Accord of February 1987 declared that the dollar had dropped enough and steps would be taken by the seven major industrial countries to stabilize its value. The Accord was reaffirmed by the finance ministers of the "Group of Seven" nations in April and once more at the Venice Summit in June. Due to complaints by America's trading partners over the size of the U.S. federal deficit, the Venice Summit developed a plan for coordinating policy via specific performance measures, including America's fiscal policy.

Given the already tight money and an environment of rapidly rising stock and commodity prices, Treasury Secretary Baker's proposal at the World Bank - IMF Meeting in September 1987 was to prove the precursor to the financial turmoil of October. The Baker proposal was simply that a basket of commodities – including gold – be used as a measure of the international effort to coordinate economic policy. A rise in commodity prices in dollar terms, for example, would indicate an overly stimulative policy in America and would argue in favor of a policy mix intended to moderate the rate of growth. And, in a step that was to have momentous consequences, Secretary Baker publicly chastised the Germans for forcing up interest rates and threatened a competitive devaluation of the dollar. The significance of this was not immediately appreciated. As an editorial in *The Wall Street Journal* on October 1, 1987, saw it, "Secretary Baker has done a service just by mentioning the word (gold) in public, where it now can presumably be discussed seriously."

The international stock, bond and commodity markets were in no mood to discuss the Baker plan during the month of October 1987. The traumatic drop in stock prices that followed the proposal immediately switched the focus of economic policy to priority No. 1: provide liquidity to the banking system. The dollar quickly resumed its decline, falling from 1.82 deutschemarks on October 22 to 1.70 deutschemarks on November 4. And nobody was in a mood to interfere. As Mr. Baker himself said in the wake of the crash, he wanted to "make sure" that the Fed kept "sufficient liquidity in the system."

As the eighties drew to a close, the Fed reverted once again to a tight monetary policy, and the dollar rose moderately until 1989. However, after domestic interest rates peaked in mid-1989, international capital found more tempting returns in Europe and Japan, and the dollar resumed its decline, posting new record lows against the deutschemark and Swiss franc by early 1991. As the U.S. dollar index plumbed new lows, it appeared that the Fed was actively abetting the process. Federal Reserve data indicated that the Fed's holdings of foreign currencies had risen from $13 billion at the end of 1987 to over $51 billion by October 1990. This could not have occurred unless the Fed had been actively selling the dollar to suppress its value.

The active Fed policy of dollar depreciation led to a new policy dilemma in the early nineties. As the Fed acquired increasing amounts of foreign currency, it was obtaining the funds needed for doing so by selling a portion of its portfolio of government securities. However, by law, the reserves the Fed holds against Federal Reserve notes – the paper currency Americans consider cash – must be backed by Treasury obligations, gold, or special drawing rights issued by the International Monetary Fund. The Fed policy of selling the dollar and offsetting or "sterilizing" the worldwide inflationary effect by selling government securities was threatening the Fed's ability to meet its legal collateral requirements. And, as the credit crunch worsened, the public demand for currency was soaring. Unless the rules changed, the Fed would eventually be faced with the requirement to increase its purchases of Treasury securities or allow the dollar to appreciate.

As the 1990's began, the Fed was effectively pursuing a "beggar thy neighbor" policy. On the one hand, domestic growth and inflation were restrained by anemic growth in bank reserves and the regulatory action taken to increase bank capital requirements. At the same time, the Fed was encouraging a lower dollar to stimulate growth in exports. The depreciating dollar led to rising import prices, while domestic prices were kept stable via tight money. Worse yet, in the new spirit of international cooperation, America's trading partners were abetting the depreciation of the dollar rather than combatting it. Foreign official institutions barely increased their holdings of U.S. Treasury securities from 1988 to 1990, and rising interest rates abroad actively pulled private funds from America to capital markets abroad.

In effect, the spirit of economic cooperation among the world's major industrial countries in the eighties and early nineties was an *ad hoc* policy of crisis management followed by intermittent periods of beggar thy neighbor policies. The central banks of the world – each for its own reasons – were following a policy of tight money as the decade began. The Fed was encouraging a gradual drop in the dollar to restore balance in the trade account while destroying money and wealth in the domestic economy. Meanwhile, Europe was tying its currencies together in a European Monetary System (EMS) which, for better or for worse, would be dominated by the German mark. The Bundesbank was keeping money tight to counter the stimulative effects of reunification. Meanwhile Japan was maintaining a tight clamp on money growth to counter the speculative excesses of the eighties. Money was scarce the world over. America would get precious little help from its economic allies.

III

"Mit diesem Übergang, beginnt das alte Herz Berlins wieder zu schlagen."[5] Thus spoke Walter Momper, mayor of Berlin, with the opening of a passage through the Berlin Wall at Potsdamer Platz on November 12, 1989. With this passage, said the mayor, the old heart of Berlin beats once again. What had occurred was truly earth-shaking. *Ein Land, Ein Volk.* It was just a matter of time. Germany would soon be reunited.

The political reunification of Germany shattered any remaining doubt as to leadership of the increasingly integrated European economy. The European Community had already stated the objective of Economic and Monetary Union, and the tumbling barriers between East and West served to accelerate the European sense of unity, with Germany at its center. The European Monetary System (EMS) was the first and most crucial piece in the European puzzle, and Germany's central bank, the Bundesbank, was set to play the lead role.

The business of fighting inflation is indelibly etched into the consciousness of the Bundesbank. One need only read the wording of a ten million mark note issued by the German Reichsbank during the Weimar Republic's hyper-inflation of 1923. The note was issued on August 22 and was subject to recall after October 1, 1923. Ten million marks would buy no more than one mark would have bought a few years earlier – about one loaf of bread. The disenfranchisement of the German middle class which occurred as a result of this loss of purchasing power – many families saw their life savings wiped out – did much to propitiate the rise of National Socialism. Later, after World War II, the German economic miracle couldn't get off the ground until Ludwig Erhard overstepped his authority under the Allied military government and implemented a far-reaching currency and market reform. Therefore, in the collective German mind, worthless currency is the epitome of economic failure and political chaos.

As a result of the traditionally conservative German attitude toward monetary management, and the traditional British reticence to relinquish the United Kingdom's political prestige, the development of an Exchange Rate Mechanism (ERM) as the first step toward EMS has been a remarkable achievement. In its early years, from 1979 to 1987, EMS suffered through 10 separate currency realignments. With the entry of Britain, however, the pound sterling was pegged to the mark, and the system seemed to gain cohesion and stability. For their part, the British saw the pegging of the pound as adding credibility to Britain's anti-inflationary stance. Germany's other trading partners have also shown a preference to use the mark as the chosen tool for intervening in the currency markets to stabilize their own currencies. Thus, as John Major said, when he was Britain's Chancellor of the Exchequer, "Increasingly, (the ERM) has functioned like a modern gold standard, with the D-mark as the anchor."[6]

What tactics the EMS would take in further integrating the disparate European currencies was still being debated in the early 1990's. On the one hand, the British argued for a new currency, the European Currency Unit (ECU) in the "hard ECU" plan. This plan called for new terms and conditions for the settlement of transactions by using repurchase obligations issued by the individual central banks and the establishment of a European Monetary Fund. The Delors Committee – a group of 12 EC central bankers – also favored adoption of the ECU – not as a theoretical unit but for actual settlement of intra-European trade accounts.

For their part, the Germans tended to favor the creation of a single and independent European Central Banking System (ECBS) to manage a unified European currency. Karl Otto Pöhl outlined the conditions which such an institution must satisfy. "In the ECBS ... it will not be possible for the national central banks to have any autonomous monetary policy powers of their own: they will only be the operational arm of the European Central Bank."[7] Mr. Pöhl's recommendation seemed to imply selection of a single dominant institution from among the existing European central banks, and the ceding of power to that one institution. Moreover, he recommended that the integration process be undertaken in one step, when all members were able to irrevocably fix the exchange rates of their currencies.

As a result of EMU, European monetary policy appeared to be heading down the same road in the nineties that Britain and France had taken in the twenties. At that time, European currencies were pegged to gold at an unsustainable rate. Gold flowed from Europe to America, and the European economy never fully recovered from World War I. In similar fashion, as the nineties unfolded, Germany adhered to a tight monetary policy despite the massive expenditures imposed upon it by the rebuilding of Eastern Europe and the integration of East Germany into the Federal Republic.

Noting the obvious similarity of the German stance to the road taken by the U.S. in 1981, Alan Meltzer dubbed this policy of increased spending financed by increased borrowing "Reaganomics on the Rhine." Despite recession in Britain, and a virtual economic standstill in France, Italy, and Spain, the Bundesbank raised its discount rate to 6.5 percent in January 1991, the highest level since 1982. Within hours, the central banks of Austria and the Netherlands followed suit. European currencies rose in tandem against the dollar, which was setting record lows against some of its European counterparts. By some estimates the dollar was as much as 40 percent undervalued against the European currencies. Moreover, to prevent a further drop in the dollar, the Fed was restrained from fighting the recession in America. The tight-fisted Germans were dragging Europe and North America into a common grave of high real interest rates, falling commodity prices, and declining economic activity.

The world appeared to have learned little from economic history. As Swiss Banker Felix Zulauf pointed out, a similar set of conditions had precipitated the Great Depression. In 1930 the Fed cut the discount rate repeatedly. At the beginning of 1931, a run on the dollar developed which resulted in the Fed's reversing its interest rate cuts. As Zulauf put it in early 1991, "The big question is whether this is a recession or a depression, and whether we (the Fed) are prevented from easing. The Bundesbank is the one true disciplinarian in the entire world structure... as long as they continue those policies, it forces the Fed to stop easing." Like the retailer who finds the cheapest suppliers, Germany was threatening to drive its competitors into bankruptcy. World capital flows had become unstable, and this was a problem that would affect the economy of every industrialized nation.

IV

Like Germany, Japan found itself coming to grips with its own success during the eighties. At first glimpse, the Japanese economy appears to have had no problem whatsoever. In a world where shoddy workmanship was the rule, Japan produced high quality goods in large volume and at lower cost than the competition. The success of Japanese automakers' American-built products demonstrated that it was not purely due to lower production costs or some innate productivity of Japanese workers. It was, rather, a case of better management. However, like Germany, Japan gathered the momentum of its success under the umbrella of an undervalued currency. The tables were turned after the dollar peaked in 1985, as the value of the Japanese yen quickly doubled by the end of 1987. Japan found itself with the embarrassment of riches.

Despite the tremendous increase in the value of the yen, Japan's trade surplus with America proved to be an intractable and potentially destabilizing problem. For example, Japan's 1990 bilateral surplus with America was $38 billion – the lowest since 1984, yet still above the $33 billion surplus of that year. Thus, at an exchange rate of 130 yen to the dollar, the Japanese were accumulating dollars even faster than they had six years earlier at 250 yen to the dollar.

Japan's performance in trade with the rest of the world was no less spectacular. The country ran an overall surplus of $52.4 billion in 1990, which was higher than the $46.1 billion surplus of 1985, when it undertook an active program of opening its markets to foreign goods. Indeed, had it not been for a sharp rise in the price of oil, the 1990 surplus would have been significantly higher.

As a result of its consistent ability to sell more than it bought, Japan was visited with the eternal problem of the *nouveau riche*: how to spend the money. One solution which seemed consistent with the objective of long-term market dominance was to build manufacturing plants in those foreign markets where Japan was active. In the most obvious example, Japanese autos, this program enabled Japan to cut the percentage of U.S. auto sales that were imported from Japan from 1985 to 1990. However, when cars built by Japan's American subsidiaries are included, Japan's share of U.S. auto sales rose from 20 percent in 1985 to 28 percent in 1990. By 1993, Japanese companies planned to have a total of ten completely owned or joint venture assembly factories in America. Nissan Motor Company alone had committed nearly $2 billion to its U.S. production facilities, including a $600 million engine plant to begin production in Tennessee in 1992.

The Japanese effort to build production facilities in America met with a warm acceptance, and was generally viewed as a sincere attempt to reduce the trade imbalance and improve the competitiveness of

American industry. Not so the Japanese effort to acquire existing U.S. companies. Japanese takeovers rose from insignificant levels in 1985 to over $10 billion each year from 1988 to 1990. The $6.1 billion purchase of recording industry giant MCA, Inc. by Japan's Matsushita Electric Industrial Co. in 1990 was a case in point for what many considered a one-way street. Due to regulatory restrictions imposed by the Federal Communications Commission, most potential American bidders in the telecommunications industry couldn't even consider such a deal. Meanwhile, tight restrictions on foreign investment in Japan limited American acquisitions in Japan to a total of just $3.7 million in 1990. On the other hand, Matsushita had paid $6.1 billion for a company whose stated net worth was only $2.5 billion – and even on this lower equity figure it was able to show a return of only eight percent.

A key factor in the success of Japanese industry and the desire for foreign acquisitions was the availability of cheap capital for Japan's major industrial corporations. When Sony bought Columbia Pictures in 1989, it borrowed $3 billion of the $5 billion price tag. The plan was to replenish the till with a low interest convertible bond issue. However, the 1990 plunge in Japanese share prices slammed the window shut before Sony could act. Similarly, Bridgestone Corp.'s $2.6 billion purchase of Firestone, as well as the $1.5 billion needed to overhaul Firestone's obsolete factories, was partly funded by convertible bonds in the Japanese market. Unfortunately, Bridgestone did not obtain long-term financing and would be forced to refinance its debt in the tight money market of the early nineties. Thus, as the nineties began Japan's appetite for foreign acquisitions was sated, and a huge overhang of liabilities from the eighties remained.

Despite the abuse they received from Japan-bashing Congressmen and TV anchormen, the Japanese were a far smaller force than the British during the acquisition mania of the late eighties. British investment peaked at $32 billion in 1988, more than double the total for Japan. On a cumulative basis the British owned $119 billion of the $401 billion in foreign-owned corporate assets in the U.S. in 1989. By contrast, America owned $373 billion in overseas assets, including $67 billion in Canada. Total Japanese assets in America amounted to just $70 billion. However, public obligations were another story: the U.S. Treasury's debt to Asian countries, mainly Japan, exceeded $153 billion in 1989.

The bilateral trade and payments imbalance between Japan and America, while perhaps not as serious a problem as the public perceived, was nevertheless a paradigm for a wider malaise that affected world currency and capital markets in the eighties. Huge disparities in wealth and productivity were present and growing despite the best efforts of public policy. Despite the imbalance, the governments of all major industrial nations, including Japan and Germany, relied heavily upon deficit financing during the eighties. And the preference for leveraging a small capital base to acquire unwieldy and inefficient assets was worldwide. As worldwide economic growth slowed in the nineties, it would become increasingly difficult to service the burden of the enormous debt that the world economy had created.

CHAPTER 9

Sic Transit Gloria:
The Decline and Fall of Junk Bonds

As the War Between the States went against the South, the Confederate government relied ever more on deficit financing, and the printing presses stamped out an enormous supply of fiat currency. The supply was so great and the quality of the printing so poor that it was often possible to apprehend counterfeiters by the superior quality of their work. The financial mania of the eighties would identify transgressors in much the same fashion. The most successful operators – such as Ivan Boesky and Michael Milken – were often victims of their own success. In fact, in Milken's case, a body of evidence suggests that he was more the victim of his own enormous financial success than of the magnitude of the offenses for which he was eventually sentenced to federal prison. Nothing attracts a crowd – or the scrutiny of an ambitious district attorney – like a vast sum of money which has been acquired quickly by mysterious means. The criminals of the eighties were merely acting out the karma of an epoch of unbridled avarice and the financial environment it spawned. But this can only be said with the benefit of hindsight. The legacy of junk bonds and bankrupt companies that remains, like old Confederate notes, is of a bold idea that failed.

The central force in the heavy issuance of junk bonds during the eighties was greed. The junk bond buyer was motivated by an interest rate premium vs. investment grade bonds. The junk bond issuer was willing to pay this premium because he expected to earn an even higher premium when the proceeds were re-invested in business operations, mergers, or acquisitions. Finally, the brokers who introduced buyer and seller received enormous fees for developing and promulgating an inherently flawed and self-serving investment theory. Let it be known as the Theory of Junk.

The Theory of Junk runs counter to the widely held theoretical view of "efficient markets." In essence, the Efficient Markets Theory holds that rational investors will seek out and accurately interpret all available information and then take appropriate action. In aggregate, this places an interest rate premium into investments, representing the market's consensus view of their risk vs. risk-free investments, such as Treasury bills. By this theory, if the market prices the interest rate on a ten-year corporate bond five percent higher than on a ten-year U.S. Treasury note, the inference is that investors require a premium of five percent per annum to compensate for the increased risk. Thus, if the market is efficient, empirical data should show that, over time and a relatively large number of issues, the actual default losses suffered by high yield bond investors approximate the interest rate premium reflected in market prices.

The Efficient Markets Theory seems to contradict the essence of the Theory of Junk. The junk theory held that the actual default loss experience of high yield securities was less than the premium offered by the market, and this yield increment would provide a real net gain for investors. In other words, the interest rates on junk bonds were higher than they should have been if the market was, indeed, efficient. Accordingly, purveyors of junk bonds in the eighties pointed out studies which indicated the fairly low default losses of non-investment grade bonds in the fifties, sixties, and seventies. For example, if the average historical default loss rate on all junk bonds was three percent vs. the five percent yield premium offered by a specific issue, one might readily conclude that investors could reap a pure profit of two percent per annum. In the long run, this was not necessarily incompatible with the Efficient Markets Theory. Increased investor buying of junk bonds would soon reverse the inefficient pricing of junk bonds; their prices would rise and yields fall to the long-run equilibrium level, where risk-adjusted yields are uniform. Indeed, this is the essence and objective of all active investing: to find investments which have not been properly priced in view of their true returns. Buy the ones that are priced too low and wait for everyone else to wake up to reality. An active and affluent group of investors follow this approach, called "value investing," and their success stands as powerful testimony to the fact that an inefficient price structure will tend to attract the funds needed to correct the problem. Prices that are out of touch with reality will not persist forever, due to the collective force exerted by value-conscious investors.

If the Theory of Junk provided a rationale for junk bond buyers, a small twist of the theory could buttress the hopes of junk issuers as well. Here it was necessary to play upon the eternal hope of all debtors:

inflation. If a corporation's $100 million in assets produced $15 million in pre-tax operating income (before interest), any interest rate below 15 percent would provide a positive net return if the borrowed funds could generate the same earnings. In this example, a doubling of corporate assets at an interest cost of 12 percent would increase pre-tax earnings by $3 million *on the existing capital base.* As an added bonus, the new assets might soon be sold for a quick capital gain, the bonds retired and the profit retained. It is easy to see how junk bonds came to play a major role in the wave of mergers and acquisitions of the eighties.

The problem with the Theory of Junk was that it was contradicted by a vast body of historical experience, which should have been obvious to any serious investor. From 1920 to 1989, the average annual increase in the consumer price index was three percent and the average top-rated bond yield was 5.6 percent. For those who were not satisfied with the resulting 2.6 percent real return on bonds, the Dow Jones industrial stocks provided an average earnings yield of 4.8 percent after inflation.[1] Moreover, real growth in output (GNP) has been less than four percent per year over long periods of time. For example, from 1870 to 1960, real income in the United States grew approximately 3.5 percent per year.[2] One might, therefore, expect both borrower and lender to ask a common question: if the average real return in the U.S. economy over time has been less than four percent, what is so different about this place and time?

II

The 1980's were indeed different from normal times, but only to the extent that all great market booms are different. There was an abundance of liquidity in the financial system and a commensurate rise in the gullibility of investors; it seemed to many that the economy would continue to grow forever. Optimistic assumptions about business prospects were the driving force behind a flood of new high yield bond issues, and the august investment house of Drexel, Burnham, Lambert, Inc. built a financial empire from junk bonds with super-salesman Michael Milken as commander of the Praetorian Guard.

Most of what is publicly known about the junk bond operations of Drexel comes from the transcripts of the many legal complaints which have been litigated in the aftermath of the collapse of the junk bond market and Drexel's bankruptcy petition. From these, it emerges that

Mr. Milken relied upon a stable of investors, including certain insurance companies and thrift institutions, to develop what appeared to be a liquid market for the many new issues which Drexel underwrote. Later, the Resolution Trust Corporation and the Federal Deposit Insurance Corporation alleged that Drexel had used a scheme of coercion, extortion, and bribery to obtain the funds of thrift institutions for these investments. "The liquidity of the markets for junk bonds was an illusion resulting from extensive manipulation through a variety of deceptive devices," according to the FDIC complaint. According to the suit, 44 thrifts which were subsequently taken over by the FDIC suffered losses of $1.25 billion as a result of their bond investments through Drexel. In addition, the agency alleged that Drexel reaped $750 million in unlawful profits due to the manner in which trades were arranged.

In addition to Mr. Milken and other Drexel employees, several executives of the failed institutions were accused of conspiring "in the plunder of their respective institutions." These included employees of Lincoln Savings and Loan Association of Irvine, California; CenTrust Savings Bank of Miami; and Columbia Savings and Loan Association of Beverly Hills, California. One defendant, Donald Engel, a former managing director of Drexel, was responsible for hosting parties at the company's junk-bond conferences. According to FDIC, "During the annual sales meetings...called 'The Predators Ball' and at other times Engel provided various forms of illicit entertainment and other favors to personnel of actual and potential Drexel clients with the purpose and effect of inducing the acquisition of junk bonds and other actions." Ah, the staid and hallowed corridors of high finance!

Drexel was by no means the only firm to benefit from the funds of junk bond investors. An example of how bondholders' funds were used to finance a financial pyramid was provided by Meshulan Riklis' acquisition of E-II Holdings, Inc. Mr. Riklis owned Faberge-Arden, which he sold to finance his 1988 acquisition of E-II. American Brands, Inc. had previously acquired E-II in a so-called "Pac-Man" defensive maneuver against an attempt by a third party to acquire the company. When E-II bondholders balked at selling their bonds to American Brands at 103 percent of par, ownership was transferred to Mr. Riklis. A swift chain reaction of financial transactions relating to Mr. Riklis' other financial interests followed. Mr. Riklis received $3 million a year from E-II for management services, while another Riklis company received $12.5 million for computer and communications services. In addition, E-II paid $15.9 million plus assumption of debt to acquire a TV business partnership from Riklis. A tax-sharing agreement which consolidated E-II in the Riklis family's consolidated tax return provided that Riklis get the direct benefit of any tax savings – potentially as much as $50 million. Riklis also extracted about $600 million in cash from E-II when it bought another Riklis-owned company, the unprofitable McCrory Corporation. Shortly after Mr. Riklis severed his relationship with E-II in December 1990, the E-II bonds, which had traded at 100 percent of face value in 1988, were changing hands at prices of 12 cents to 24 cents on the dollar.

After reality had set in and the house of junk was falling apart in the early nineties, chastened investors were raising complaints about the way many of the buyout deals of the eighties had been handled. A case in point was Revco D. S. Inc., whose court-appointed examiner outlined grounds under which legal action could be initiated against former shareholders and advisers from an attempted leveraged buyout directed at the retailing concern. Two years after Revco went private in 1986, it filed under Chapter 11 of the federal bankruptcy law. The bankruptcy court examiner later alleged that Salomon Brothers, Inc. had provided overly optimistic earnings projections. The lead bank in arranging buy-out financing, Wells Fargo, had doubled its fees in the course of the negotiations. Further, the examiner alleged that Revco's auditors, Peat Marwick Mitchell, destroyed important work papers. And, finally, Revco's chairman negotiated a severance contract shortly after the buyout, which apparently included his acquisition of certain corporate assets at prices which appeared to be less than fair market value.

Another case of payback for the crazy eighties was Interco, Inc., a furniture and shoe company based in St. Louis. Interco took on nearly $2 billion in debt in 1988 to ward off a hostile takeover, and by 1989 had already defaulted on some of its high-yield bonds. After the company filed for Chapter 11 protection in 1991, it sued its former investment banker, Wasserstein Perella & Co. for negligence. The suit charged the investment bank with delaying the sale of Interco's Ethan Allen furniture subsidiary and causing it to accept a lower price than could have been obtained.

The finger-pointing phase of the business cycle had started. A growing list of bankrupt companies would begin looking for scapegoats to explain their woes. However, what was often overlooked in these suits was the possibility that the officers and directors of America's largest corporations and financial institutions should have been prudent and circumspect enough to avoid the troubled waters in which they had foundered. In the case of Interco, it would probably be difficult to prove that the company was "forced" to sell Ethan Allen. But, from the bondholders' viewpoint, the issue was moot. Interco's 13.75 percent junk bonds were trading at four cents on the dollar. Had the loss been due to incompetence, gross negligence, or outright fraud? Regardless of cause, a vast amount of wealth had been wiped out and a viable enterprise was in danger of being shuttered.

One immediate effect of the junk bond debacle was the new attitude of financial prudence it evinced from investors. One example which demonstrated how "old money" tends to survive was provided by Fred Trump, father of the self-proclaimed entrepreneurial legend, Donald Trump. During the eighties, the younger Trump came to epitomize financial gunslinging with his successful use of leverage to build what – to all outward appearances – seemed to be an awesome New York real estate empire. His flashy lifestyle and widely publicized acquisition of an airline, gambling casinos, and the world-famous Plaza Hotel made him the darling of the gullible news media. Later, after it had become apparent that Trump's empire was built upon a house of debt and default on some of the junk bonds issued by his gaming interests seemed a distinct possibility, he was able to rely upon his father's help to meet one of the scheduled interest payments on the Trump Castle bonds. The crafty elder Trump merely sent his agent – with a suitcase of cash – to the casino to purchase $3 million in chips. By doing so, the senior Trump avoided lending funds directly to his son, which would be a violation of New Jersey's gambling regulations. As the holder of the casino's chips, Trump had no need to compete with other creditors for his money. Of course, his funds bore no interest, but in the nineties Will Rogers' old admonition regarding return *of* capital was increasingly taken to heart. Mr. Trump could at any time merely redeem his chips at the casino for cash. As one observer noted, "It is the ultimate first mortgage."

It was beginning to seem that the only investors who still had cash were the ones who were steeped in the capitalist tradition of self-defense, and they would clearly be the ones who would dictate the terms under which credit would be available in the nineties. Optimistic assumptions were no longer made. Capital was committed on the basis of the worst-case scenario, which ever more often seemed to be borne out by experience.

III

By 1990, it became apparent that most issuers of junk bonds had sold investors passage on a "Ship of Fools." The deceleration in economic growth, which had started in 1988, had turned into a full-blown recession by the end of 1990. With recession and weakening sales, the high fixed interest obligations incurred during the eighties would prove to be the shoals on which many a ship foundered. The pages of the financial press were littered with tales of the wreckage of those companies who had considered their prospects bright enough to service long-term debt at interest rates of 12-16 percent. A look at a few of the victims is sufficient evidence of the folly of the ebullient investment climate which had produced an excruciating burden of debt.

The first gasp for air in the process of financial strangulation was usually an attempt to cut the debt burden. Burlington Holdings, Inc., whose 1990 interest expenses of $251.9 million swamped operating profit of $162.7 million, found itself selling assets. As often occurred, this was not enough to impress investors, who were widely offering Burlington's 13.875 percent bonds for resale at 42 cents on the dollar. After all, the book value of corporate assets is a poor proxy for their market value, which is – in part – dependent on a liquid market for that corporation's equity. And that market is, in turn, dependent on the company's ability to generate profits from those assets.

Since the prospects for asset sales and stock issues were increasingly limited, a frequently attempted alternative was to restructure debt. Often, asset sales and restructuring of debt were part of the same package. Ambase Corp., an insurance holding company, finding itself running short of the cash needed to make coupon payments on its 14.875 percent notes of 1999, offered 25 cents on the dollar to repurchase half of the outstanding notes. To get the cash needed, the company was expecting an advance from TVH Acquisition Corp., which had offered to buy Ambase's Home Insurance subsidiary. By buying back its bonds at such low prices and selling assets, Ambase was achieving the same result as it would by selling assets at high prices.

While the Ambase offer surely seemed like a bad deal to bondholders who had bought the bonds at par, many junk bond owners would have been happy to get out at 25 cents on the dollar. Owners of USG Corp. bonds, for example, found the company missing principal and interest payments as their 13.25 percent bonds sank to 20 cents on the dollar. In an oft-repeated error, USG had taken on $2.4 billion in debt to deter a hostile suitor in 1988. However, in this case, the company's principal unit, U.S. Gypsum, was vulnerable to asbestos-related claims if it filed for Chapter 11 protection. Thus, USG bondholders found themselves with a depreciating asset but could only aggravate the problem if they attempted a forcible seizure of assets through bankruptcy. So USG struggled to sell assets and reach an agreement with its bondholders to restructure its debt. An excessive debt burden was once again the culprit. An otherwise viable company, that had sales over $1.9 billion in 1990, could simply not generate enough cash flow to service its debts.

Many a dream of building a financial empire on a sandy foundation of debt would be washed away in the tidal wave of the nineties. Such was the case of Robert Campeau, self-made Toronto real estate investor, whose Campeau Corp. engineered the takeover of retailing giant Allied Stores Corp. in 1986 and of Federated Department Stores, Inc. in 1988. The combined price tag of $10.1 billion resulted in a $7 billion debt burden, which was too large for the combined entity to profitably service. By 1991, Bank of Montreal was petitioning a Canadian court to declare Mr. Campeau bankrupt. The bank's move was taken to recover some of the $29.7 million in personal loans it had extended. As a proxy for how the market's sentiment for speculative investments had changed, the Campeau stock which the bank held against these loans as collateral had sunk from 31 Canadian dollars in 1986 to 48 Canadian cents in 1991. By forcing Mr. Campeau into bankruptcy, his creditors would at least have a claim on his $10 million Toronto mansion. The dazzling success stories of the eighties would dazzle equally – but in a different way – as the nineties unfolded.

As the Persian Gulf War held petroleum prices up and air travel down, the debt binge of the eighties wreaked more financial havoc on the airline industry than ten years of plotting by Abu Nidal and his entire coterie of trained terrorists. Continental Airline Holdings, Inc. filed for bankruptcy court protection shortly after Iraq invaded Kuwait, and was soon followed by the venerable Pan Am Corp. Meanwhile, an eager United Airlines, in trying to buy Pan Am's lucrative route to London, agreed to guarantee one-third of the $150 million debtor-in-possession loan extended to Pan Am by Bankers Trust. Despite the possibility of a successful reorganization, Pan Am bonds sank to nine cents on the dollar. Chastened investors were obviously not holding out much hope for Pan Am to survive its crash landing.

Pan Am's demise was soon followed by Eastern Airlines. In Eastern's case, most of the more profitable assets had already been sold by the time the company filed under Chapter 11 in January 1991. In fact, the airline industry was disintegrating so fast that it was weakening the competitive structure of the industry. The U.S. Justice Department indicated that it was concerned that the sale of Eastern's Atlanta hub operation would concentrate 87 percent of that market in the hands of Delta Air Lines. A debt-laden industry had dissipated its liquidity in fare wars, and the survivors were ready to divide the spoils of victory.

Nowhere were the effects of the eighties' buy-out binge more readily apparent than in the troubled retailing sector. Carter Hawley Hale Stores, Inc. took on $1.3 billion in debt to ward off a 1987 takeover attempt by Limited, Inc. By the time Carter Hawley filed for bankruptcy protection in 1991, it had already sold some of its most profitable assets. Nevertheless, a 30 percent contraction in trade credit – the financing retailers receive from their suppliers – pushed the company over the brink. A similar case of financial quarantine had dealt the *coup de grace* to the big catalog retailer, Best Products Company. As trade credit contracted, so did inventories and sales, which suffered an almost immediate drop of 23 percent. The prosperity of the eighties had been built on credit, and when the credit disappeared so did the prosperity.

Every bankruptcy which occurred due to an excessive debt burden was to result in financial strain for a wide circle of bondholders, bank creditors, and suppliers. In the Best Products case, Equitable Life Insurance Society and Metropolitan Life Insurance were owed a total of over $290 million, while Rockefeller Group was left trying to collect nearly $100 million. Nevertheless, Manufacturers Hanover Corp., which was forced to place $181 million in loans to Best on a non-accrual status, immediately combined its efforts with Chemical Banking Corp. to extend new loans of $250 million in debtor-in-possession (DIP) financing. Chemical was evidently making a policy of using shell craters for foxholes: the bankruptcy filing by Carter Hawley was immediately followed by a DIP loan of $800 million from Chemical. The new lending credo seemed to be that nothing succeeds like failure.

IV

The rising tide of corporate bankruptcies became an increasing source of worry to investors as the enthusiasm of the eighties gave way to the circumspection of the nineties. An index of junk bonds compiled by Salomon Brothers indicated a negative "total return" of seven percent in 1990, when both interest payments and resale value are counted. However, the market was drawing sharp distinctions among the various gradations of junk – from "quality" junk at the top to toxic waste at the bottom. For example, the next lower grade of bonds below the BBB rating, Standard and Poor's lowest investment grade, is BB, or "double B," which actually returned a positive 5.8 percent in 1990. However, two steps down in the non-investment grade spectrum, CCC-rated bonds, produced a negative total return of 36.5 percent. The market was making an emphatic statement that the most highly leveraged firms with unstable cash flow from their primary lines of business were in imminent danger of default.

By opting for the higher grades of junk, investors were tacitly acknowledging the rapidly deteriorating quality of America's corporate debt. A total of $510 billion of corporate debt was downgraded in 1990, nearly three times the already high 1989 figure. The number of corporations downgraded by S&P in 1990 was more than four times the number upgraded. In this environment, the trend toward further deterioration of corporate balance sheets was obvious, and investors were placing steep discounts on the lowest-rated bonds. And, as the U.S. economy receded in 1990, the rapidly deteriorating market continually added to the supply of junk bonds. Even though the bond market window had been slammed tightly shut for new issues, new junk bonds were created from investment grade credits which were downgraded to junk status.

The increasing number of so-called "fallen angels" actually represented a return to the historical norm for the junk bond markets. Before Michael Milken re-shaped the market for junk bonds in the eighties, bonds were infrequently rated at junk levels at the time of issuance. Instead, junk bonds were created when former investment-grade bonds were discounted as the issuers fell on hard economic times. There they languished, offering tempting yields to secondary market investors who were willing to assume the obvious risks of ownership and bet on recovery. The innovation of Milken was to capitalize on the euphoric investment climate of the eighties by underwriting new issues which were junk-rated *from the very time of issuance*. These issues were the financial fuel for the leveraged buy-out boom of the eighties, when as much as $30 billion of junk bonds were issued in a single year. It seemed during the eighties that some investors would buy anything. Often, junk bonds were bought less from ignorance than necessity. The returns on investment grade paper were simply too low to meet the cash flow required by a financial system which was itself highly leveraged, and so junk bonds became the preferred poison for insurance companies and thrifts that were already mortally wounded.

As the nineties began, a once and future fallen angel, Chrysler Corp., demonstrated the tenuous condition of many of America's most reputable firms. Chrysler, which had been the beneficiary of a government-sponsored bailout in the early eighties, had emerged from the precipice of looming bankruptcy with the assistance of voluntary import quotas on Japanese autos. The company then rode the coattails of the surge in consumer spending during the eighties with the enormous success of its innovative minivans. However, the huge cash hoard the company acquired was soon frittered away on such projects as the acquisition of the Italian automaker, Lamborghini, whose $175,000 automobiles were hardly compatible with the American automaker's traditional middle class market. By early 1991, Chrysler had amassed a debt burden of nearly $21 billion, and Moody's as well as Standard and Poor's (S&P) both officially relegated the company's bonds to junk status. As Moody's noted, the company's "already limited financial flexibility may impair its ability to fund the large product development programs" it would need to remain competitive. Evidently, S&P was taking an only slightly less jaundiced view of America's other big automakers: both General Motors Corp. and Ford Motor Company debt were downgraded to single-A, just one rung above the lowest investment grade. The huge pile of cash the auto industry had acquired in the eighties was rapidly disappearing; the debts were not.

The most immediate problem confronting Chrysler and other companies who faced credit downgrades was the increased cost of obtaining financing. Many institutional investors are prohibited by charter from owning below-investment grade bonds, and must therefore divest their holdings of bonds which are downgraded to junk status. The continued deterioration of the market in 1990 thus led to an ever increasing supply of bonds offered for resale in the secondary market. And the pressure of increasing supply was exerting its inevitable effect on prices. Despite the steadily increasing number of downgrades, due to sharply falling bond prices the market value of junk bonds traded in the secondary market declined to $150 billion in 1990 from $220 billion in 1989. Contributing to the bleak landscape was the Resolution Trust Corporation, which by early 1991 had sold nearly $3 billion of the junk bonds it had acquired from failed thrifts. Moreover, those thrifts which remained healthy found that the 1989 FIRREA law had, in effect, required them to sell their junk holdings, a block which represented seven percent of total junk bonds outstanding.[3]

V

By the end of 1990, the resale market for junk bonds had become so weak – and yields so high – that it was bound to attract a new group of investors willing to take a flyer on the resurgence of America's economy, or, at least the prospect that collapse was not yet imminent. After all, at 28 percent – a rate which was not unheard of in the secondary market for junk bonds – money doubles itself in three years. At these returns, even a weak company would be a good bet if it appeared able to survive the recession. Besides, the simple arithmetic of falling bond prices had restored a large measure of the financial prudence which business managers themselves seemed to lack. For example, if a company was fully leveraged and its debt traded at 50 cents on the dollar, the *market value* of the company's debt was but half its assets. With many companies' bonds trading as low as 20 cents on the dollar, the possibility of a new wave of buyouts and restructuring did not escape the market's collective imagination. The collapse of the junk bond market, therefore, created the conditions for yet another wave of corporate takeovers.

An example of the new generation of optimists was the Water Street Corporate Recovery Fund I, managed by the investment bank of Goldman Sachs. The fund raised $650 million in the second half of 1990, and immediately put it to work in such troubled issues as those of Interco and USG. Other investors were less hasty: Chicago's Sam Zell raised $1 billion, while Trust Company of the West amassed $300 million earmarked for distressed securities. While Zell and Trust Co. were weighing their opportunities, Salomon Brothers' index of returns on defaulted bonds dropped by 30 percent in the latter half of 1990. Market observers estimated that the Water Street Fund's premature foray into the market resulted in a paper loss of over $130 million during this time. Clearly, this was no market for widows and orphans.

By early 1991, the takeover potential of many junk issues was beginning to attract the interest of an increasing circle of investors. Bonds of Fort Howard Corp. soared by 17 percent in the closing days of 1990, as the company announced plans for a $250 million equity infusion. Southland's bondholders realized similar gains when they approved the company's Chapter 11 reorganization plan. At the same time, Harcourt Brace Jovanovich, Inc.'s 13 percent bonds jumped by 20 percent on General Cinema's buyout offer. Unfortunately, some operators still seemed to be up to their old tricks: in all three cases, the bonds started their price rise in advance of official announcements. To all appearances, insider trading was alive and well on Wall Street.

Regardless of what insiders might have known, Harcourt surely looked like a bargain to General Cinema. The buyout offer called for Harcourt's bondholders to redeem their bonds at prices ranging from 32 cents to 93 cents on the dollar. Since the bonds had been trading at far lower prices, investors gave the offer a warm acceptance. And, from General Cinema's viewpoint, it was acquiring Harcourt at a total cost of about six times cash flow, less than half the going rate during the takeover craze of the eighties.

Not all bondholders received such generous terms as those offered by General Cinema. Troubled Charter Medical Corp. attempted to reduce its massive $1.7 billion in debt by offering bondholders a combination of new bonds and common stock. By substituting some debt for equity, the company hoped to lower its interest payments from 14 percent to 10 percent, while cutting outstanding principal by $700 million. The exchange offer would restore a healthy cushion of equity in the company, thus forcing bondholders to provide capital that the company would be otherwise unable to raise. While this may not have matched their original investment objectives, it would be preferable to holding bonds through the looming prospect of Chapter 11 reorganization.

Charter Medical's cruel logic of half a loaf being better than no loaf applied equally well to bondholders in a large number of the debt-laden ghosts of the eighties. Junk bonds traded at an average price of 75 cents on the dollar in early 1991, and as cash flow deteriorated, many investors took a more benign attitude toward selling out than enduring the lengthy process of reorganization. Salomon Brothers' junk bond gurus were rumored to have compiled a hit list of 30 junk bond issuers which appeared attractive from a takeover standpoint. A new takeover game was developing. Debt-laden companies whose basic business income remained viable would have value to someone. At some price, a company's debt was cheap enough to restore the equity which the company had lost through its operations. If the bonds were trading below that magic price, an astute speculator could realize a quick gain. The *Zeitgeist* of the eighties was dead, but the profit motive survived and many of the companies to be restructured were familiar names to the regenerated veterans of the takeover game.

One famous leveraged buy-out deal of the eighties whose junk bonds soared in the nineties was RJR Nabisco. As a takeover target which measured up to its billing, RJR was virtually unique: the company's operating profit was *increasing*. Before Kohlberg Kravis Roberts & Co. engineered the famous 1988 mother of all buyouts, RJR had just $5.2 billion in debt vs. market value of common and preferred stock of $25.3 billion. By 1990, debt was $17.9 billion and market value of the stock just $8 billion. However, the company had nearly cut its work force by half and had increased operating profit from $2.97 billion to $3.43 billion. The improved cash flow from operations was accompanied by a jump of 75 percent in the market value of RJR's 17 percent bonds, and allowed the company to pay down much of its debt. Meanwhile, the company's stock jumped from $1 in 1990 to over $6 in 1991.

RJR Nabisco was the exception. Most of the gains made by speculators in junk bonds had only been possible as the result of someone else's loss, i.e. the bonds traded to a substantial discount from face value and were then sold by their original owners. Many a sunken ship would be raised, but only after the original crew had drowned. The decline, fall, and eventual recovery of the junk bond market was playing itself out in a similar fashion to the experience of the other troubled sectors of the economy, such as banking and real estate. A misguided army of institutional investors – flush with liquidity during the aggressive financial environment of the eighties – had paid inflated prices based on overly optimistic expectations. The critical error of these investors was their failure to appreciate that debt is a two-edged sword. Interest obligations were looked upon as a normal operating expense to be paid in the course of business rather than a fixed obligation representing a prior claim on the assets of the corporation. When revenues failed to meet the devoutly anticipated rosy scenario, a vast cross-section of American business was faced with cost-cutting, asset sales, or outright liquidation. America had built an empire based on paper, but when it collapsed, the wealth it destroyed was real.

CHAPTER 10

Futures, Options, and Exponential Nirvana

We know from Greek mythology how Cassandra obtained the gift of foresight from Zeus, but then broke her bargain with the god. No double-dealer, Zeus left the gift intact, but reduced the object of his desire to a soothsayer whom nobody believed. Thus has it ever been impossible to be forewarned of Greeks bearing gifts. In perfect accord with this tradition, futures and options were the Trojan horse of the eighties. Their rapid growth presents an interesting study of how far the financial game of self-delusion divorced investment capital from its traditional role of diverting consumption in the present to production in the future. In the world of futures and options, one cares not whether he is a buyer or a seller; whether the commodity is pork bellies or rapeseed or no commodity at all; nor whether the price is already too high or too low. All that matters is the eternal hunt for the Greater Fool.

While all investments are an implicit attempt to quantify an uncertain future, nowhere is speculation a greater motivating force than in the markets for futures and options. The trader agrees to buy or sell a standard contract at some specific time, place, and price. If the price moves in his favor at any time prior to the contracted delivery date, the opportunity for profit presents itself. The futures trader is indifferent to whether these profits arise from being short or long, i.e. the opportunity to profit from selling before buying is the same as from approaching the trade in the traditional sequence (buying then selling). Buy low and sell high, but in no particular order. The game is purely and simply a bet on the direction of price movements from the time the trade is entered to the time the position is offset. Does the trader expect the price of cotton to fall between January and July? Then sell July cotton in January and buy the contract back some time before July. The contract will almost certainly be bought back before delivery is due; the number of contracts on which physical delivery is made is but a minuscule percentage of the total traded.

Like gambling, futures trading is a zero-sum game: for every buyer there must be a seller; and for every dollar won, a dollar must also be lost. The futures markets are not a mechanism for distributing capital, although wealth is clearly re-distributed in the process. Instead, the economic *raison d' être* of the market is to transfer price risk from producers who confront it in their businesses to speculators who are willing to assume the risk in return for profit. So much for theory. In reality, the two parties to a futures trade are more likely to be a buyer who is speculating that prices will rise and a seller who is equally eager to bet that prices will fall.

The art of speculation has spawned an entire body of pseudo-scientific trading techniques, some of which have been handed down by folk trading legends such as W. D. Gann. In a pattern shared by many successful traders, Gann was raised in a rural environment, and was drawn to the commodity markets at an early point in life. In his case, the cotton fields of Texas were to spark an interest in the harmony between the market and nature. In an age before computer technology, he developed a system for observing the internal harmony of each market and reconciling it with the harmony of the seasons and numerology. His system of measuring time and price was supplemented by practical trading rules for limiting losses and managing risk capital. While many a student of Gann's supposedly foolproof methods has squandered his capital, Gann himself is reported to have extracted over $50 million from the commodity markets by the time of his death in the 1950's.

The theme of harmony between markets and nature recurs often in the work of popular market theoreticians. One who has been widely read in recent years is Ralph Nelson Elliott, whose work during the 1930's described market movements unfolding in a basic rhythm: five waves up followed by three waves down. While Elliott concerned himself with the stock market, his more recent students have applied his work to the commodity, bond and currency markets as well. During the bull market of the eighties, Robert Prechter, editor of a financial newsletter known as "The Elliott Wave Theorist" became a frequent celebrity guest on financial news programs and – in many ways – became a kind of financial high priest to many investors.

There is some justification for comparing the works of early market technicians such as Gann and Elliott to those of the early scientists. Elliott, for example, popularized the work of a fourteenth century Italian mathematician, Fibonacci, who had made a study of the ancient Egyptian pyramids. The symmetry of the pyramids became a source of inspiration to Fibonacci, who developed a series of numbers and ratios which form the basis for Elliott's system to predict the magnitude of price moves.[1] For example, a commonly used Fibonacci ratio is 61.8 percent, which suggests the point to which prices will retrace after a major market move. It is easy for the modern mind to scoff at such an anthropomorphic view of the price discovery process. Nevertheless, whether professional traders find Elliott's work credible or not, they ignore it at their own risk. The widespread following of technical trading techniques such as Elliott's tends to perpetuate their accuracy as their followers draw the same conclusions from price charts and then act in unison with the obvious effect on market prices.

The advent of the computer age and the mad markets of the eighties produced a new generation of market legends. Perhaps foremost among them was Paul Tudor Jones, who left his home in Memphis to seek his fortune trading on the New York Cotton Exchange in 1979. Mr. Jones still sends a Christmas card every year to the Memphis banker who wasn't sufficiently impressed to hire him when he graduated from the University of Virginia. By 1988 Jones' personal fortune was estimated at over $50 million, and he evidently continued to add to his winnings after that time. By 1990, Jones found himself returning some of the funds he managed to his investors. Even in the enormous markets in which Jones dealt, his market positions had become so large that they were difficult to liquidate without moving prices. Nevertheless, after deducting the four percent management fee and 23 percent of profits (the incentive fee), Jones' Tudor Investment Corp. posted a 75 percent gain for its investors in 1990. In 1991, the giant Japanese investment firm, Nomura Securities Company, provided tacit recognition of Jones' expertise in the fine art of speculation by forming a 50-50 joint venture with Tudor Investment to trade commodities, currencies, and financial futures. While not yet forty, Jones still had ample time ahead to blow everything. However, his attitude gave no indication that this was likely to happen. As he himself said, "Ego is the single most destructive force you can confront in this business."

While Paul Tudor Jones used a sophisticated resource base of computers and analysts to arrive at his trading decisions in a mind-boggling worldwide array of markets, L. Thomas Baldwin III did it with his heart, his head, and his lungs trading U.S. Treasury bonds on the floor of the Chicago Board of Trade. When Tom Baldwin first appeared in the T-bond pits in the early eighties, he had a stake of $20,000 and a pregnant wife. By his calculations, he had six months to make or break his future. Make it he did. By 1991, he was personally accounting for about $2.4 billion of bond trades per day – about five percent of total volume. Most of these trades are a complete "round turn," i.e. purchase and sale, all on the same day. And there are losing days as well as winners: one day in March, 1989 Mr. Baldwin departed the pit $2 million poorer than he had entered it that morning. Nevertheless, in less than ten years in the pits, he had accumulated a personal fortune estimated to be nearly $50 million.

The experience of the eighties seemed to indicate that commodity trading was not purely art. To demonstrate that trading was a science, trader Richard Dennis formed a group of trainees known as the Dennis "turtles." Using Dennis' computerized trading techniques for spotting breakouts and then jumping on to follow the trend of major market moves, the turtles later set up commodity firms of their own. Their results were astonishing. Of the 12 Dennis protégés active in 1990, all posted positive returns through the first ten months of the year. Despite the difficult 1990 investment environment, when most money managers lost money, returns ranged from nine percent to 263 percent, with three of the twelve posting triple digit returns.[2]

For every successful futures trader, there were many more who were net losers. The commodity markets have never been a democratic means for re-distributing wealth. In fact, the opposite is true. Large, well-capitalized professionals tend to have the sophistication and staying power needed to survive in the uncertain and turbulent world of trading. Nevertheless, the hope of becoming a successful trader – like the hope of winning the Illinois lottery – has inspired thousands to plunk down their life savings and try to walk in the footprints of the few who walk away as winners.

II

While commodity traders may – with some justification – see themselves as the *crème de la crème* of private risk-takers in an increasingly managed economy, the case might be made that their fortunes are no more immune to the financial environment produced by the Federal Reserve than is a snow flake immune to the spring thaw. The relationship between the monetary environment, commodity prices, and – ultimately – the inflation rate was, on the contrary, an important indication of the extent to which, during the eighties, the traditional financial levers used by the Fed seem to have lost the power they once held over the economy.

If it ever existed, the direct relationship between monetary policy and commodity prices broke down after 1971, when freely fluctuating exchange rates were introduced. After Nixon closed the gold window, a weakening dollar on the exchange markets could and did counter the effects of slow growth in the domestic money supply by stimulating foreign demand for commodities priced in dollars. Hence, after adjusting money growth for inflation and for changes in exchange rates (with some lag for the adjustments to take effect), it appears that the money-commodity relationship remained relatively stable through the mid-eighties. For example, from 1970 to 1973, the exchange-adjusted money supply increased by approximately 15 percent, followed by a sharp rise in commodities from 1971 to 1973. Similarly, a 15 percent rise in the real money supply from 1977 to 1980 preceded the sharp rise in commodities from 1978 to 1980. The price elasticity of commodities with respect to money during the 1970-85 time period indicated that a change in the real money supply (as defined above) would yield a percentage change in commodity prices of over twice the magnitude. Thus, as far as commodity price trends were concerned, the Federal Reserve's monetary policy was the dominant explanatory variable. Traders – and policymakers – who ignored this did so at great peril.

In the mid-1980's, the economy seemed to be entering a brave new world in which the relationship between monetary conditions and the real sector of the economy began to break down. The recession of 1982 never really fully went away, as rolling pockets of hard economic times struck like winter blizzards with stochastic frequency. For a time during 1985 and 1986, it appeared that the Federal Reserve was pushing on the proverbial string in its attempt to revive the rust belt, the oil patch, and basic industries such as machine tools and durable goods. The Volcker Fed responded by adding reserves to the banking system at an unprecedented rate. For example, in the twelve month period from August 1984 to August 1985, reserves of the banking system grew by over 40 percent! At no time in the history of the central bank, before or since, has this rate been equalled or even approached. Nevertheless, commodity prices, already low, dropped 10 percent further before hitting bottom in mid-1986. In large measure, the financial boom of the eighties may be viewed as an unintended by-product of this explosive growth in bank liquidity. As far as the banking system was concerned, the Fed policy was "damn the torpedoes, full speed ahead"; the first priority of economic policy was to devalue the dollar and resuscitate American industry.

By 1987, the foreign exchange value of the dollar had declined enough to halt the erosion in America's foreign trade position, and the effects of the previous monetary stimulus were showing up in the commodity markets. Precious metals and commodity prices rose sharply during the spring of 1987, and the Federal Reserve, always operating under a game plan of undamped oscillation, immediately began leaning in the opposite direction by draining bank reserves. Bond prices fell sharply from March to October and, eventually, stock investors stopped hallucinating and woke up to reality. From August to October stock prices fell sharply, culminating in the traumatic sell-off on October 19, 1987. Of course, in the subsequent search for a scapegoat, the politicians discovered stock index futures and program trading, much as the politicians of the thirties had accused short sellers and the pernicious "money trusts." But, if anyone was discriminating enough to inquire – and few did – the true cause of the bull market as well as the subsequent crash was the same on both occasions: the high-handed and clumsy monetary policies of the Federal Reserve.

From 1987 to 1990, the Federal Reserve under Alan Greenspan seemed intent on reversing the potentially inflationary effects of the monetary policy of the mid-eighties. Indeed, there was little choice in the matter as the economy remained strong and inflation persisted. During the summer of 1988, a severe drought caused an explosion in grain prices. Commodity prices, as measured by the Commodity Research Bureau (a subsidiary of Knight-Ridder, Inc.) index of futures prices, reached the highest level since the early eighties – over 38 percent above the low in 1986. While commodity prices trended irregularly lower after mid-1988, consumer price inflation stubbornly remained above four percent – and rose sharply with higher fuel prices after Iraq seized Kuwait in August 1990. As a result, Federal Reserve policy remained extremely tight over a prolonged period, from early 1987 to the end of 1990. The feast of easy money had become a famine of tight credit as the decade drew to a close.

As 1991 began, the index of 21 commodity futures prices tracked by the Commodity Research Bureau (CRB) was plumbing four-year lows. A market basket of agricultural products whose prices are monitored by the U.S. Department of Agriculture, showed farm prices five percent below the year-earlier levels. It appeared that the Federal Reserve's efforts to restrain inflation were having the customary negative effects on commodity prices, even though consumer prices (which are heavily weighted by the price of services) continued to rise at over a five percent annual rate.

At the same time commodity prices were responding to the effects of tight money in the early nineties, they would be buffeted by the effects of the successful conclusion of the Persian Gulf War. By coming down on the side of the richest oil-producing nations, America was guaranteed access to a large source of cheap oil imports. In combination with oil producers in the Americas, U.S. allies in the Persian Gulf produced over 50 percent of world oil output. Moroever, the military expense and destruction wrought on Saudi Arabia, Kuwait, and Iraq would insure that large volumes of oil would be exported to finance the re-construction of the region, and some of the biggest lenders of "petrodollars" to the world's capital markets during the seventies and eighties would themselves be short of cash and anxious to sell more oil. America had patched together an empire that would virtually assure the world of a plentiful supply of a key industrial commodity, and this would reinforce the deflationary trend already in place as the nineties began.

III

Despite the generally tight money conditions in the latter part of the 1980's, the number of contracts and dollar volume of futures trading continued to run counter to the overall downtrend in trading volume in most investments. In 1990, futures trading on Chicago's two largest exchanges – the Chicago Board of Trade and the Chicago Mercantile Exchange – hit record volume of 257 million contracts, over $10 trillion in final market value. However, rather than evidencing an inflationary boom in the demand for physical commodities, contracts for financial instruments remained dominant. At the Chicago Board of Trade, Treasury bond futures and options volume accounted for two-thirds of the exchange's total volume.

As new contracts for financial instruments, theoretical indexes, and options were introduced, the trend away from physical commodities drew the futures markets ever further from their roots in the agricultural commodities, and this often became a bone of contention as to which federal watchdog agency should be responsible. The Securities and Exchange Commission (SEC), which had been established in the 1930's in response to abusive practices in the nation's stock and bond markets, had rules regarding short selling as well as the margin requirements for investors who bought securities with borrowed funds. On the other hand, the Commodity Futures Trading Commission (CFTC) was responsible for the futures markets, where popular stock indexes, one of the most popular financial innovations of the eighties, were traded.

Contracts based on U.S. Treasury bonds and the Standard and Poor's 500 stock index were great success stories indeed. Each Treasury bond contract stipulated delivery of a principal amount of $100,000 in standard long-term eight percent government bonds. Bonds issued by the U.S. Treasury having different coupon rates could also be delivered using standard conversion tables to determine the appropriate principal amount to deliver. Before making a trade, speculators were required to post an initial good faith margin deposit of less than five percent of the value of the contract, usually no more than $4,000. Commissions charged by futures brokers ranged from $25 to $75 per contract and bid-offer spreads on the Board of Trade were usually 1/32 of one point, i.e. $31.25 per contract. Thus, a speculator's margin and transaction costs were far less than would be required to buy Treasury bonds in the cash market, while the futures trader could receive the full benefit of any price move. Price changes of one point in a single day, which were not uncommon in the Treasury bond market, would provide a mark-to-market gain or loss of $1,000 per contract, a 25 percent return on speculative margin. This was the stuff of which dreams – and nightmares – were made. In 1990, a typical day on the Chicago Board of Trade would see 300,000 contracts change hands, evidencing an underlying principal amount of $30 billion. Since the average open interest (the number of contracts outstanding at any time) was also approximately 300,000 contracts, it appeared that most contracts were held for only one day.

Initially, the bang-per-buck attraction of stock index futures was even greater than for Treasury bonds. The Chicago Mercantile Exchange contract on the S&P 500 had a value of $500 times the number of index points. For example, with the S&P index at 300, the theoretical value of each contract would be $150,000. When the speculative mania of the bull market of the eighties was at its peak, margin deposits were less than $10,000 as against a typical margin requirement of 50 percent to trade the stocks themselves. Thus, with large daily moves in the index and the seeming unwillingness of the market to go anywhere but higher, the S&P 500 contract quickly won a large number of "players." During 1987, typical volume was 75,000 contracts per day, and this was in addition to the large volume of trading on other exchanges which offered contracts on the Value Line Index, the New York Stock Exchange Index, and the Major Market Index. The amount of money changing hands was enormous. On October 19, 1987 each S&P 500 contract lost over $40,000 in value.

In the aftermath of the Crash of '87, many observers felt that stock index futures contributed heavily to the carnage. Therefore, a system of "circuit-breakers" was introduced to limit trading once daily price limits were exceeded. Margin deposit requirements were also increased to over $20,000 for speculators. After – though not necessarily because of – these changes, trading volume declined: typical trading volume on the S&P 500 in 1990 was approximately 50,000 contracts.

In large part, the rapid rise in the popularity of stock index futures during the eighties was due to the discovery of "program trading" by Wall Street. Since stock index futures contracts were based on indices of specific stock issues, it was possible for arbitrageurs to profit from price discrepancies between the futures market and the prices of the component stocks on the stock exchange. And, with the availability of computer technology, it was possible to identify these price discrepancies almost instantaneously. With electronic access to the stock exchange and low transaction costs, the major investment banks could quickly capitalize on these trading opportunities, for example, by purchasing a market basket of stocks while selling the futures contract to lock in a favorable price spread. By the time the futures contract expired, the price discrepancy would disappear and the trade could be unwound at a profit. Thus, with sophisticated computer programs and immediate access to stock exchanges, program traders could pre-empt the general public to reap handsome profits.

Despite the malevolent motives attributed by regulators, it could be argued that program trading was actually a benefit to the stockholding public. The function of any arbitrageur is to profit from price volatility and, in so doing, the result is to add liquidity to the market and continuity to price movements. And, as to the cost advantage the big market players had over the general public, this was no different from the advantage any organized business holds over the retail public via access to wholesalers and volume discounts. Nevertheless, program trading became the political whipping boy of the 1987 crash, just as the "money trusts" of the twenties had incurred the wrath of Congressional inquisitors during the thirties.

Despite the Congressional finger-pointing, the CFTC does not seem to have made a serious attempt to limit the proliferation of new contracts after the Crash. For example, new contracts introduced in

1991 included seven separate "cross-rate" currency futures contracts, which permitted traders to speculate on the rate between two foreign currencies, without regard to the dollar.

To maintain its bureaucratic hegemony over these and other contracts, CFTC asked for broader enforcement powers to assess fines and monitor the financial status of futures clearing firms. The 1991 request was made to counter a Bush Administration proposal which would have transferred oversight of stock index futures to the SEC. At the same time, the SEC was complaining to Congress that CFTC was hindering financial innovation due to a provision of the Commodity Exchange Act which required products with futures elements to be regulated by CFTC. The Federal Reserve, meanwhile, was trying to dodge responsibility for setting margin requirements on financial futures, as called for by a Senate bill. In short, the regulatory environment remained in a state of flux as America entered the nineties. But the volume of futures trading – most of which was no longer related to physical commodities – continued to waltz about in its own private world, without regard to the deflationary financial landscape. Wealth was neither created nor equitably redistributed by this process. It was a rhyme without reason, a tempest in a teapot, very much in keeping with the brave new world of financial nirvana, which had been carried to the $n'th$ power during the eighties.

IV

As the volume of futures trading grew during the eighties, so did the level of abstraction of the new contracts approved by CFTC. The greatest growth occurred in options on futures – a virtual second derivative on reality. In 1980 there were no exchange-traded options on futures. True, options on stocks and bonds as well as those on physical commodities had been traded on formal exchanges as well as in the informal over-the-counter market for some time. But the idea of creating options to buy or sell futures contracts seems never to have been seriously considered before America's great decade of financial degeneracy. Options on futures were indeed the perfect idea for the eighties: the potential rate of return on options is stratospheric and they quickly attracted a new flock of financial lambs to the eager wolves of the commodity pits.

An option simply grants its owner the right to buy (in the case of a call) or sell (in the case of a put) some specific item at a stipulated exercise (or strike) price. European-style options can only be exercised on a specified date, while American-style options – which are the type traded on the futures exchanges – may be exercised at any time up to the expiration date. The owner of a call option on gold futures, for example, might have the right to purchase one contract of December gold futures at $380 per ounce at any time prior to November 12. Should he exercise this option, the owner would then find himself with a long gold position, i.e. he would be obligated to purchase one contract of gold – 100 ounces – in December at a price of $380 per ounce, a total contract value of $38,000. Any time prior to expiration of the option, it could be sold at the prevailing market price to some other trader who is willing to pin his hopes on rising gold prices. And, if the option is held to maturity and exercised, the futures contract obtained could still be sold prior to the date for taking delivery of the gold. The options trader has sufficient opportunity to avoid taking or making delivery, which would interfere with his essentially speculative motives.

While the option trader is waiting to cash in on the desired price move, he is the owner of a "wasting asset" – one that will eventually be worthless if the price of the underlying futures contract does not reach the level required to be "in the money" by the time the option expires. The fee he has paid for a call option is a bet the price will rise; the fee paid for a put is a bet the price will fall before the exercise date. And, even if prices move in the desired direction, the trade could end in a loss if prices don't move far enough through the exercise price to exceed the fee paid to own the option. To evaluate the probability of an option's expiring in the money, a variety of mathematical models have been developed and these are often used as a guide by traders in establishing a continuous market for trading options. However, the essence of the commonly used pricing formula is that option owners pay a premium based on the recent price volatility of the underlying futures contract. In doing so they are betting that prices will move in the desired direction, far enough and fast enough, to increase the resale value of the option. If the desired price change occurs, a quick profit is possible. For example, the December 380 gold call option might cost, perhaps, $1,000 in September when gold was trading at $360 per ounce. The same option would have an intrinsic value of $10,000 if the price of gold rose to $480 per ounce by expiration. In this case, the gold price has increased by one-third, while the call option has increased by 900 percent! And, even if the price of gold drops to $300 per ounce, the option trader can lose no more than his $1,000 fee. It is a business proposition not unlike betting on a dark horse at the race track and will generally appeal to "investors" of a roughly similar mindset. And sometimes it works: owners of put options on the S&P 500 stock index reaped enormous profits during the market crash on October 19, 1987.

While every widely traded futures contract – commodities, currencies, financial instruments, and indexes – featured a companion set of put and call options by 1990, the trading of options on stocks was nearly as widespread. Often, options became an important tool in takeover attempts as well as for "bear raids," a maneuver to trash a company using roughly the same tactics as the legendary manipulator, Jay Gould. During the rapidly deteriorating stock market of 1990, bear raids were often made on shares of banks, thrift institutions, and those companies whose fortunes were tied to a rapidly weakening retail environment. In a typical transaction, a raider might buy a large block of shares but an even larger block of put options. As the market weakens, the raider steadily increases sales of his shares, further depressing the market. By the time the drop in share prices has turned to an all-out rout, the raider has disposed of all his stock and can sell his put options at a handsome profit. When he has sold his shares in a falling market, the bear raider has effectively circumvented the spirit of the Securities and Exchange Commission's "uptick rule," which only permits short sales of stock when the price trades higher ("ticks up") from the previous price. The profits from this type of maneuver were so quick and so easy that traders referred to it as a "slam dunk." However, it is only fair to note that a slam dunk can only be successful in a stock which is already fundamentally weak. The bear raider is simply accelerating the process by which the price reaches a more realistic valuation of the company's prospects.

Option traders often find that they can be right and still lose money, purely due to the timing of their trades. This occurs when the price moves in the desired direction, but not far enough to compensate for the cost of the option. Sometimes, even when the desired price move does happen the machinations of brokers on the floor of the exchanges where options are traded can still turn the trade into a money-losing proposition. Such was the experience of many investors who bought options on crude oil futures during the Persian Gulf War. To their chagrin, many who had purchased put options when the price of oil soared as high as $40 during the pre-War crisis found that floor brokers were not required to execute "limit" orders, i.e. at the price specified by the customer. Exchange rules only required brokers to accept "market" orders, to be filled at the prevailing market price at the time the order is executed. Unfortunately, in fast-moving markets, a difference of opinion arises as to what the market price is at any particular time. As viewed by George Perk, President of American Futures Group (a firm that places option orders for retail accounts), "If you own a $25 put (on a contract of 1,000 barrels of crude oil) and the market's trading $20 (a barrel), you should be able to sell it for $5,000. When you can only sell it for $1,000, you feel cheated." Of course, a more sophisticated and well capitalized trader would merely buy the underlying futures contract and exercise his option to lock in the $5,000 profit, less commissions. But this is exactly the point: neither the trading public as a whole nor the commission merchants who handle their trades are generally savvy enough to escape the predations of the skilled professionals who roam the floors of the exchange. Floor traders or "locals" are there to trade at the time and price of their choosing, not to perform a public service.

The practices of floor brokers on the New York Mercantile Exchange (NYMEX), where options on crude oil futures are traded, prompted over 50 complaints from oil options customers during the three months leading up to the Persian Gulf War. The response of NYMEX Chairman Z. Lou Guttman to the situation in his statement to Congress was that "The public had access to full and open price discovery, and a forum for shifting risk during particularly volatile times." This was a predictable response; commodity exchanges are organized and operated by the same people who – directly or indirectly – make their living trading in the pits. Thus, the president of a commodity exchange might be compared to the madam in a house of prostitution, who is concerned about her clients' welfare and happiness, but only to a degree. Unlike the SEC's restrictions on stock specialists, CFTC's rules tend to be a rubber stamp on proposals made by the individual commodity exchanges. The small speculator, who is drawn by the hope of fast profits from the usually mistaken belief that he knows more than market professionals, enters the market bereft of protection and generally exits bereft of his risk capital.

V

The vagaries of trying to beat local floor traders and other more sophisticated speculators and commercial accounts at their own game was to be the bane of many a small-fry speculator during the eighties.

One futures industry consultant estimated that 300,000 individual retail trading accounts were active in 1990. However, fully two-thirds of those would trade no more than four contracts during the year, and half of the existing accounts were closed within six months from any particular point in time.[3] This is consistent with the widely held view that 70 percent or more of small speculators eventually lose their risk capital and exit the market. Yet, if small speculators were losing, someone had to be winning. In the eighties, it appeared to be the professionally managed pools of futures funds known as "managed money."

From $500 million in 1980, managed accounts grew to $12 billion by 1990 as more and more small traders sought professional help. Nor were they generally disappointed. During 1990, for example, the average futures fund showed a net profit to investors of 20.8 percent, while the investor in common stocks generally lost money. Over longer periods of time, however, the stock buyer fared somewhat better. From 1986 through 1990, a period which included the Crash of 1987 and a significant stock price decline in 1990, managed futures pools returned 14 percent per annum as against 13.1 percent on Standard and Poor's 500 stock index, when dividends were reinvested.

And who were these fleet-footed pool managers who could consistently win at a zero-sum game? Funds were managed by an unlikely group of former floor traders, money managers, doctors and dentists – those who have both the time and the capital to gain expertise at the fine art of speculation. For example, the champion for publicly issued funds in 1990 was an emergency room physician, Dr. David Druz, who split his time with patients in Alaska and Hawaii while managing his $2.8 million in two separate computer-guided funds. Each of his funds returned nearly 100 percent in 1990, a year in which his trend-following system told him to jump on and buy crude oil, even as it hit new highs shortly before Iraq invaded Kuwait. A similar strategy was followed by Elizabeth Cheval, whose 133 percent gain for the year was second best among privately owned commodity pools. Ms. Cheval, one of the celebrated "turtles" of super-trader Richard Dennis, claimed to have made money in five markets – Eurodollars, Treasury notes, Treasury bonds, gold, and yen. "I made money in both directions ... when prices rose and fell," she said. Her system evidently capitalized on the old trading saw, "the trend is your friend."

One of the problems confronting traders who use computers to spot emerging commodity trends is the whipsaw effect of having to liquidate positions when the trend doesn't materialize and everyone else's computer system is generating the same signals at the same time.

Often, the reversals are traumatic. Tom Shanks, who turned in the best performance for a privately owned commodity pool in 1990 (up 250%) saw his capital drop by 30 percent on January 17, 1991 after the Persian Gulf War began. Dr. Druz also saw his fund's equity drop by nearly 20 percent that day, while fund manager Dinesh Desai saw his $170 million in managed money decline by 25 percent. Mr. Desai was on the wrong side of all markets: he had bought gold, silver, crude oil, and heating oil, while selling foreign currencies and U.S. Treasury bonds.

Despite success by some fund managers, commodity trading remained a dangerous road to riches for small investors. The investor who was unwilling to fork over his risk capital to a professional manager would probably not have been satisfied if he chose the alternative of following a commodity newsletter. The trades recommended by the newsletters followed by Bruce Babcock's *Commodity Traders Consumer Report* during 1990 would have generated a net loss of five percent of capital, following on the heels of a 15 percent loss during 1989. While the newsletters generated profits of 44 percent in 1987 and 19 percent in 1988, the volatility of futures returns is difficult for most investors to manage. Some Wall Street brokerage firms have attempted to overcome investor reticence to the volatility of commodity trading by sponsoring "guaranteed funds." By investing two-thirds of its assets in zero-coupon Treasury securities, Shearson's Futures 1000 Plus fund was able to guarantee that investors would get back at least 100 percent of the contributed capital at the termination of the fund. Once again, Wall Street was pandering to an ignorant investing public. Any investor who cared to think about it could dedicate two-thirds of his capital to Treasury securities and trade the final third with the personal resolution to stop trading when his capital had been lost. But this would not generate the eight percent fee for Wall Street to sell him the idea!

When all the pieces of the futures and options puzzle are put together, the commodity markets of the eighties appear to be but one piece of an even larger picture of financial innovation and speculation. The result – if not the intent – of committing funds to futures and options was to separate the small American investor from his capital. Large blocks of managed money generated fees for professional managers and commissions for brokerage firms and floor brokers. While claiming to offer liquidity and transfer of price risk to make the markets more accommodating to commercial traders, the general tendency toward computer-guided trend-following may well have increased the volatility of commodity and financial markets. In a larger sense, the rising popularity of futures and options exemplified a national trend away from responsible long-term investments in favor of the "get rich quick" psychology which pervaded all markets. Whether one bought or sold and what it was he traded was not important. The technical dementia of trading – such chart formations as inverted head and shoulders bottoms, key island reversals, Fibonacci retracements, and exhaustion gap bottoms – replaced such concepts of the real world of business as rate-of-return, market-to-book, and price-earnings ratios. America had entered the age of 24-hour real-time financial delirium. Like the Californian who swallows the philosophy, "you are what you drive," the financial markets had taken a long road away from traditional values.

CHAPTER 11

The Arteriosclerotic Stock Market

"How's the market doing?" This question will almost invariably elicit a response indicating whether stock prices have been going up or down and by how much. Despite the fact that the dollar volume of stocks traded is dwarfed by the volume of bonds, mortgage securities, and foreign currencies, the stock market remains "the market" to most Americans. And this is an understandable misconception, for if equity capital is the lifeblood of America's economy, then the stock market is the circulatory system through which its life-giving power is fed to *Corpus Oeconomia*. The stock market is, therefore, a widely followed barometer of just how our economy is doing. It tends to reflect the sentiments of the public as well as the financial prospects of business. With good reason, the Commerce Department includes movements in New York Stock Exchange prices as one component of its Index of Leading Economic Indicators.

As America's economy boomed through the middle part of the eighties, the stock market marched to the same tune, and it soon became popular in investment circles to compare the market's performance with the great bull market of the 1920's. Indeed, the parallel between the twenties and eighties extends well beyond the stock market. In both periods, the early warning signs came from agriculture, where falling farm prices caught farmers owning land at inflated prices and high levels of debt accumulated during the prior decade. There was also a reversal of traditional roles in the international capital markets: America and Great Britain changed places as debtor and lender during World War I, while Japan and America were reversing roles as the eighties began. In both cases, the newly rich nations – America in the twenties and Japan in the eighties – struggled with their new roles and failed to fully open their markets to imports, thus creating bottlenecks in world capital markets. Finally, and most important as far as the stock market is concerned, the rapid rise in the availability of credit in both periods greatly favored financial assets in a predominantly deflationary or "disinflationary" environment. During the eighties, the rate of inflation was declining as were interest rates, while federal tax rates were being cut. Under these conditions, the stock market attracted vast sums of equity capital from the public. The economic environment of the twenties was very much the same.

As far as the stock market is concerned, the similarity of the eighties to the twenties was as much a similarity of form as of substance; stock prices reached unprecedented levels in both periods and followed remarkably similar paths to their objectives. The Dow Jones Industrial Average rose from 63.9 in 1921 to a high of 381.2 in 1929 – a compound annual growth rate of 25 percent! During the 1980's, the Dow advanced from 759.1 in 1980 to 2722 in 1987, a compound annual rise of 20 percent. Of course, it is possible to carry the parallel too far; stock prices declined sharply for three straight years after 1929, losing 90 percent of their peak value, while the Dow was setting new record highs three years after the Crash of 1987. Nevertheless, behavior of the stock market during and after the Crash of 1987 provides a useful means of exploring the dilemma which confronted policymakers in both periods. The picture of the economy that emerges from the stock market in both eras is one of declining earnings growth, deteriorating balance sheets, and widespread investor unrest with fraudulent or deceptive practices by stock issuers and securities dealers. The immediate impact was felt, if not in declining prices of stocks, in declining earnings, layoffs, and – ultimately – the liquidation of insolvent banks, insurance companies, and broker-dealers. Finally, in both periods, the public seemed to lose touch with the market; stock prices eventually departed from reality and marched to the beat of their own mysterious drum, without regard to traditional measures of value.

II

As America entered the nineties the choleric attitude of consumers was beginning to be felt by virtually every company that dealt directly with the retail public. As 1991 began, retail sales were lower than the year-earlier level, the first time this had occurred in thirty years. This was not an inflation-adjusted decline; the *absolute* number of dollars spent was lower. Meanwhile, nonfinancial credit grew only three percent in 1990, a huge drop from the double-digit growth rates of the eighties. Despite the slowdown of credit growth in the early nineties,

America's consumers entered the 1990 recession with record debt levels. Installment debt, for example, was a third higher than in previous recessions while the savings rate, at four percent of income, was but half the level of the two previous recessions. Meanwhile, the number of insurance company failures more than doubled from 1984 to 1989, while bank failures rose tenfold from 1980 to 1990.[1]

There seemed to be no safe haven for money in the nineties. Executive Life Insurance, a unit of First Executive Corp., withdrew its operations from two states under pressure from regulators. Eventually, the company's entire operation was taken over by insurance regulators. Money market funds, the repository of more than $500 billion in liquid assets, were told by the SEC to limit their investments in companies rated below the top credit grade to a maximum of five percent of their assets. Investors found themselves in search of a place to park their funds and increasingly lighted upon the previously overlooked shares of small companies. Many of these companies had avoided debt, and a Merrill Lynch study indicated that low-leverage stocks outperformed the broader market by an increasing margin after 1989. As the stock market rebounded from its initial drop in the emerging 1990 recession, small stocks outstripped the performance of larger ones. The National Association of Securities Dealers' (NASDAQ) 100 index of the largest over-the-counter issues soared by nearly 40 percent in the three months from October, 1990, while the Dow Jones average was up by a less dramatic 16 percent.

Why were investors avoiding the big names? One reason was the ever-rising popularity of Chapter 11, the portion of the 1978 Bankruptcy Reform Act that applies to reorganization of corporations. During the eighties, a long list of household names had filed for Chapter 11 protection: A. H. Robbins, Allegheny International, Braniff Airlines, Continental Airlines, Johns-Manville, LTV, MacGregor Sporting Goods, Osborne Computer, Texaco, Wheeling-Pittsburgh Steel, and many others. Several of these bankruptcies had little to do with the distressed companies' viability as economic units. Manville had $2 billion in asbestos-related claims facing it in the courts; Robbins was the victim of suits regarding its Dalkon Shield; LTV was contending over pension liabilities; Continental was attempting to void its labor contracts. By stopping lawsuits, abrogating labor contracts, and eliminating interest payments to creditors, many of these companies hoped to emerge as stronger companies, cleansed of past misfortunes and misdeeds. Laurence Kallen, who witnessed many of these events first-hand in bankruptcy litigation, viewed the process as a type of welfare program for corporate America. As the economy turned sour in 1990, he predicted an increase in Chapter 11 filings from pollution liability, the savings and loan mess, and the worsening plight of the domestic auto industry.[2]

Indeed, the auto industry found itself walking on a thin layer of ice as it entered the nineties. Domestic auto production in the first quarter of 1991 was the lowest since 1956. In the fifties, what was good for General Motors was considered good for the U.S.A. In 1991, what would be good for GM would certainly not be good for its stockholders' cashflow; the company's $1.8 billion dividend would need to be cut to conserve cash. Meanwhile, Ford Motor Company, which had accumulated a huge cash hoard during the mid-eighties, had a cash outflow in 1990 which was greater than the total drain for the three recession years of 1980-82. Ford spent $2.5 billion to acquire Britain's Jaguar PLC, a company that required 300 labor-hours to build a car, ten times the figure for Ford's Taurus. And, as if the auto business was not already highly dependent on the credit cycle, Ford "diversified" into the financial sector. Over $500 million was spent to acquire several troubled thrift institutions and $3.3 billion was doled out to acquire The Associates, a consumer and commercial lender. No doubt Ford's management knew more about lending money than its new subsidiaries did about building cars. Nevertheless, Ford found itself increasing loan-loss reserves by $115 million in the third quarter of 1990, at the same time it was paying a $1,000 rebate to anyone who would buy the U.S. version of its Ford Escort. The idea probably occurred to some investors that there was something basically wrong with a business that needs to bribe its customers to do business.

Safety was no longer to be found in even the most respected names. Sears, Roebuck and Company – virtually the symbol of the American retailing business – had its debt ratings downgraded by Standard and Poor's as it struggled under the weight of $10 billion in debt. Like Ford and GM, Sears found itself cutting costs, and 21,000 unhappy Sears employees were to receive pink slips in 1991. The company's earnings for 1990 were the lowest since 1982, and upstart competitor Wal-Mart found itself replacing Sears as the nation's largest retailer in 1991. The success of Wal-Mart was a sign of the times; as a discount retailer, Wal-Mart followed a policy of mass-merchandising aimed largely at the lower middle class in rural America. The American consumer was operating under a tight budget constraint and Wal-Mart never lost sight of this fact.

While it became fashionable to trash the quality of American products in the eighties, building a good product was not sufficient to insure a company's success. Maytag Corp., which had built an enviable reputation for the high quality of its appliances, put its own balance sheet through the wringer as it diversified during the eighties. In 1986, Maytag bought Magic Chef, Admiral, and Norge, companies whose quality control programs were somewhat spotty. In 1989, Chicago Pacific Corp. and Hoover Company were acquired. Long-term debt, almost non-existent before these acquisitions, soared to over $800 million by 1989. Though sales increased, earnings declined. Maytag's stock dropped nearly 40 percent during 1990. Maytag shareholders had been put through the spin cycle.

III

If investors were disillusioned by the financial performance of their "household name" investments in the eighties, their pique was no less than what some felt toward the securities industry itself. In American society, no profession – with the possible exception of attorneys – could match the record of securities salesmen in terms of high compensation for questionable and – sometimes – negative economic contributions. By one estimate, the cost of regulating America's 80,000 stockbrokers reached nearly $1 billion per year, more than $10,000 per head. This amount included regulatory compliance expenditures of the SEC, CFTC, New York Stock Exchange, the National Association of Securities Dealers, the Federal Reserve Board, and compliance boards of the individual states. But, for all this purported protection, small investors were generally leaving the stock market in the latter part of the 1980's – a trend which had continued intermittently for two decades. In 1989, individuals were net sellers of 3.5 million shares per day.

Had the market become too complex for the little people? Were they handing their money over to mutual fund managers who better understood the confusing array of options, warrants, and derivative products? Perhaps they were just tired of losing. In support of the latter possibility, Mark Skousen, an independent investment strategist, spoke the words that would have been taboo in the securities industry. Noting the tendency of brokerage firms to concoct unctuous titles for their brokers, such as "first vice president" or "account representative,"

Skousen stated what should be obvious to anyone who aspires to becoming a successful investor: "these 'financial consultants' like to pose as independent, objective financial advisors. But the cold, hard truth is that they are *salespeople*, and their first goal is to *make commissions*, not give you objective advice." Dan Dorfman, a popular financial columnist, noted that "a study of stock recommendations by 147 investment advisors and brokerage firms found that no brokerage firm placed in the top 50."[3] Not one! Little wonder that nearly all brokerage firms were still bullish on the eve of the October 1987 market crash.

An internal memo circulated to Dean Witter Reynolds Inc.'s 500 branch managers in 1991 serves to bring the economics of the securities business into sharper focus. The memo chided the managers for not encouraging the firm's 7,500 brokers to sell more of the mutual funds managed directly by Dean Witter. These funds, on which the firm collected annual management fees, represented about 60 percent of Dean Witter's mutual fund sales in 1990 vs. management's goal of 75 percent. Lipper Analytical Services, which tracks mutual fund performance, indicated that only seven of Dean Witter's 17 funds outperformed the average for their investment categories. Nevertheless, Dean Witter's sales management team was able to overcome the mediocre record of its funds through the studious use of sales incentives. The initial "front end" fees for buying a mutual fund, which range as high as 5.5 percent of the invested amount, form the basis for brokers' commissions. At Dean Witter, internally managed funds generated a commission payout of 35-41 percent of the front-end fee vs. 30-39 percent for outside funds. With this commission structure, a Dean Witter broker who acted with his client's interests foremost could well find himself cutting his own commission when he recommended an outside fund which had demonstrated superior performance.

Big customers were as readily victimized by the Street as small ones. Salomon Brothers, Inc., which did not build its huge capital base through good works alone, was fined $1.3 million by the New York Stock Exchange for diverting profits from six of its customers during 1987. The record fine resulted from Salomon's execution of program trading, the computer-assisted index arbitrage trades in which large baskets of stocks are traded against one another. In essence, Salomon's violation involved the underpayment to customers for stocks sold and overcharging for stocks purchased. By not reporting price corrections to customers in October, 1987, for example, Salomon kept $240,000 of funds due their customers. Of course, Salomon fired the employees involved in the scam and installed an automated system to prevent its recurrence. But one wonders if this action would have been taken had the matter not been investigated by the Exchange. The tendency of Salomon's senior management to condone abusive practices was to visit grief upon the firm and its shareholders in the nineties

Investor complaints regarding investment banking practices apply to activities in the bond market as well as stocks. Noteholders of Ames Department Stores, Inc. filed a class-action lawsuit against Wertheim, Schroder & Co. for an allegedly fraudulent scheme to artificially inflate the price of Ames' senior subordinated notes. The suit accused the investment banker of making false and misleading statements about the company's condition and prospects. Once again, the buyout boom of the eighties was the fountainhead of investor discontent in the nineties. Ames had issued the notes in 1989 to pay off short-term debt taken on during its acquisition of Zayre Corp. Zayre had proved too big a meal for Ames to digest, and the combined entity filed for Chapter 11 protection in 1990. Of course, in this case, the investment banker was the investors' only hope for redress; federal law did not permit a company to be sued while it was undergoing Chapter 11 reorganization.

In 1990, the courts were flooded with more securities-related class-action suits than in any of the previous 20 years. At an average hourly billing rate of $360, this provided something of a bonanza for the legal profession. One study by a Yale Law School Professor, Roberta Romano, indicated that plaintiff attorneys ended up with cash far more frequently than their clients. Pay for performance was certainly not the rule. Janet Cooper Alexander, a Stanford law professor, studied shareholder suits arising from the 1983 surge in initial public offerings from Silicon Valley companies. Most cases were settled for about the same percentage, regardless of the losses suffered by investors. In Ms. Alexander's view, the settlement process appeared "fundamentally sick." Thus, the aversion to the stock market by small investors may well have been a rational response to predatory business practices – by public companies as well as their investment bankers – and an inability to obtain suitable restitution through the court system.

IV

The disenchantment of small investors was to serve as a backdrop to a sharp decline in profitability of the securities business after the 1987 Crash. The price of a seat on the New York Stock Exchange is a useful barometer of the decline in the Street's fortunes after the deluge of October 19. Shortly before the Crash, a seat changed hands at $1 million. On March 5, 1991 – with the Dow Jones Industrial Average nearly 10 percent above the 1987 high – the price of a seat was $350,000. The financial boom of the eighties – which had brought a huge increase in employment and profitability in all financial services – had sharply reversed itself after 1987 and was continuing to point downward in the nineties.

Salomon Brothers, traditionally one of Wall Street's most profitable firms, indicated how inhospitable the investment climate had become. Earnings for 1990 dropped sharply as the firm took a $155 million loss on sale of its commodity unit, Philipp Brothers, Inc. Return on equity fell to 8.3 percent, no better than what an investor could get from U.S. Treasury bonds. The problem at Salomon, as well as at competing firms, was an industry-wide drop in fees. The $8.9 billion in commission receipts in 1990 was off 30 percent from the 1987 peak of $12.7 billion. The drop in fees was consistent with an overall drop in the "value of trading," i.e. share volume times share prices. At an average of $5.3 billion per day in 1990, the value of trading in stocks was the lowest in five years. By contrast, the average daily trading volume in corporate bonds was $15.7 billion in 1990. In the new era of financial moderation, investors seemed to be backing away from the casino tables to put their money into long-term investments.

For the securities industry as a whole, 1990 was a year of going backwards: approximately $50 million in pre-tax losses, the worst year since 1974. The industry had kept itself profitable after the 1987 Crash by a boom in mergers, acquisitions, and junk bond financing. However, in 1990, all of this came undone. Many of the temporary "bridge" loans that some firms had extended their clients remained on the books when the investment banks were unsuccessful in completing buyouts and restructuring transactions. Like their fellow travelers in the banking industry, Wall Street firms such as CS First Boston, Inc. and Paine Webber Group, Inc. found themselves absorbing huge losses in "writing down" these loans to their true value.

The quickest way for Wall Street to return to profitability was to cut the exorbitant bonuses which had become common during the Boom of the Eighties. However, Main Street could hardly become lachrymose in viewing Wall Street's version of paycuts. Morgan Stanley and Co. paid total compensation to investment bankers with two years experience somewhat over $150,000 in 1990. Even less profitable firms such as CS First Boston and Merrill Lynch and Co. paid comparable employees over $100,000. Nevertheless, even at these compensation levels, bonuses for 1990 were estimated to be down 40 percent from 1989 levels. Senior investment bankers, whose total annual compensation typically exceeded $1 million in 1989, found their pay down by 35 percent in 1990. Considering the ludicrously high level of compensation even after these putative austerity measures, Wall Street's version of "Down and Out in Beverly Hills" said much about what had happened to America during the eighties.

Of course, "cutting" the pay of 28 year-old investment bankers to $100,000 would not be enough to restore profitability. Staffs were trimmed as well. Fidelity Investments, a discount broker that was also the nation's largest mutual fund company, cut employment to 6,700 employees from 7,000. Before the Crash of 1987, Fidelity had employed as many as 8,100. Industry-wide, securities firms cut their payrolls by nearly 70,000 in the three years following the Crash, a decline of approximately 20 percent in total employment. Meanwhile, employment in the securities industry's supporting armies of attorneys and accountants was also falling. The fourth-largest U.S. accounting firm, KPMG Peat Marwick, found itself taking the unusual step of cutting partners to boost profitability. The average pay and benefits of the 265 partners who got walking papers was $250,000. However, the firm was unlikely to realize immediate benefits from the cuts, which were estimated to cost $52 million in severance expenses.

Despite the cost-cutting measures, many Wall Street employees found themselves worrying whether their employers would survive the downturn. To demonstrate the short life expectancy of investment banking firms, in 1991 Merrill Lynch and Company produced a fictional "tombstone" ad announcing the sale of common stock by American Motors Corporation in 1969. The ad named 47 firms in the hypothetical underwriting syndicate, including such respected names as Burnham; Hutton; McKinnon; and Bache. The point of the ad was that, in addition to American Motors, all but one of the investment bankers — Merrill Lynch, of course — had disappeared as an independent entity by 1990. However, the true magnitude of the changes that had taken place was demonstrated, not so much by the lengthy list of defunct firms, but the manner in which the ad was reported by *The Wall Street Journal*. The world's foremost financial daily reprinted the ad, representing it as factual, though correcting its error in a later edition.[4] That so editorially punctilious a publication could assume such a high attrition rate without question was ample evidence of how bad conditions had become.

V

If the decline of Wall Street's fortunes during the latter part of the eighties was due to the setback investors had suffered during the Crash, at least one may suppose that they learned something from the experience. As the legendary stock speculator of an earlier age, Jesse Livermore, is supposed to have said, "being broke is a very efficient educational agency." Nevertheless, to judge by their dismal performance at the onset of the nineties, professional money managers and advisors still had some to learn and some to lose. During 1990, the average stock fund fell by over six percent, the worst performance since 1974. Adding insult to injury, most advisors were caught going the wrong way as the market opened 1991 with a scorching rally inspired by America's victorious performance in the Persian Gulf War. Richard Fontaine, one of the few who out-performed the market – and nearly outperformed Treasury bills – in 1990, was looking for a 20 percent decline in the Standard and Poor's 500 as the year began. Two months later, the index had not fallen, but risen by 25 percent.

Neither were Wall Street's major investment advisors any more prescient than usual. As the Dow Jones Industrial Average dove with the onset of the 1990 recession, investment newsletters turned increasingly bearish, with over 55 percent offering negative recommendations when the market bottomed in October. By February 1991, with the Dow 25 percent higher, 55 percent of the same group were offering bullish sentiments. With the market poised to rally in early 1991, Robert Salomon, Jr. of Salomon Brothers was looking for the stock market to "trade down by at least another 15 percent." Ditto that for Merrill Lynch's Robert Farrell. Morgan Stanley's Barton Biggs, who had also been bushwhacked by the rally, put the matter into perspective. "What it just proves," said Biggs, "is that despite all the intellectual conceits, all of us professional money managers are just strictly momentum players. We buy them when they're strong and sell them when they're weak."

One stock watcher who was not a momentum player was Richard Russell. This respected proponent of the so-called Dow Theory seemed to represent the attitudes of an unseen army of individual investors as they perused the investment climate of the nineties. "One of the best ways to get rich is to identify a major bear market bottom," said Russell in early 1991. "We haven't had one...I am going to let others play it." All over America, investors were coming to the same conclusion. Let others play it. The equity markets, the great emporium of productive capital where the savings of the past come together with the ideas of the future, had lost touch with its constituency. Debt had been readily substituted for equity during the eighties. During the nineties, equity had decided to quit fighting, take a long vacation, and return when the market regained its senses.

CHAPTER 12

Human Capital

"Imagine there's no country. It's not so hard to do. Nothing to kill or die for, and no religion too." The lyrics of John Lennon's song extolling the purported advantages of atheism – and nihilism in general – is an apt metaphor for the rapid departure from traditional values and lifestyles which changed the nature of the American labor force during the seventies and eighties. Perversely, the defeat of America's foreign policy – but not its army – in Vietnam seemed to many to signal the dawn of a new Age of Enlightenment. Through his inherent goodness and reason, man could perfect himself, his society, and, ultimately, a One World Brotherhood would evolve. Humanism, the belief that man is the measure of all things, had entered a period of ascendancy. The Judeo-Christian ethic and the rule of law appeared to be in secular decline. Look not to Cotton Mather or St. Augustine for the purpose and meaning of life. The eighties featured their own guiding lights: the Moonies, the New Agers, even Jim Bakker. While society reassessed its mores, it was tacitly re-shaping the nature of human capital – the ultimate raw material of all output.

The social science of economics is virtually devoid of literature on the role society's cultural values play in the productivity of its labor force. That two landlocked economies at the extremes of the economic spectrum – Switzerland and Upper Volta – could differ principally with respect to the quality of their human capital, seems not to motivate the dismal science toward a rigorous analysis of the interaction of cultural values with economic activity. On the contrary, the unparalleled economic success of the industrialized nations has not motivated America's universities to study how successful cultures could best be emulated in the third world. Instead, "liberal" education at an American university during the eighties tended more toward the cynical phenomenon known as "deconstruction." The essence of deconstruction is that "what we normally regard as the reality of things, whether in a work of literature, a code of law, or even the differences between the sexes, is nothing but a fiction, an ideological construct that has been imposed upon us by malevolent social and linguistic traditions."[1] That such a repulsive philosophy could be permitted to survive in the halls of academia is evidence of the changing assumptions that buffeted American labor in the eighties. Laissez-faire capitalism only works well in a society that is ethical and highly disciplined at its lowest level, yet a large contingent of the academic world seemed to be hell-bent on destroying America's dominant cultural heritage.

The use of Affirmative Action to replace the invisible hand of Adam Smith pointed the direction in which the new morality directed employment of America's precious human capital in the nineties. Rather than rely upon the laws of Ricardian economics, it was deemed appropriate, for example, by the bill proposing "the Civil Rights and Women's Equity in Employment Act of 1991" to create incentives for employers to use racial, ethnic, and religion-related quotas. Many employers were already living in fear of the landmark 1971 Supreme Court decision, Griggs v. Duke Power. Here it was decreed from Mount Olympus that hiring practices which appear fair can still be unlawful under the 1964 Civil Rights Act if they disproportionately harm one group. Under the so-called "disparate impact" standard of Griggs v. Duke Power, employers worried that their pursuit of high standards might inadvertently cause a segregated racial/ethnic mix which would subject their companies to costly litigation. This was not enough; the 1991 bill sought to further restrict hiring practices to meet the whim of the courts. As a result, the pernicious effects of "civil rights" quotas would extend well beyond the cost to employers in lost worker productivity and legal defense. David Duke, a racial demagogue from Louisiana, quickly capitalized on the backlash of resentment from those who felt threatened by government-sponsored discrimination. And voters appeared to be sincerely concerned. Jesse Helms, the firebrand of Southern conservatives, used the fear of racial quotas to win re-election to one of North Carolina's seats in the United States Senate, perhaps setting the tone for politics in the nineties.

Minority rights was but one of many moral issues with which America was confronted. Another clear threat was AIDS – the first disease in history which was to be accorded the status of civil rights. How could this be? A study of those afflicted with AIDS in Haiti and Africa indicated a fairly even distribution with respect to sociological factors, suggesting that the disease was, perhaps, being transmitted in these regions by natural phenomena. In America, the disease was heavily concentrated in homosexuals, intravenous drug users, and prostitutes – which suggests that lifestyles were the primary risk factor. But the traditional historical response, i.e. to quarantine those who were likely carriers, would clearly be an inappropriate measure in the 20th Century Age of Enlightenment. As a result, the disease spread rapidly to the general population during the eighties. The World Health Organization estimated that as many as 100 million people would be infected worldwide by 1991. It was easy to become hysterical with figures like these. Extrapolating from historical growth rates, scientist Iben Browning estimated that the world population would be reduced by 50 percent over 25 years.[2] Though at the extreme, Browning was not the only person frightened by his research. The National Institutes of Health spent over $28,000 on AIDS research for every AIDS-related death in 1989. Meanwhile, heart disease, the leading killer, got $953 worth of research per victim.

While the AIDS epidemic was reducing the number of workers and increasing the cost of providing them health insurance, America's law schools were hard at work eviscerating the traditional entrepeneurial *élan* of American management. For example, a National Bureau of Economic Research Paper by Kevin Murphy, Robert Vishny, and Andrei Shleifer studied economic growth and work force composition in many countries before reaching the unsurprising conclusion that engineers are good for growth and lawyers bad. The study divided college graduates into two groups, rent-seekers (who get most of their income from redistributing the wealth of others) and entrepreneurs (who seek to create wealth by introducing new production techniques or better organizing existing technologies). Of course, lawyers are simply the most obvious example of an entire rent-seeking class which includes bankers, stock brokers, and government employees. America's universities churn them out by the millions. But who could blame the eager young graduates? The financial rewards of rent-seekers were great during the eighties and the perquisites of power lunches, power ties, and one-minute management were far more inviting than the study of integral calculus. Traditional standards of excellence need not apply. Or so it seemed.

II

Though economists inquired little into the changing value system of the work force, the traditional focus of labor economics – supply and demand for labor – nevertheless provided a pregnant area of research. Here the results of a weakening manufacturing base and an aging labor force were apparent. Much of the decline in the fortunes of American labor could, of course, be put down as incident to the cyclical decline in output as the recession of 1990 was transmitted to the labor market. Demand for senior executives by U.S. corporations fell by 17 percent in 1990, according to a study by Korn/Ferry International, an executive search firm. Finance and real estate professionals were particularly hard hit. Everyone, however, had good reason to be concerned. A survey by Manpower, Inc. of 15,000 companies indicated that, nation-wide, hiring plans were the weakest since the 1982 recession, while some regions such as the Northeast were well below the depressed levels plumbed in the previous decline. The drop was greatest in the region's construction, wholesale and retail trade, and government. Yes, even government employees found themselves waiting for the axe to fall.

The labor market also found itself under the dark cloud of declining productivity as employers struggled to bring payrolls in line with falling output. Productivity at nonfinancial companies registered back-to-back declines in 1989 and 1990, the first time that had occurred in 10 years. Factories trimmed their hours by 6.4 percent in 1990's final quarter, but still were unable to keep unit labor costs from rising by 4.3 percent in 1990 and 3.9 percent in 1989. Yet, while employers were getting less output from their employees, workers were also getting less consumption from their paychecks. Real compensation per hour, i.e. earnings adjusted for inflation, dropped 1.8 percent in 1990 after declining 1.5 percent in 1989. In nominal terms, average weekly earnings in early 1991 were up just 2.5 percent over year-earlier levels. This continued a fifteen year trend of disinflation in wage rates. Annual increases in hourly compensation peaked at 11 percent in 1975, declined for three years, and then reached double digit rates once again in 1980. Wage inflation has not since approached these high levels. Despite the persistent creeping inflation of the eighties, American labor found it necessary to settle for annual raises which were common in the stable price era of the 1950's and 1960's.

Perhaps one reason for the declining fortunes of the American worker could be found in the incipient decline of the service sector of the economy. Whereas the rising share of labor-intensive services in national output had cushioned the decline in jobs in previous reces-sions, the service industry behaved increasingly like a mature industry in the 1990 recession. John B. Trammell, an economist at A. Gary Shilling & Co., calculated that the percentage of business cycle-related service jobs lost for each 0.1 percent decline in GNP was 0.58 percent in 1980, 0.42 percent in 1981 and 2.29 percent in 1990. Since the service sector comprised 75 percent of all American jobs in 1990 and Mr. Trammell estimated that 75 percent of these jobs were business cycle-related, the sharp declines in employment in airlines, advertising, financial services, and general merchandise trade in 1990 struck fear in the hearts of America's highly leveraged work force.

While demand for America's labor force was declining, demographics insured that the country would have an abundance of mature, well-educated job seekers for years to come. As the post-World War II baby boom swelled the work force in the 1970's, the annual growth rate in the adult population soared above 1.5 percent and remained high through 1990. In addition, a sharp decline in the percentage of women who were married provided additions to the labor force well beyond what could have been expected from population growth alone. This had been consistent with the ongoing de-industrialization of America in the eighties as manufacturing employment accounted for an ever smaller share of the work force; the steady increase in adult job-seekers was accommodated by the rapid growth in service industry employment.

As the nineties began, a closer look at demographic trends provided tea leaf readers with some worrisome omens. First, for those baby boomers who had finally bought their dream house in the eighties, it appeared it would be difficult to find a buyer when the time came to sell. Household formations dropped below 0.6 percent of total households in 1990, down from a high of 2.2 percent in the seventies and 1.5 percent in the eighties. One prominent student of demographic trends, Richard Hokensen, forecast that the 1990 recession would actually see an outright decline in the number of American households – the first time that had occurred in the twentieth century. A primary reason for the decline was the fivefold increase in the percentage of the population that never married. In 1989, 13.4 percent of all men over 25 were living in a household headed by another man or by a woman. George Bush, who was slandered by some as a "wimp" earlier in his career, was apparently presiding over a new age of rampant nationwide wimpism. These modern households may have considered themselves more caring and sensitive, but they were not generating the same levels of outlays for suburban housing, furniture, and automobiles which had been common fare for their parents.

Along with the decline in the traditional household, America was experiencing a "baby bust." From an average of 4.1 million births per year during the baby boom, births declined to 3.1 million per year in the 1970's. As these babies matured in the nineties – and proportionately fewer formed traditional households – the birth rate could be expected to continue its secular decline. Thus, while the baby boom generation provided a large and well-educated pool of labor for the economy, it was evident that shortages of younger workers would begin showing up as the nineties progressed. As proportionately more of the job-seekers of the future would come from the less well-educated minority groups, America was faced with the challenge of revamping its education system to meet the demands of the world marketplace. Would it also be possible to provide the workers of the future with the strong moral values which could be taken for granted in Americans of an earlier generation? The face of the American family had changed dramatically in the seventies and eighties; the labor market would feel the impact in the nineties – and beyond.

III

The inability of America's education system to generate world class quality became increasingly evident during the eighties. Chairman John Akers of IBM, for example, decried the inability of America's schools to satisfy its primary customer: business. Mr. Akers noted that his company's Japanese plant provided better yields and turnaround times than similar plants in the U.S. Another American corporation found it necessary to spend $200 to $2,000 to bring its stateside employees up to the technical proficiency of those in its Japanese plant. Employee training in Japan cost but $1 per employee – the cost of providing the employee a manual.

America's school system seemed to provide the worst of all worlds: poor results *and* high costs. American educators had better ideas than their forebears. Not only was prayer out of the schools, but so too, it seemed, was anything that smacked of traditional American values. Courses seemed more geared toward exposing what was wrong with America and its ruling elites. Probably nowhere was there a better measure of the dismal failure of the new approach than in New York City. The city's public school system served 900,000 students at an average yearly cost of $6,700. In some New York high schools, as few as 25 percent of students graduated and the dropout rate averaged 30 percent city-wide. A study by the Rand Corporation found that only the top one-sixth of students took the Scholastic Aptitude Test (SAT) but, nevertheless, performed poorly: an average score of 632 out of a possible 1600.

It would be consistent with the *Zeitgeist* of the seventies and eighties to excuse the abominable performance of New York schools on the basis of the same frequently used crutches: non-representative racial and ethnic mix and low income levels. Unfortunately for the "anything goes as long as you're poor" crowd, New York also provided a shining example of how these factors could be overcome through discipline, dedication, and strong moral values. New York's 140 Catholic schools, many of which were located in the economically depressed areas of Harlem and the South Bronx, enrolled over 51,000 students, 85 percent of whom were black, Hispanic, or Asian. The Catholic schools had a one percent high school dropout rate, sent 90 percent of their graduates to college and spent just $1,900 per student. The same Rand study which examined public school performance found that three-quarters of the Catholic school students took the SAT, and achieved an average score of 804. While New York's public schools employed 7,000 bureaucrats to administer their authoritarian version of academic freedom, the Catholic school system employed just 35 people in its central office.

Despite their unquestionably superior performance, America's private schools were fighting a government-subsidized monopoly. While the Archdiocese of New York found itself having to solicit $100 million from the public to keep its tuition affordable, the public system found it had enough money to try again on those students whose education did not take. New York Telephone, a division of NYNEX, had to test 57,000 applicants in 1987 to find 2,100 qualified for training as operators and repair technicians. The public school system, therefore, found itself contemplating whether to offer warranties on its graduates. Chancellor Joseph Fernandez proposed in 1991 that any employer who found New York's graduates unable to read, write, or calculate proficiently be permitted to return the worker for remedial education at no additional cost to the employer. Similar plans were already in effect in Prince Georges County, Maryland and the Plymouth-Carver school district in Massachusetts.

America's substandard performance in educating its children implied lower worker productivity and declining real incomes in the future. Unfortunately, many young graduates found themselves in the same position as marginal business enterprises which had issued junk bonds; they had high contractual liabilities which did not permit them the luxury of accepting reduced pay. With a decrepit or non-existent system of public transportation, most American workers were not fully equipped for employment without an automobile. This accessory alone drove the worker's subsistence wage higher by thousands of dollars. For example, NFO Research, Inc. found in a nationwide survey of households that the average cost of auto insurance alone was $923 in 1990.

But the high cost of commuting paled against the debt service on the highly leveraged diplomas of many new sheepskin holders. The number of student borrowers nearly doubled – to 4.5 million – from 1980 to 1990. Outstanding student loans amounted to $12.3 billion, of which $2.4 billion were in default. Many students had simply borrowed more than their degree would be worth in terms of increased earnings potential. While the average graduate from a private college in 1986 owed $10,000, many found themselves owing over twice that amount. A study by the Massachusetts Higher Education Assistance Corp. found that 20 percent of recent college graduates were forced to postpone big-ticket purchases due to high levels of student debt. Worse, many could not afford to take the normal low-paying entry-level positions in their career fields. One recent graduate in English literature with $15,000 in student loans hanging over his head decided that a $6-an-hour job in a publishing house would not leave enough to meet his $150 per month student loan payments. Instead, he took a job as a sheet metal fabricator.

In short, America's human capital was finding it difficult to compete – either on the basis of cost or quality – in the world marketplace in the nineties. The integration of the world's capital markets had made capital far more free to move across national borders. On a national basis, however, human capital remained a relatively immobile factor. This was especially true of American workers, who speak only one language, and are generally unwilling to learn a second. If America's workers were unable to provide high quality output at a reasonable cost, then American capital would seek higher returns elsewhere. While public education operated as a monopoly in the domestic market, the ultimate requirement for American labor to remain competitive demonstrated that the system's performance fell far short of the economy's requirements. The problem was widely recognized; the solution was not.

IV

One of labor's tried and true solutions from the past, which had become a dinosaur in the nineties, was the labor union. The grandfather of the movement, the AFL-CIO, reported total union membership of slightly over 14 million in 1990. But despite an intense organizing effort, which recruited 250,000 new members, total membership was down by 15,000 for the year. This continued a multi-decade decline in the importance of the organized labor movement. Indeed, it appeared that the movement had outlived its original purpose of organizing factory workers. In 1990, AFL-CIO unions represented just 12 percent of the private-industry work force, while unions representing teachers and government employees represented 35 percent of the public payroll. Of course, the critical flaw of public employee unions was that the public as a whole would little notice or care if union members felt sufficiently oppressed to invoke strikes. At any rate, the evidence did not seem to contradict this idea: major work stoppages hit a record low of 40 in 1988, and changed but little in the following two years.

One reason the strike weapon was rarely invoked was that workers were too fearful of losing their jobs, not just temporarily, but forever. A prime example was the 1991 bargaining between the United Steelworkers of America and giant steel-maker USX. The steelworkers were not anxious to repeat the mistake of their six-month strike during 1986. Striking as they did then, at a time of severe financial strain for the domestic steel industry, was successful only in achieving smaller pay *cuts* than the company had originally proposed. Moreover, the union lost its automatic cost-of-living wage adjustments which had been such a boon to steelworkers during the seventies. By 1991, however, union pay scales at USX were still $1 an hour below 1982 levels. Ever mindful of the damage these high wage rates had done to the company's competitiveness, USX was unwilling to grant life-of-contract increases in 1991. Moreover, USX – which also owned giant Marathon Oil – was mulling a plan to concentrate its steel operations in a separate subsidiary. By separating its labor contracts and pension obligations from the parent company, USX would enhance its own value at the same time it was making the steel operations more readily marketable. The union was clearly nervous about this prospect.

An example of where the newfound concern over job security might lead was provided by the United Auto Workers. Demonstrating its poor understanding of the business cycle, General Motors inked an accord with the UAW in the fall of 1990, just as recession was impending. Ford and Chrysler were forced to follow suit in contracts which guaranteed UAW members 85 percent of their normal take-home pay for up to three years. While employment at the "Big Three" auto-makers had shrunk from 750,000 hourly workers in 1980 to 450,000 in 1990, it would shrink no further in 1991-1993. For all practical purposes, the new contracts made labor a fixed cost. Yet, despite their pride in the new pact, union members had achieved nothing that was not available to their non-unionized brethren. The 22,750 American workers at U.S. assembly plants of Japanese automakers were kept on the job, despite falling production, in keeping with the Japanese firms' traditional no-layoff policy. It was little wonder that UAW efforts to organize workers in these plants had been unsuccessful. American labor saw no reason to marry the cow if the milk was free.

One union that never quite understood its impotence in the face of a weak economy was the Amalgamated Transit Union, whose members struck against ailing Greyhound Lines, Inc. Greyhound maintained it couldn't afford the union's pay demands and proceeded to replace striking workers with non-union employees. This led to several violent incidents, including some buses being fired upon while transporting passengers. Ultimately, the company filed for Chapter 11 bankruptcy protection. Yet, the spectre of Christmas past continued to cast a pall over the company. The union filed suit through the National Labor Relations Board (NLRB), accusing Greyhound of illegal activities in its bargaining with the union. Thus, the possibility arose that the NLRB could award back pay and benefits to the union, impairing the claims of the company's other creditors. This contingent liability was a significant impediment to the company's reorganization effort. Once again, the courts would cast the deciding ballot: Greyhound's creditors asked the U.S. Bankruptcy Court to place a maximum on any back-pay award to the union.

As U.S. companies increasingly found unionized labor too costly or too hostile and embarked for friendlier climes, unions found themselves turning ever more frequently to the court system for recourse. The Machinists Union charged that McDonnell Douglas Co. and General Dynamics Corp. failed to give proper 60-day notice under the 1988 federal plant closing law. The irony of this situation was that the two firms in question had laid off workers on the heels of the Defense Department's cancellation of the A-12 attack aircraft contract. A kind of vicious cycle of rip-offs was in prospect: the unions could "stick it" to the employers for not giving proper notice because the same government which passed the plant closing restriction had stuck it to the contractors. However, given the short list of competent aircraft manufacturers, the afflicted concerns need merely wait until submitting their next contract bid to Defense, thus taking the opportunity to recover their losses. Meanwhile, the taxpayer who would foot the bill for all this chicanery, remained oblivious to its cause, if not its effects.

The 1988 law regarding plant shutdowns was not the only serious impediment to companies that were straining to improve the efficiency of their operations. American Home Products Corp. acquired A. H. Robbins Co.'s over-the-counter drug business in 1989 and moved to close its Elkhart, Indiana plant to streamline operations. The Oil, Chemical, and Atomic Workers Union charged that the company was wrongfully taking advantage of tax benefits offered by the Common-wealth of Puerto Rico in relocating its manufacturing operations. The union evidently placed far greater value on the services of its members than did the company. While the suit requested $100 million on behalf of its 575 affected members, the company stated that the tax benefit of moving to Puerto Rico was just $500,000. To companies like American Home Products, labor unions were often an albatross, an unwanted but ineluctable reminder of the unpleasant past.

V

Better an albatross than a millstone, which is what labor's "safety net" had become to the economy in the nineties. It appeared that much of the patchwork of government and privately sponsored programs intended to succor the American worker in time of need had been weakened materially by the economic and demographic changes which had occurred during the eighties. American workers had, nevertheless, become complacent in their tendency to identify some of these pro-grams as immutable. Worried about job security? Well, there would always be unemployment compensation. Health care costs rising? So what! The company insurance plan covered just about everything. Save for retirement? With social security and the company pension plan, why bother?

Anyone who cared to look further into the matter would find that these safety net programs were essentially funded on a pay-as-you-go basis. As a result, the impending economic strains of the 1990 recession placed ever greater pressure on the economy's ability to support the American worker in the style to which he had become accustomed during the previous generation. The unemployment insurance system was a good example of how the changing face of the economy had left many workers vulnerable. As new claims for benefits soared past a half million per week in early 1991, it became apparent that many of the individual states, which were responsible for administering claims for workers within their borders, would not have sufficient funds to meet the emergency. Worse yet, many workers found that they were not covered at all. The eighties had witnessed a surge in contract employment of labor, by which many remitters evade unemployment insurance premiums. In addition, many of the marginal workers who had been absorbed by the labor market in the economic boom did not have sufficient seniority to collect the level of unemployment insurance benefits they might have expected.

Many of the newly jobless found themselves uninsured in another equally daunting area, that of medical care. As employment lapsed, so too did health insurance coverage. Yet, even those who remained employed learned that their companies would be cutting back on health benefits. The sharp general rise in the cost of medical care, which had increased by one-third from 1985 to 1988, had caused health insurers to raise their rates accordingly. But the premium increases were still not enough to match the sharp increase in benefit payments. By 1988, the capital reserve of all Blue Cross plans nationwide had fallen to $3 billion, which many deemed inadequate to meet rising claims in the ensuing cyclical downturn. The New Jersey plan, which had been running deficits for four years, sought a 47 percent rate increase in 1991. And increasing numbers of workers would find that their health status would deny them employment. Mountain States Blue Cross and Blue Shield planned to raise health insurance premiums by 50 percent for those individuals it considered high risk.

For those workers who thought they were comfortably insured, there was a stark tale to be heard from Glennis Hammack, who also thought he was covered through his company plan with Blue Cross & Blue Shield of West Virginia. Instead, the 32 year-old gas-line repairman found himself stuck with $36,000 in unpaid medical bills when his health carrier filed bankruptcy in 1990. With the $23,000 per year he earned from two jobs, Mr. Hammack was at a loss to determine how he could ever make his debts good. All over West Virginia, his fellow mountaineers were wondering how to handle the $50 million that was left unpaid when the West Virginia chapter of Blue Cross went under.

One source of pressure on private health insurers was the restraint placed on benefit increases by the federally sponsored Medicare and

Medicaid programs. Medicare payments, which increased by 14 percent from 1989 to 1990, were a $107 billion equivalent of crop price supports for the medical field. Though Medicare and Medicaid payments rose steadily during the eighties, their failure to meet the total cost of medical care was beginning to throw physicians into the cold embrace of the free market. For example, Medicaid payments covered only 78 percent of the cost of treatment to its beneficiaries in 1989. Nevertheless, the Bush Administration's 1992 budget proposal included a $23 billion cut in payments over a five year period. As federal payments fell short of the total cost of treatment, the health industry would increasingly try to recoup its losses by raising rates to privately insured patients. Thus, in the nineties, the burden of support for America's not-too-effective system of health care would increasingly shift to private insurers – and the employers who supported it. Constrained by rising costs, falling output and declining revenues, employers could be expected to continue shifting the burden of health care to their employees during the nineties or, in some cases, eliminating health coverage altogether. Adam Smith's invisible hand would soon be at work at the operating table.

As to pensions, most retired workers would still say that Social Security was the best financial deal they had ever made. Hardly anyone put as much into the pot as he later drew out. But emerging trends were worrisome. Real per capita benefits the retired worker was projected to receive from Medicare and Social Security peaked at 45 percent of per capita gross national product in 1982, and dropped to 37 percent by 1988. Congress voted to begin taxing some benefits in 1984, and the eligibility age for full retirement benefits was scheduled to begin increasing in the year 2000.[3] Despite the ominous demographic trends which made these changes necessary, a bipartisan effort was underway in Congress to cut the payroll tax which funded the Social Security program. New York's Senator Moynihan, who showed himself more adept in the art of politics than the science of mathematics, proposed a 16 percent cut in the social security tax. The Moynihan plan proposed to compensate for some of the lost revenues by raising taxes on the affluent. Senator Moynihan, who had tried unsuccessfully to cut the payroll tax in 1990, seemed to have better prospects for his 1992 budget proposal. If his effort succeeded, the social security trust fund would almost surely begin placing financial demands on the general revenues raised by the Treasury, a complete reversal from the fund's role as a major buyer of Treasury bonds during the eighties.

The problem of how – and at what level – to fund the social security retirement fund was similar to the problems facing many private pension plans. The Pension Benefit Guaranty Corp. (PBGC) reported losses of $780 million from companies terminating underfunded pension plans in 1990. The agency, which indemnified workers affected by such defaults, reported that the loss left it with negative net worth of $1.8 billion. Despite a federal court decision to relieve it of the $3 billion in liabilities left by default of LTV Corporation's pension plans, the agency estimated that it faced as much as $8 billion in potential losses from underfunded plans. The 1990 federal budget permitted PBGC to increase its premiums by $120 million annually for five years, but total annual premium income would still amount to no more than one-tenth of its total liability.

Thus, as the nineties unfolded, American labor found itself assailed on all possible fronts. The basic manufacturing strength which had financed the continually rising expectations and lifestyle of the American worker had declined dramatically. The service-based economy, which depended on small and poorly capitalized businesses, was unable to fund the high level of long-term benefits which had been considered every worker's right. The days of John Wayne's patriotism, Chester A. Riley's assembly line, and Dagwood Bumstead's home life were over. Everyone was deemed to have a right to a college education, but most college graduates could not identify the Bill of Rights, nor appreciate the wisdom of doing so. Meanwhile, emerging demographic trends were pushing a less skilled, less educated and less productive work force into one end of the labor pipeline while the number of retirees coming out the opposite end grew – along with their demands – at an exponential rate.

CHAPTER 13

The Indentured American Consumer

"The scales are tipped slightly in favor of suggesting that the current downturn may well prove milder than the typical postwar recession." Thus spoke the master of equivocation – if not prevarication – Alan Greenspan. The date was March 6, 1991 and the occasion was the Federal Reserve Board Chairman's testimony before the House Ways and Means Committee regarding the conduct of monetary policy. Next in the witness chair was Robert Reischauer, Director of the Congressional Budget Office, who indicated that the recession which had begun in the second half of 1990 was likely to be mild and of short duration. Thus, as America struggled through an economic decline in which consumer finances were strained more severely than at any time since the Great Depression, the ostrich seemed more appropriate than the eagle as the national symbol. The benign attitude of America's economic policymakers in the face of rapidly crumbling consumer confidence was something akin to the attitude of the League of Nations in the face of Hitler Germany's truculent foreign policy. The aftermath of an official policy of insouciance to impending danger was likely to match the Churchillian assessment: never was so much owed by so many to so few.

Partly to blame for the decline in consumer psychology as the 1990 recession set in was the uncertainty caused by the Persian Gulf War. This explains why policymakers were loath to try to correct the problem. If war was the problem, victory would be the solution; economic policy need not be tailored to the crisis at hand. Indeed, the quick military success against Iraq did provide a sharp boost in consumer confidence, which had dropped from a high above 120 in 1989 to the manic-depressive level of 54 in January, 1991. A partial recovery in this widely followed index of consumer sentiment, which is compiled monthly by the Conference Board, carried to the low 80's immediately after the hostilities concluded. But the decline had been too great and had persisted too long to be written off purely to war phobia. When the data were examined on a regional basis, it was evident that many consumers were all but suicidal. In the New England States, the confidence reading plummeted to 26.9 in December, 1990, barely a quarter of the 1985 base index of 100.

The morose attitude of the American consumer was indeed rooted in causes far less transient than anxiety over what ultimately became a turkey shoot in the Mideast. Annual increases in disposable income, after subtracting price inflation, peaked in the second quarter of 1988 and declined steadily thereafter into the 1990 recession, by which time incomes were declining in real terms. Consumer spending marched to the beat of the same drum. Meanwhile, the percentage of disposable income dedicated to mortgage payments and installment debt rose to new records. This continued a trend which had been in place for thirty years. In 1960, debt payments were slightly over nine percent of disposable income; by 1990, the figure was approaching 14 percent. And the rise could not be blamed solely on higher interest rates. Outstanding mortgage debt, which was less than 40 percent of disposable income in 1960, had risen above 60 percent of income in 1990.

As the American consumer retrenched in line with his falling income to meet the economic decline, it should have been evident that the bloom was off the rose of the ebullient attitude of an entire generation. Ideologically, the Baby Boom generation had progressed from "Hell, no! We won't go!" to "Support our Troops." The rebellion of the sixties had spawned the confusion of the seventies, which begot the concupiscience of the eighties. The economy had responded by growing to meet the demands of each personality change. But as the Boomers passed 40 and thoughts began to turn toward grandchildren and retirement, the atavism of the nineties brought new challenges which argued in favor of less housing, more saving, and less spending. In short, the assumptions on which 50 years of economic policy had been based were as anachronistic as hula hoops, Nehru jackets, and pet rocks.

From the mid-sixties to 1990, the number of Americans in the all-important group of consumers aged 25-34 rose from 23 million to nearly 44 million. Meanwhile, the less exuberant group in the 45-54 age group grew from 17 million to 25 million. During the nineties, however, the 45-54 age group was projected to rise from 25 million to 37 million while the 25-34 group *declined* by seven million. The economic ramifications would be significant; it is the younger adults who borrow and spend disproportionately to acquire housing, automobiles, and household goods as they establish their adult lifestyle. For example, in

1988 the 25-34 age group spent nearly 2.5 times as much as the 45-54 group on debt payments as a percentage of income.

As America's population became older during the nineties, its attitude toward consumption and saving was sure to change. In autos, Fords or Toyotas might do just as well as Mercedes or BMW's. In apparel, Levi Strauss could retain the pre-eminent position which once seemed to be threatened by fashionable upstarts like Gloria Vanderbilt. And, as far as housing is concerned, was not a bigger home just more work? Yard work and window washing were never chores one willingly accepted purely on the basis of their own merits. As their own children grew, the Baby Boom would find that it needed less housing. And as the cost of college education for the new generation rose and the prospect of retirement came ultimately into consideration, the need for increased saving would become obvious. Thus, the Baby Boom generation, which had been an economic locomotive ever since it spawned the initial post-World War II housing boom, would no longer borrow and spend. It would pay down its huge debt and begin saving.

II

If Americans really were about to go on a saving binge in the nineties, it would be at least as much out of necessity as preference. The $2.7 trillion of mortgage debt and $740 billion of credit card balances consumers were carrying in 1990 had turned America into a nation of working poor, much like indentured servants. While consumer spending was up by six percent from the previous year in 1990 – the same increase as recorded for personal income – shoppers found themselves pinching pennies like never before. Due to increased taxes and stubborn inflation, the median real income of the typical family declined from 1989 into 1991. The "typical family" of two wage-earners and two dependent children saw its income peak at $41,572 in 1989 and drop by over one percent in 1990, if federal taxes, social security taxes, and the "inflation tax" are deducted. State and local taxes as well as federal excise taxes, which are not counted by the Tax Foundation, which monitors this data series, reduced real family income by an additional but unknown amount.

The economic pinch of declining real after-tax incomes stimulated some remarkable changes in consumer behavior. The premium placed on cash was perhaps best demonstrated at the annual IRS tax refund ritual. Many tax preparers offered instant cash in the form of refund anticipation loans for those customers who filed their tax returns electronically. *The Wall Street Journal* reported that most filers were willing to pay the $30 fee in return for immediate cash rather than wait two weeks for the automatic bank deposit from IRS. On the average cash refund due of $916, this computes to an annual interest rate of 85 percent. The additional electronic filing fee of $20 would push the effective interest rate well beyond most states' usury limits. Yet, even at these rates, John Hewitt of Jackson Hewitt Tax Service estimated that 75 percent of his customers would opt for the instant cash.

Why the high premium on cash? Often, it was needed to pay overdue utility, telephone, or credit card bills. Regardless, for many Americans the IRS refund was the biggest pile of cash they would see during the entire year, and many just could not wait to get it in their hands. Used car dealer Randy Leonard in Memphis, Tennessee reported that he did approximately 50 percent of his annual sales during the three month period when the tax refunds were rolling in. Leonard explained that the typical cash down payment of $800 was simply too much for most of his customers to handle from their usual cash balances. Only during "tax season" could most of his clientele afford the down payment. The manager of the Cash America, Inc. retail outlet next door would probably agree. Cash America, which operates a retail chain of pawn shops throughout Texas and the South, was making hay from hard economic times. The company, which capital- ized on its expertise from the economic bust in Texas, saw its annual sales increase from $5.3 million in 1985 to over $100 million in 1990. The pawn business is essentially the business of making small collateralized loans (at an annual interest rate that exceeds 200 per- cent!) to consumers who generally do not have strong enough credit to borrow from a financial institution. Therefore, as money tightened and consumer creditworthiness deteriorated during the late eighties, Cash America found its business booming.

Many of those consumers who had not yet resorted to pawning their wedding rings found themselves clipping coupons – the kind one finds in the Sunday newspaper, not those on bonds. D'Arcy Masius Benton & Bowles, a New York ad agency, reported that manufacturers distributed 267.6 billion coupons in 1989, with a total potential savings of $132 billion. The typical coupon shopper was a middle-aged married working white woman with household income of $29,000. By assidu- ously clipping coupons, she was able to save $6 on her average weekly grocery bill of $74. D'Arcy opined that many of these stout-hearted souls got a sense of satisfaction from "beating the system."

Whether they were trying to beat the system or just preventing it from beating them to death, American consumers were definitely becoming more value-conscious. Sears, Roebuck & Co. launched a value pricing campaign in March 1989, featuring "everyday low pricing." This was right in step with the more conservative shopping habits of Baby Boomers like Raven Wallace of Ann Arbor, Michigan. "I don't ever buy anything at the first price I see," said Mrs. Wallace, whose hard bargaining got her one-third off the price of an Apple Macintosh computer and 20 percent off the sticker price on a new Chevrolet Suburban. Mrs. Wallace was just one of millions; the bargaining and buying habits of Americans had clearly changed. Conspicuous consumption was out. An economy which had over-invested in catering to the consumer provided fertile ground for customers to shop for value. Indeed, parsimony was becoming fashionable.

III

One reason buying habits were changing in the early nineties was the reaction to the enormous growth in the use of all forms of consumer credit during the eighties. Credit cards, auto loans, and home equity loans were used to finance a major portion of the prodigious growth in spending during the eighties, and this naturally led to a marked deterioration in the quality of existing consumer debt, while it stemmed the appetite of consumers to go further into hock. From the standpoint of the finance industry, however, many institutions had made huge investments to enter the consumer finance business and, therefore, had a vested interest in pushing ever greater mountains of debt on those still willing to assume it.

The rapid growth of the credit card industry bears witness to the abandon with which the purveyors of plastic dealt their wares during the eighties. Citicorp led the way when it set up its Citibank subsidiary in South Dakota, with the express purpose of issuing credit cards that would be subject to higher usury rate ceilings than in the operation's previous domicile in New York State. The company further expanded its consumer lending operations by purchasing Diners Club and Carte Blanche. Citicorp was soon followed by other banks and thrifts intent on increasing their consumer lending businesses. By the end of the eighties, such unlikely competitors as Sears and AT&T were significant players in the credit card business, while the Big Three automakers were driving their finance subsidiaries from zero to sixty in three seconds via auto loans and home equity loans. Air bags and security alarms were not offered as extra cost options, either for the borrower or the lender.

Plastic became the preferred poison of an economy that seemed willing to swallow the inevitability of the "cashless society." The number of Visa, MasterCard, American Express and Diners Club cards outstanding had grown to 268 million by 1989, more than one for every man, woman and child in America. Families earning over $75,000 per year had an average of 7.4 credit cards. Debt outstanding on bank cards grew from $25 billion in 1980 to $132 billion in 1989, while bad debt on bank cards soared from $500 million to over $4 billion. Consumer purchases by credit cards amounted to $328 billion in 1989, nearly one-tenth of the $3.5 trillion in total personal outlays.

Expanding competition led to deteriorating conditions in a business which had once been highly profitable for banks. Donald Auriemma, the owner of a Garden City, New York, consulting company which bears his name, indicated that banks generally needed a three percent pre-tax return on their credit card assets, while non-bank issuers could make money at far lower spreads. And there were other incentives for non-bank competitors. Sears' Discover card and AT&T's Universal card could stimulate business or protect market share in other profit centers. Many issuers waived annual fees or offered reduced interest rates. Meanwhile, the unrelenting search for ever more marginal customers led to an industry-wide increase in credit losses. The American Bankers Association disclosed that 4.5 percent of bank card balances were overdue at the end of 1990, a rise of nearly 40 percent from the year earlier. As a percentage of their credit card receivables which banks had sold to investors in the form of asset-backed securities, charge-offs hit 4.5 percent in November, 1990. These data were compiled by Moody's Investor Services, Inc., which examined all credit card-based securities which had been outstanding at least twelve months. The Moody's study also seemed to indicate that consumers were stretching their repayments out longer; slightly over 10 percent of debt outstanding was paid down each month, a decline from the repayment rate recorded in 1989.

If credit card issuers were having increasing difficulty recovering receivables, their experience was shared by those who had jumped into the auto loan business. The Snatch Man, as the lender's auto recovery agent is known in the inner city, found his services in ever greater demand. Car-loan repossessions climbed to 1.2 percent of outstanding loan dollars in 1990 from 0.7 percent in 1989, according to the Consumer Bankers Association. Leased autos were being snatched at a still more rapid rate, 1.5 percent of outstanding contracts in 1990. Meanwhile, delinquencies in excess of 30 days on auto leases soared to 2.1 percent, despite the fact that lease payments are generally lower than standard auto loan payments. Duly chastened by their increasing loss rates, the Association indicated that its members approved just 51 percent of auto loan applications in 1990. No wonder Randy Leonard, the used car dealer in Memphis – and others who offered to "tote the note" for their customers – were finding an increasing number of buyers who had been turned away by traditional lenders.

As lenders tightened guidelines and consumers balked, total consumer credit actually declined with the onset of the 1990 recession. For the year as a whole, credit rose a modest three percent, after increases of 7.8 percent in 1989 and 8.9 percent in 1988. In 1990, automobile credit outstanding fell by 1.9 percent for the year as a whole. All of this made for a far less buoyant attitude on the part of lenders such as Household International, Inc., whose debt ratings were downgraded two times in one year. In justifying the downgradings, Moody's stated that it was "based upon growing uncertainties about the company's asset quality." While company officials indicated that the increased cost of borrowing would not affect loan pricing, it was obvious that the industry-wide experience of rising credit loss would have an effect on underwriting guidelines and the availability of consumer credit.

While lenders re-examined their lending guidelines, many of America's credit junkies decided to go cold turkey. The Ward family of Manchester, Connecticut, provided a good case study for many consumers who had obligated themselves to a mountain of debt and were struggling to make drastic changes in their previously spendthrift lifestyles. With a combined annual income of $60,000, they jumped on the real estate bandwagon by signing a $152,000 mortgage note. Mr. Ward, unbeknownst to his wife, amassed 25 credit cards and ran up a balance of $35,000 with pricey clothing, vacations, and sundry luxuries. When he got to the point of kiting payments on some cards via advances on others, Mrs. Ward stepped in to demand a return to fiscal responsibility. On the advice of a credit counselor, the Wards destroyed all but one credit card, which they deemed necessary for identification purposes in the credit-happy American economy, and consolidated their payments in a lump sum of $1,200 monthly. That left the family of four with a monthly budget of just $300 for food and $50 for clothing.

As lenders sought increasingly to identify those consumers who were in danger of over-extending themselves, the information gathered by America's credit reporting agencies became a critical factor in lenders' decision-making. Many credit card issuers made it a practice to request credit reports on existing customers – regardless of payment history – to identify those that were having problems with other lenders. Credit reports also gained new importance as a screening device for employers. Often the legal data gathered by credit bureaus showed inaccuracies in the work histories claimed by prospective employees. Equally important, an applicant's ability to meet contractual debt obligations was deemed important information regarding character – often a difficult attribute to assess from interviews or professional references. Unfortunately, with two billion credit information inputs each month, errors often crept into the reporting bureaus' automated data bases. On examining their credit reports, which most consumers failed to do, many people found themselves identified with adverse information belonging to others with the same or similar name. Minor errors by unseen clerks could jeopardize an application for a loan, employment, or apartment rental. Thus, those who had generated a history of shirking their obligations – and some consumers who had not – found it increasingly difficult to operate in the highly automated "cashless" economy of the nineties.

Ultimately, the only recourse for many consumers who had leveraged themselves beyond the hope of satisfying their creditors was to file a petition under the U.S. Bankruptcy Code. The number of Americans choosing this last resort to restoring financial order more than doubled between 1986 and 1990, when it reached a record of 685,249. Most of these were under Chapter 7 of the Code, which permits debtors to keep some assets while liquidating others to satisfy creditors' claims. Others, who were simply too deep in debt to keep their payments current, filed for so-called "wage earner protection" under Chapter 13 of the Code. The bankruptcy court appoints a trustee to supervise payments by wage earners under a three to five year payment schedule. When payments specified by the court have been satisfied, the debtor's remaining obligations are cancelled by the court and the bankrupt emerges free from all debts except federal income taxes, child support payments, and certain other excluded items.

As bankruptcy became ever more popular in the eighties, many lenders and merchants found they could not afford to pass up the opportunity to write off this rapidly growing base of potential customers. Many banks began offering "secured" credit cards, in which the customer posts a cash deposit with the card issuer, against which card transactions are credited. Many used car dealers also started offering loans to bankrupts, especially those who had faithfully made payments under Chapter 13. Sears, Roebuck & Co. offered to continue extending credit to customers who went through bankruptcy – as long as they agreed to continue paying off any pre-petition account balances.

Regardless of what gimmicks lenders chose to delude themselves to continue doing business with those who had defaulted on their past debts, the willingness of business to consider dealing with bankrupts demonstrated that financial sanity remained a distant goal for the American economy. Intellectual dishonesty, which is the root cause of all dishonesty, remained an integral part of strategic planning. America's business community had not yet reached the point of understanding that a hamburger today is real, while the prospect of being paid next Tuesday is not. Yet when Wednesday arrived and payment had not, hamburgers continued to be produced and consumed, while the bill continued to mount, with interest. Thus, as the American consumer struggled under a crushing burden of debt, declining real income, and the frightening prospect of unemployment, lenders and accountants failed to see that the emperor was not wearing a fine suit of new clothes but was, in fact, naked – and shivering.

CHAPTER 14

Whither America?

The catalog of ills facing American society as the nineties began was well-known, yet almost too painful for most Americans to express. From a European's perspective, it appeared to Werner Meyer-Larsen that the decline of a superpower was imminent. Writing in Germany's *Der Spiegel* magazine, Meyer-Larsen listed a litany of problems he found incompatible with world leadership:[1]

- Two million Americans leave school each year without having learned to read and write, while 24 million adult Americans can not locate their own country on a map of the world.

- Thirty-seven million Americans have no health insurance.

- America pays $700 billion per year for medical care, yet is in last place in the industrialized world in terms of child mortality, life expectancy, and visits to physicians.

- One-fourth of all American children under six live in poverty.

- Americans save less than six percent of their income and – as a nation – consume 3-4 percent more than they produce.

- Some 3.7 million Americans were in prison.

- In 1990 in New York City one in 100 was homeless; one in 300 had AIDS; someone was murdered every five hours; someone was robbed every six minutes; and, a car "disappeared" every four minutes.

The natural response of a concerned citizenry is to clamor for action to correct such frightful conditions. Unfortunately, calling upon the U.S. government for corrective action is the rough equivalent of hiring a mercenary army of Ostrogoths to beat back the incursions of the Visigoths. To a large degree, the problems of inferior education, crime, poverty, a bankrupt financial system, and deficient capital formation were due either to the failure of government in its traditional aegis of providing for the public weal, or in some non-traditional area in which it had chosen to pre-empt the private sector.

Neither of the two major American political parties seemed able to perceive how a free society should operate. The Democrats, once identified as the party of preference for the working class, seemed intent on alienating their basic constituency by a formless and mindless adherence to "liberal" causes. For example, to confront the great S&L fiasco – which was only made possible by the New Deal plan of government guarantee of private debts – Democrats found themselves sponsoring minority employment and low-income housing amendments to thrift bailout legislation. Perhaps it was reasoned that once the taxpayer realized he had lost $500 billion in the deposit insurance boondoggle, largely to subsidize white collar "good ole boy" incompetence, he wouldn't notice the likely waste of the few billion more that would result from requiring 25 percent of the contractors to be women and minorities. Not so! *The Wall Street Journal* reported that the Leadership Conference on Civil Rights suppressed a poll that showed working class whites thought "civil rights" legislation had little to do with the original intent of the movement. Civil rights bills had come to be viewed as government-sponsored quotas, both by those who identified themselves as Democrats and by the public as a whole.

The fairness issue cuts both ways in the American economy. On the one hand, to acquire wealth from hard work and one's own native ability is the traditional American dream. On the other hand, the gap between the "haves" and "have-nots" appeared to widen during the eighties. In 1989, the share of income received by the highest quintile of households was 46.8 percent, vs. 44.2 percent in 1979 and 43.0 percent in 1969. This was quite likely due to the low income and increasing number of single mothers. One-half of all households headed by a woman found themselves in the lowest income quintile. Thus, despite – or because of – the vociferous efforts of women's rights activists, the rise in such households from 10.8 percent of all families in 1970 to 16.5 percent in 1990 was attended by greater variability in family income, indicating that the "rights" women were attaining, whatever they might be, were inversely related to their economic standing. Yet, the Democratic Party's cries of "soak the rich" would further burden an already progressive tax system. Effective 1991 federal tax rates for the poorest income quintile were 8.5 percent, rising to 26.8 percent for the "richest" quintile and 28.9 percent for the top one percent. The much ballyhooed Reagan tax cuts had reduced the effective tax rate of the top quintile by less than one percent from the 1980 rate, while the poorest group saw its rate virtually unchanged – though down significantly from the 1985 level. Thus, the rich were already getting soaked and there were strict limits to the powers of social engineers to redistribute income via the tax code.

If fiscal policy was the only yardstick, the Republican Party was no more effective as an advocate of free markets than were the rival Democrats. George Bush presided over both the greatest tax increase and the most rapid growth in federal spending during the post-FDR era. It would be facile for Republicans to blame the explosion in spending on the thrift bailout, yet every one of the 10 major domestic spending programs grew faster than inflation from 1989 to 1991. With the $170 billion 1990 tax increase, which was billed as a "Budget Compromise," domestic spending would rise by 10 percent, while all federal taxes as a percentage of GNP would be the highest since World War II. Worse, due to the hard and fast rules of the 1990 tax accord between Democrats and Republicans, tax rates would be rigidly controlled over a five year period. The government's fiscal policy would not respond to the business cycle as it often had in the past.

As Washington's power and influence grew during the post-War era, so did the feeding frenzy of special interest groups. It was the fulfillment of the fondest expectations of Robert Ely, the nineteenth century founder of the American Economic Association, who once stated that "we regard the state as an educational and ethical agency whose positive aid is an indispensable condition of human progress." Ely's dream has certainly been a boon for the career prospects of economists, and for anyone else who makes his living from Big Brother. By 1990 there were some 1,200 "think tanks" — liberal and conservative alike — trying to influence what the Heritage Foundation has identified as "the 6,000 people who count." The 6,000 elect included members of Congress, 1,500 of their staffers, 700 executive branch officials, 1,000 academics, 1,000 journalists, and sundry talk show hosts. It had become a government of the people, by the people, and for the people, via a carefully selected, narrowly based, non-random sample.

II

As self-government receded under the weight of the technocracy and the 6,000 "people who matter," an equally important aspect of America's tradition of self-determination, morality and ethics, declined in lock-step. The data which portray the rising crime rate were familiar: homicide and incarceration rates nearly doubled from the fifties to the eighties; in 1990, 23 percent of black men aged 20-29 were behind bars, on parole, or on probation; and, over half of black families with children under 18 were headed by a woman, usually never married. In America's schools, such problems were usually not discussed out of fear the discussion might impart some bias or – perish the thought – values to impressionable youths.   Thus, the oxymoron of a "value-neutral" education was building a society which was morally and ethically bankrupt.

The problem of declining morality was not unique to any particular class or stratum of American society. It was evidenced by investment advisors like James D. Donahue, a church-going family man who garnered millions from gullible investors with his alleged track record of 15 percent annual growth in Hedged Investment Associates of Englewood, Colorado. Of the $290 million Hedged Investments raised from 1980 to 1989, $17 million was wrapped around the axle of failed California windmills, $129 million disappeared in the stock market in purportedly "hedged" investments, while Mr. Donahue paid himself $3 million. Another $125 million was disbursed to investors who were smart enough to demand their alleged "profits." After having lost virtually all the remaining capital in a risky options play, Donahue called an investors' meeting and reported the sorry fact that their funds were all but depleted.   Too embarrassed to face the group of faithful supporters, who had repeatedly been told their investments were growing rapidly, Donahue simply left his recorded videotape confession for their viewing.

The role played by the greed and incompetence of many thrift and banking executives is the hackneyed tale of the age. Yet one wonders whether the sad truth would ever have come to light were it not for the post-bankruptcy finger-pointing of red-faced, cover-it-up regulators trying to exonerate themselves. Thus, the corruption which infects the many government-regulated industries which have not yet failed goes largely unnoticed. Physicians have used the Medicare and Medicaid programs as their own "welfare for the rich" feeding trough to transform a profession whose stated purpose is to heal the sick into one which preys upon their health. The government happily pays excessive or fraudulent claims. Padded medical bills are absorbed with similar alacrity by an equally insouciant health insurance industry, while employers are ultimately forced to cut the costly benefits they provide their workers. Meanwhile, clinical labs such as the Hanlester Network sold limited partnership interests to doctors who then referred Hanlester their business. Whether this type of arangement can legally be considered a kickback or not, it does not pass the smell test: it is unlikely that Hanlester would have been willing to pay the reported annual returns of $200 to $532 per $500 share to any of the investor-doctors' patients who might have expressed a desire to get in on this high-yielding gravy train.

Morality implies behavior under rigid ethical rules, even when it hurts. The obvious case in which America falls far short is the practice of sexual morality. The proposed solution to AIDS and teen pregnancy is free distribution of hypodermic needles and condoms, because "they're going to do it anyway." The assumption is made that America's values are not sufficiently strong – or can not be sufficiently strengthened – to alter behavior. More ominous, values are already so sorely lacking that there is no conviction to condemn promiscuous and even self-destructive behavior. Anyone who tries will be vilified with something far more damaging than a scarlet "A." America is more tolerant of immorality than it is of morality.

If American morality fails in the fairly objective norms which can be applied to sexual behavior, how can it be expected to fare in the more difficult subjective ethical issues? Michael Milken, before his conviction, was loudly cheered by a large group of investment professionals as he entered the courthouse. Milken was but the sacrificial lamb of a system gone wild with greed. Nobody knew how many floor traders on the Chicago Mercantile Exchange were making pre-arranged trades at artificial prices before the FBI conducted its sting operation. And, incredibly, many traders accused the FBI of a "witch hunt," as if the few trades apprehended were not evidence of a much broader problem. How many investors have been fleeced so often in so many markets that they have given up and simply refuse to invest? Thus, the dishonesty of comparatively few constricts the lifeblood of capital while worthy industry stagnates.

In the nineties, the next great axe to fall will be the liquidation of the government's ill-advised attempt to subsidize the dream of a single family detached home with a white picket fence for every American who wants one. Homebuilders who bribe FHA's appraisers and inspectors naturally find that they can realize a sizeable profit on sale of a house. It then merely becomes a question of pressuring an eager loan officer to approve credit on a marginal buyer who is not strong enough to get a loan from a private lender – of whom there are few left – or smart enough to buy a home with better value. The loan officer may find it necessary to alter credit reports or income verification forms. Likewise, the closing attorney must be heavily leaned upon to cover up untoward legal discrepancies that might dissuade the buyer. The FHA office meanwhile churns out government insurance certificates with purblind indifference. And any real estate professional who tries to rock the boat in this foul process is a trouble-maker, who will soon find his services in very little demand. Sadly, in the fashion of American politics, it will require a huge financial loss to the FHA insurance fund before anyone even bothers inquiring into these practices.

America is a great nation only if it is a free nation of strong, moral individuals with freedom to choose. Yet every time government spending grows by another dollar it has sucked another dollar vote from the free market. Is pornography a subjective issue? Then vote on it with your hard-earned dollars by avoiding prurient literature and art. Ah, but how can you if the object of your distaste has already been subsidized by the National Endowment of the Arts? And how can the next generation be taught ethical values in a costly and inefficient government-controlled education system which finds not only values but also achievement standards to be inappropriate and even "biased." In the words of Nancy Amuleru-Marshall, director of research for Atlanta's public schools, "any tests that emphasize logical, analytic methods of problem-solving will be biased against minorities." During the national debate over civil rights during the fifties and sixties, this is exactly the line of reasoning used in support of segregated schools. Now that separate education has been accepted as inherently unequal, do America's educators want to revisit the issue by assuming blacks are inherently less analytical than whites? Is it possible we have sunk so low that we no longer recognize the value of objective standards of achievement to the future of society? Whither America?

III

It would be natural to conclude from this somber recitation of the ills affecting the American economy that doom is imminent and government action is needed to avert an all-out catastrophe. This would be a natural response for most Americans, conditioned as we are by sixty years of government-prescribed remedies, government-sponsored insurance, and government-financed bailouts. Two generations of politicians, economists, and businessmen have repeatedly demonstrated the economy's ability to spend its way out of recession. And perhaps there is still one more battle left in the old war horse. Maybe the taxpayer can swallow yet another spoonful of the poison of the private market's hot potato bad debts. Maybe government budget deficits can be kicked up in one last Weimar-inspired increment before the government's interest burden on its accumulated debt overwhelms the stimulative impact of deficit spending. Indeed, this is the crucial question which has faced every debtor from time immemorial: at what point does the cash flow turn negative? When does it start costing me more to satisfy my creditors' claims than I can get from increased borrowing? In other words, until the businessman owes the bank $1 million, the bank has leverage over him. But after $1 million, the businessman has leverage over the bank. This is when the true test of morality occurs.

As the nineties began, America's economy was in the twilight zone between increased use of leverage and widespread repudiation of debt. Clearly, the consumer was already in the process of repudiation. From a moral standpoint, he never had any intention of repayment unless the general economy and real estate markets remained buoyant. Debt was not widely considered a moral obligation which must be quickly and frugally met. The young graduate did not borrow money only to buy his first automobile to commute to his new job. He financed *every* auto he acquired throughout his business career – in ever higher amounts and over ever longer repayment periods. Everybody did it. It became a way of life for America's gullible generation of future deadbeats, who assumed that their paychecks would expand exponentially to meet the continually rising burden of debt.

America's highly leveraged real estate mania was based on an even more dangerous set of assumptions than those that fueled the boom in the consumer durables market. Principal amortization was usually stretched out over an entire career, if it was required at all. Down payments were often insufficient to cover the transaction cost of buying, not to speak of selling the property. Under these circumstances, continual inflation in property prices was not just assumed on the part of the borrower; from the standpoint of the lender, it was necessary. Borrowers did not sign up with the idea that they might lose money, nor did lenders require sufficient reserves to cover falling property values.

As real estate inflation ground to a halt in the early nineties, the easy alternative for those who could not get the price they needed to satisfy their debts was to "mail in the keys." And they did so in alarming numbers as the rising tide of foreclosures mounted ever higher.

American businessmen were no more prudent than America's consumers and homeowners, for they had gamely abetted the profligacy of the consumer. Balance sheets were over-leveraged and liquidity was kept to a minimum. Employers agreed to expensive labor contracts along with unaffordable employee pension and health benefits. If inflation drove costs higher, it was assumed that revenues would rise at an even greater pace. Into the shoals of this already raging sea, the rocket scientists of Wall Street introduced the unrestricted submarine warfare of leveraged buyouts via junk-bond financing. Corporate assets were bid up on the basis of "break-up value," while corporate liabilities were ignored. And when everything was fully leveraged up, bid up, and – finally – forked over to its new owners, the economy – and the banking system on which the market values of these business assets were based – began to founder.

The falling fortunes of America's financial system in the nineties would thus have a negative and incontrovertible impact on business activity – which would in turn further exacerbate the banking system's own woes. Lenders had long overlooked the same problems as businessmen and consumers. A shortage of cash to service debts was never viewed as important in the inflationary economy of the seventies, nor was it yet critical in the continuing rampage toward debt during the transitional economy of the eighties. Bankers themselves had overleveraged. The ratio of commercial bank capital to bank assets dropped below ten percent, while the capital of thrift institutions and insurance companies was disappearing altogether. Ever riskier loans were advanced to generate the fee income which would be needed to offset the rising tide of loan defaults. Thus, portfolios degenerated from garbage to toxic waste. The banking system in the nineties found itself with insufficient capital to extend new loans, nor was capital sufficient to support the existing asset base. Even if good credits could be found – and few were – the major task confronting bankers was to shrink their assets, not acquire new ones.

Government would inevitably be drawn into the vortex of this financial whirlpool. State and local governments depended upon sales and property taxes, which would suffer as retail sales ebbed and property values plummeted. Government spending at all levels was programmed for years in advance under the pork barrel process of purchasing ever more fat to get a continually declining volume of meat. Administrators and educators had been cowed by long years of brow-beating into sycophancy toward the vocal and counterproductive demands of minority and special interest groups. The federal government's ever-widening social safety net had assumed a burgeon-ing mountain of liabilities that no private investor was willing to touch. The assumption was repeatedly made that the taxpayer would assume these burdens for the "greater good" of society. These were the same tenuous assumptions on which George III had bet Britain's colonies and Marie Antoinette's husband had bet her coiffure, and everything under it.

The burdens which had been placed on America's economy were not unique. For all their self-righteous criticism of America's fiscal irresponsibility, the other major industrial nations faced their own formidable problems. Germany had assumed the problems of its forlorn eastern states, and had financed its burden by debt. Japan had built its prosperity by preying on its trading partners and over-leveraging its banking system. The British and Canadian economies operated under the immutable assumptions of a falling currency, high interest rates, and heavy borrowing. In Western Europe, debt burdens were everywhere at oppressive levels. In Eastern Europe and the Third World, the economic oxygen of foreign capital could not be coaxed in at any rate. As to OPEC, even the oil-rich countries of Saudi Arabia and Kuwait had switched roles from lender to borrower. Indeed, the shortage of capital and the wave of debt repudiation were worldwide phenomena.

Once again, Kondratieff's long wave had turned full cycle. The world economy had been playing Russian roulette with a six-decade handgun. Five decades had come up blank, and now the sixth chamber was here, fully locked and loaded, and the hammer was ready to strike. Not everyone would perish. Those who had not lost faith in the work ethic, who had not deluded themselves by chasing after pipe-dream investments, who had not lost sight of the "worst case scenario" in their financial planning would survive. Such has been the beauty and the power of the capitalist process since the origin of the species. Those who survived would write the history and the laws for the next generation. And so, as T. S. Eliot foresaw, the world would end, not with a bang, but a whimper.

FOOTNOTES

Chapter 1

1. *The Commercial Appeal*, Memphis, Tennessee, April 13, 1991, pg. A-2.
2. Werner Meyer-Larsen, "America's Century Will End With A Whimper," translated and reprinted from *Der Spiegel* in *World Press Review*, January, 1991.

Chapter 2

1. Arthur E. R. Boak and Wm. G. Sinnigen, *A History of Rome to A.D. 565* (New York: MacMillan Co., 1964, 5th ed.), pg. 92.
2. Kondratieff's 1925 paper was edited and translated in the November, 1935 edition of the *British Review of Economic Studies*.
3. LCdr. David Williams (Ret.), *Financial Astrology* (Tempe, Arizona: American Federation of Astrologers, Inc., 1982), pp. 59-76.
4. LCdr David Williams, *ibid.*, pg. 66.
5. Data were obtained from Milton Friedman and Anna Schwartz, *A Monetary History of the United States, 1867-1960* (Princeton, N.J.: Princeton University Press, 5th ed., 1971), pg. 37.
6. Friedman and Schwartz, *ibid.*, pg. 68.
7. At its low point in 1864, it took $12.50 to purchase one British pound. By 1879, when specie payments resumed, that $12.50 could be exchanged for over 2½ British pounds.
8. Friedman and Schwartz, *ibid.*, pg. 121.
9. Friedman and Schwartz, *ibid.*, pg. 91.
10. Friedman and Schwartz, *ibid.*, pg. 108.
11. Friedman and Schwartz, *ibid.*, pg. 156.
12. Friedman and Schwartz, *ibid.*, pg. 206.
13. Friedman and Schwartz, *ibid.*, pg. 232.

14. Ravi Batra, *The Great Depression of 1990* (New York: Simon & Schuster, 1987), pg. 107.

15. Joseph A. Schumpeter, *History of Economic Analysis*, ed. by Elizabeth Boody Schumpeter (New York: Oxford University Press, seventh printing, 1968), pg. 687.

Chapter 3

1. Senator Theodore Burton, *Crises and Depressions.* Reprinted in J. R. Levien, *Anatomy of a Crash - 1929* (New York: Traders Press, 1966), pg. 59.

2. John Kenneth Galbraith, *The Great Crash, 1929* (Boston, MA: Houghton Mifflin Co., 1988), pg. 47.

3. *Ibid.*, pg. 50.

4. The data for 1929 are from J. R. Levien, *ibid.*, pg. 31-55.

5. Eugene N. White, *Crashes and Panics: The Lessons of History* (New York: Dow Jones-Irwin, 1990).

6. Commodity Research Bureau, *Futures Market Service* (New York: Knight-Ridder Business Information Service), Vol. LVII, No. 1, January 4, 1991.

7. Galbraith, *ibid.*, pg. 192.

8. Ravi Batra, *ibid.*, pp. 116-119.

9. Friedman and Schwartz, *ibid.*, pp. 712-14.

10. *Ibid.*, pg. 423.

11. *Ibid.*, pg. 421.

12. *Ibid.*, pg. 470.

13. Jacob Oser, *The Evolution of Economic Thought* (New York: Harcourt, Brace & World, Inc., 1963), pg. 327.

14. John Maynard Keynes, *The End of Laissez-Faire* (London: Hogarth, 1926).

15. John Maynard Keynes, *ibid.*, pp. 47-48, 52-53.

16. John Maynard Keynes, *The General Theory of Employment, Interest, and Money* (New York: Harcourt, Brace and World, 1936).

17. John Maynard Keynes, *op. cit.*, pg. 131.

18. Catherine Drinker Bowen, *Miracle at Philadelphia* (Boston: Little Brown and Co., 1986), pg. 45.

Chapter 4

1. Julius Caesar, *The Gallic War*, with English translation by H. J. Edwards, C. B. (Cambridge, Mass: Harvard University Press, 1986), pg. 343.

2. *Ibid.*, pg. 347.

3. Schumpeter, *ibid.*, pg. 905.

4. Internal Revenue Service, *1990 Form 1040 and Instructions* (IRS: Bloomington, Il, 1990), pg. 23.

5. Adolf Hitler, *Mein Kampf*, translated by Ralph Manheim (Boston: Houghton-Mifflin Co., 1971), pg. 213.

Chapter 5

1. Eustace Mullins, *The Secrets of the Federal Reserve* (Staunton, VA: Bankers Research Institute, 1983), pg. 1.
2. *Ibid.*, pg. 3.
3. Friedman and Schwartz, *op. cit.*, pg. 412.
4. Walter Wriston, "No Wonder Banks Fail," *The Wall Street Journal*, December 19, 1990.

Chapter 6

1. Friedman and Schwartz, *ibid.*, pp. 556-7.
2. *Ibid.*, pg. 668.

Chapter 8

1. Thucydides, *The Peloponnesian War*, The complete Hobbes Translation, ed. by David Grene (Chicago: University of Chicago Press, 1989), pg. 47.
2. Lenny Glynn, "Global Debt," *Global Finance*, September, 1990, pg. 31.
3. Lenny Glynn, *ibid.*, pg. 32.
4. *Ibid.*, pg. 39.
5. Walter Momper, *Vier Tage im November* (Hamburg, Germany: Stern-Buch, 1989), pg. 51.
6. Karl Otto Pöhl, "On the way to EMU: The Bundesbank View," *Futures* Magazine, March, 1990.
7. *Ibid.*
8. *Value Line Investment Survey*, edition 12, December 7, 1990, pg. 1765.

Chapter 9

1. "A Long-Term Perspective," chart produced by Value Line Publishing, Inc., 1990.
2. Friedman and Schwartz, *op. cit.*, growth rate interpolated from Chart 62.
3. Estimate of Assoc. Professor Glen Yago, State University of New York, in February 14, 1991 letter to *The Wall Street Journal*.

Chapter 10

1. J. D. Hamon, *Advanced Commodity Trading Techniques* (Brightwaters, N.Y.: Windsor Books, 1986), pg. 23.
2. *Futures* Magazine, January, 1991, pg. 50.

3. *Futures* Magazine, January, 1991, pg. 48.

Chapter 11

1. Data on insurance companies from the National Association of Insurance Commissioners. Data on bank failures from the Federal Deposit Insurance Corporation.
2. Laurence H. Kallen, *Corporate Welfare: The Mega Bankruptcies of the 80's and 90's* (Lyle Stuart, 1990).
3. Mark Skousen, *Forecasts and Strategies*, April, 1991, pg. 5.
4. *The Wall Street Journal*, February 25, 1991, pg. C-1.

Chapter 12

1. Hilton Kramer, "DeMan at Yale," *The Wall Street Journal*, February 25, 1991, pg. A-9.
2. *The Browning Newsletter.*
3. Richard B. McKenzie, "The Retreat of the Elderly Welfare State," *The Wall Street Journal*, March 12, 1991, pg. A-18.

Chapter 14

1. Werner Meyer-Larsen, *ibid.*

The Bankruptcy of America may be ordered
from Publishers Distribution Service by
calling 1-800-345-0096 (toll free)

or 1-616-929-0733
(in Michigan and outside the U. S.)

or by FAX 1-616-929-3808

or by writing to:

Publishers Distribution Service
121 East Front Street, Suite 203
Traverse City, Michigan 49684

Visa and MasterCard accepted
Quantity discounts available

Notes

Notes